SOCIOLOGY
A complete introduction

T0385176

SOCIOLOGY
A complete introduction

Paul Oliver

British Library Cataloguing in Publication Data: a catalogue record for this title is available from the British Library.

Library of Congress Catalog Card Number: on file

Paperback ISBN 978 1 47361 166 5

eBook ISBN 978 1 47361 167 2

5

Cover image © Shutterstock.com

Typeset by Cenveo® Publisher Services.

Printed in Italy by Elcograf S.p.A.

John Murray Learning policy is to use papers that are natural, renewable and recyclable products and made from wood grown in sustainable forests. The logging and manufacturing processes are expected to conform to the environmental regulations of the country of origin.

Hodder & Stoughton Ltd
Carmelite House
50 Victoria Embankment
London EC4Y 0DZ
www.hodder.co.uk

The authorized representative in the EEA is Hachette Ireland,

8 Castlecourt Centre, Dublin 15, D15 XTP3, Ireland (email: info@hbgi.ie)

Also available
in ebook

Contents

About the Author   ix
How to use this book   x

Part One: Theoretical issues and sociology
1   Introduction to sociology and the
    social sciences   3
    The origins of sociology
    Differentiation in society
    The scope of the social sciences
    The social basis of knowledge

2   The role of theory in sociology   21
    The nature of a theory
    Theories, perspectives and paradigms
    Sociological perspectives

3   Sociological research methods   37
    Using the methods of the physical sciences within sociology
    Using interpretive approaches within sociology
    The positivist approach to collecting data
    Interpretive techniques for collecting data
    Questions of sampling
    The analysis of data
    Social research ethics

Part Two: The Social Environment
4   Urban and rural contexts   59
    The Industrial Revolution
    The development of urbanization

5   Social and work organizations   73
    Organizations and society
    Social action and organizations
    The construction of knowledge

6 The political control of social existence   89
The sociology of politics – concepts and theories
Pluralism and political power
The concept of elites
Social class and politics
Post-structuralism and political power
The media and political control

7 Religion and secularization   105
The sociological study of religion
Secularism and religion
Classical perspectives on the sociology of religion
The sociology of new religious movements
Constructionism and religion

8 Society, the mass media and the Internet   121
The nature of the mass media
Theoretical perspectives on sociology and the media

9 Health and social policy   133
The sociology of health
A Marxist perspective on health
A functionalist analysis of health
The social construction of health and illness
Occupational health

Part Three: The Global Society

10 Ethnicity, culture and the movement
of peoples   149
The origins and causes of migration
Migrants as refugees
European expansion

11 Differential economic opportunity   163
The influence of geography
Rapidity of change
Poverty, deprivation and exclusion

12 The changing nature of work   175
Different approaches to work
Work in the electronic age
The nature of work tasks

13 Transition in the natural world   187
Social influences on the environment
Risk and the environment
The environment and equilibrium

14 Globalization and the world state   199
The concept of globalization
Globalization and communication networks
Globalization and risk
Supply chains and outsourcing
Anti-globalization
A knowledge society and globalization
Globalization and commodification

15 Caste, class and strata in society   215
Different types of social stratification
The concept of social class
Caste in Hindu society
Social class and education

16 Evolving concepts of gender   233
The nature of patriarchy
Women and education
Women and employment
The treatment of women
Equal pay

17 Law, crime and social order   249
Crime, deviance and social norms
Environmental explanations of crime
The origins of crime in social conflict
Marxist viewpoints on crime and deviance
The relationship between the media and crime
Crime and statistics

18 Sociology and citizenship   265
The concept of citizenship
Duties and rights
Citizenship and the movement of people

19 The sociology of educational
achievement   277
The causes of educational achievement
Family factors affecting achievement
*Strategies to improve the achievement of children
from poorer families*

20 Postmodern society 291
The nature of postmodernity
Postmodernity, power and knowledge

Answers 305
References 309
Index 317

About the Author

Dr Paul Oliver was formerly a lecturer at the University of Huddersfield. He was course leader for the Doctor of Education programme, and has wide experience of supervising and examining doctoral theses. He has published 20 books, 7 of these having been translated into other languages. Dr Oliver has taught sociology of education on teacher-training courses, sociology in a further education college, and sociology of multiculturalism at the State University of New York, while on a staff exchange visit.

How to use this book

This Complete Introduction from *Teach Yourself®* includes a number of special boxed features, which have been developed to help you understand the subject more quickly and remember it more effectively. Throughout the book, you will find these indicated by the following icons.

 The book includes concise **quotes** from other key sources. These will be useful for helping you understand different viewpoints on the subject, and they are fully referenced so that you can include them in essays if you are unable to get your hands on the source.

 The **case study** is a more in-depth introduction to a particular example. There is at least one in most chapters, and hopefully they will provide good material for essays and class discussions.

 The **key ideas** are highlighted throughout the book. If you only have half an hour to go before your exam, scanning through these would be a very good way of spending your time.

 The **did you know?** boxes give you some additional information that will liven up and focus your learning.

 The **test your knowledge** questions at the end of each chapter are designed to help you ensure you have taken in the most important concepts from the chapter. If you find you are consistently getting several answers wrong, it may be worth trying to read more slowly, or taking notes as you go.

 The **dig deeper** boxes give you ways to explore topics in greater depth than we are able to go to in this introductory level book.

Part One

Theoretical issues and sociology

1

Introduction to sociology and the social sciences

This first chapter will act as an introduction to the broad themes of the whole book. It will discuss the nature of sociology as being arguably the foundational discipline of the social sciences. In so doing it will analyse related subjects such as economics and psychology. The chapter will also include a discussion of inter-disciplinary subjects, such as education, which incorporate a significant element of social thought. There will also be a discussion of the nature of the concept of 'science' in social science, and whether sociology can be considered analogous in terms of scientific thought to the 'natural' sciences.

The origins of sociology

Sociology is a relatively new subject, having developed from the work of European social philosophers of the early 19th century. As the industrial and scientific revolutions gathered pace, there was an increasing assumption that similar rational approaches could be used to analyse human society. At the forefront of these ideas was the French philosopher Auguste Comte (1798–1857), who did not favour a traditional religious interpretation of society but preferred a scientific approach.

Sociology has since evolved into a broad-based subject which analyses all aspects of human behaviour in society. It can treat as its subject matter the behaviour of large groups of people, or of individuals and the way in which they relate to organizations and institutions. Sociology is very much an empirical subject in that it relies upon the collection and analysis of data in order to further an understanding of society. The data, and the methods used to analyse them, may be quantitative, qualitative or a combination of the two.

Sociology is a scientific discipline in the sense that it adopts rational, systematic thought processes to the investigation of society. Sociologists conduct research on many aspects of social phenomena, ranging from factors affecting social stability to the reasons for change in society.

In its early days, sociology was influenced by the Enlightenment and by the approach to rationality and logic typified by such figures as Voltaire (1694–1778) and David Hume (1711–76).

Did you know?

In 1726 the French writer and philosopher Voltaire had exchanged some humorous and perhaps slightly rude remarks with a rich aristocrat called the Chevalier de Rohan. The latter apparently told some of his servants to attack Voltaire. Although Voltaire threatened legal action, the Chevalier used his influence to have Voltaire imprisoned in the Bastille. Voltaire pleaded to be sent into exile instead of being imprisoned, and was hence allowed to travel to England. He spent three years in London where he became popular and well known in literary and philosophical circles. Eventually he returned to Paris where in 1734 he published a book praising the freedom of expression which he had found in London, thus further upsetting the French élite.

The rise of sociology as a discipline coincided with the many changes brought about by the Industrial Revolution in Europe during the late 18th and early 19th centuries. The new manufacturing processes resulted in the transformation of society, notably in relation to employment patterns.

Key idea: The Enlightenment

The Enlightenment was a philosophical and intellectual movement of 18th-century Europe that emphasized the use of reason, observation and science, in contrast to the dogmatic beliefs that had previously held sway.

The growth of industrialization during the 19th century led to a migration of people to the cities, both in Europe and in the United States. The new urbanization, combined with the fusion of people from different cultures and social classes, had many consequences for society.

These changes became of increasing interest to academics, who were working in the new field of sociology, leading to the establishment of university departments devoted to this area of study. William Graham Sumner (1840–1910) gave lectures at Yale University in 1876 on the work of Auguste Comte, and in 1892 the first postgraduate school of sociology was established at the University of Chicago. The latter university became well known for encouraging its sociology students to conduct empirical research in Chicago and its environs, on the many different cultural groups who had made their home there.

The Chicago School of Sociology

In the mid-19th century Chicago was a very small town. However, by the early 20th century its population was measured in millions. This large increase in population was due to rapid industrial expansion, which brought many workers and their families to Chicago. This large-scale migration was partly from Europe, and partly consisted of black people from the southern states of America who were trying to escape the endemic racism there.

Almost inevitably, Chicago was unable to provide the infrastructure to support this influx of people, and during the period of heaviest immigration, facilities such as housing, health care and other social services were inadequate. It is perhaps not surprising that groups of immigrants from the same European or American region tended to live in the same area of Chicago, and hence to sustain the sense of community they had felt in their original home.

The School of Sociology at Chicago had a reputation for recruiting some of the leading social scientists of the period, including W. I. Thomas, Florian Znaniecki and George Herbert Mead. Moreover, the School developed a deliberate policy of researching the city of Chicago itself, and in particular the social diversity brought about by the large-scale immigration.

Researchers in the School used a combination of existing data collected on the city, with new qualitative data that reflected the social problems and social mobility within Chicago. The researchers there became well known for their use of a range of qualitative methodologies, including life history and autobiographical accounts, and ethnographies. The Chicago researchers demonstrated that sociologists did not need to stray very far in search of interesting social data. Very often the people and communities on one's doorstep could provide data and insights which were of much wider relevance.

The study of sociology was also thriving in European universities, and in 1895 Émile Durkheim (1858–1917) established the Department of Sociology at the University of Bordeaux.

The early sociologists were inclined to employ empirical – and notably quantitative – methods in their studies. They felt that such approaches gave a scientific legitimacy to their research. In a seminal piece of work, Durkheim studied suicide rates among Catholic and Protestant communities. In general, he found lower suicide rates among the former and higher rates among the latter. He explained this by suggesting that in Catholic communities there was normally an increased sense of social solidarity and social cohesion. This would provide a sense of support for individuals that would render them less likely to want to take their own lives. In Protestant communities, on the other hand, Durkheim hypothesized that there was less of a sense of social solidarity, and that people had to be more reliant upon themselves, than upon support from society. Despite criticisms of his methodology by some academics, this was an epoch-making study in that it sought to explain the action of individuals, not on purely psychological grounds, but upon the basis of the social context in which people found themselves.

This has remained an important insight, and even to this day still influences thinking about human behaviour. Within liberal societies, for example, we do not seek to explain criminal behaviour in an individual by genetic factors or simply feckless behaviour. We also try to take into account something of the social context of the criminal behaviour, and the upbringing of the individual.

Differentiation in society

Early social thought was also concerned with stratification in society. It was evident from observations of the new social order in industrialized cities of the 19th century that there were great distinctions in terms of wealth, power, social status, education and living conditions. In short, social class had become a major factor affecting the lives of individuals.

Karl Marx (1818–83) wrote extensively on the subject of social class, arguing that the members of a social class were linked through a shared concern with their own socio-economic priorities. Marx argued that the most important factor in relationships between social classes was the way in which each class was connected to the 'means of industrial production'.

Financiers, investment bankers and factory owners provided capital for the manufacturing process and to a large extent controlled the lives of those who laboured in the factories. Marx used the term 'bourgeoisie' for the capital-owning social class. The ordinary workers who sold their labour to the bourgeoisie, by working in the manufacturing process, were referred to by Marx as the 'proletariat'. For Marx the proletariat or working classes were exploited, and never fully reimbursed for the work that they provided for the manufacturing process. Industrial workers therefore created a 'surplus value', which was kept by the capital-owning class as profit.

'Marx's transformation of the social question into a political force is contained in the term "exploitation", that is, in the notion that poverty is the result of exploitation through a "ruling class" which is in the possession of the means of violence.'

Arendt, Hannah (1973), *On Revolution* (p. 62).

Marx argued that members of the proletariat would ultimately recognize their shared role in the appropriation of capital by the bourgeoisie, and hence would become aware of their class solidarity. Ultimately, only a sweeping away of this fundamentally unethical economic relationship would open up the benefits of society for all.

Key idea: Working-class system

Within a Marxist analysis, the proletariat were members of the social class who worked under adverse conditions within a capitalist system with the result that the capital-owning class could enhance their wealth and status.

In more recent times, Marxist ideas were applied by sociologists to an analysis of what became known as 'social reproduction'. The study of social class appeared to demonstrate that members of the wealthier, more advantaged classes were able to pass on not only their economic capital, but also their social advantages to their children and grandchildren. On the other hand, members of the working classes found it very difficult to escape from their social position. There appeared to be few opportunities for the children of working-class parents to improve their social status or life chances. Sociologists began to investigate the mechanisms of social reproduction, partly from an academic perspective, but also with the purpose of helping working-class children to improve their life chances.

It is perhaps not surprising that by the mid-20th century, when sociology was becoming established as a mainstream curricular subject, that it was seen as being preoccupied with change in society, and as being a source of radical social ideas for young people. This was perhaps slightly unfair, as the principal role of sociology was to analyse society and to try to explain the different factors affecting it. Indeed, the early sociologists had if anything been more concerned with understanding stability in society, rather than advocating social change.

Marx thought that it was possible to understand society in terms of broad, sweeping paradigms, which could be used to explain individual social events. By the early years of the 20th century, however, some sociologists were turning to more individualistic ways of understanding society.

Notable among these was the German sociologist Max Weber (1864–1920). While acknowledging that universalistic explanations of society were very desirable, and indeed useful, Weber cautioned that they would always be of limited validity. Individual human beings, Weber argued, would always look at the world in their own unique way, and form their own interpretation of the social world. Society could not be expected to behave in the same uniform way as a scientific environment in a laboratory. Suppose, for example, that we were to measure the melting point of a metal in the laboratory, we would expect all other samples of that metal, assuming the same degree of purity, to have the same melting point. However, just because one human being behaves in a certain way under certain specific circumstances, we would not expect all other human beings to behave in the same manner.

Weber thought that it was a laudable aim to try to develop testable hypotheses and theories in relation to sociological research, but that we should simultaneously accept that the subjective viewpoint of individual human beings would always remain important in sociology.

By the 1960s the influence of Marxist ideas in particular had popularized the idea of radical changes in society. There was a widespread feeling that only major changes in society would produce the kind of world to which people aspired.

There were significant protest movements in the West, against the Vietnam War in the United States, and against government policies in France. Young people, and students in particular, used a Marxian analysis to point out that it was not only the working class which was exploited in society. Other groups, such as black people, gay people and women, were also seen as being exploited and disadvantaged. This type of analysis was adopted by sociologists, who increasingly saw society as the site of major conflict between economically advantaged social groups, and other groups who consistently suffered from inequality. This type of analysis was particularly notable during the mid-1960s and early 1970s, with sociologists examining concepts and models that would help them understand the mechanisms operating in society.

MOBILITY IN SOCIETY

From the 1960s onwards, French sociologist Pierre Bourdieu (1930–2002) developed new analyses of society, often using the concept of 'capital', although he employed this in a different sense to Marx.

> 'Bourdieu likes to present life as a game. Capital is the currency. Whereas classical Marxism sees capital as purely economic, Bourdieu extends the concept – as Adorno extended the term "industry" – to include the cultural'
> Brooker, Will (1998), *Cultural Studies* (p. 90).

Bourdieu was interested in trying to explain the way in which some people were successful in society, and rose to positions of power and influence, while others failed to advance their lives to any significant extent. In particular, he explored the factors that might result in some children doing well in the education system, and others not succeeding. He was implicitly looking for factors that were not purely genetic, or in other words concerned with 'intelligence', but rather seeking explanations that were sociological in nature.

Bourdieu argued that children acquire a range of forms of capital, which help them in their progression through life and help to determine their level of achievement. One of the most obvious forms of capital some children possess is 'economic capital'. Such capital will normally be inherited from their parents, but can be exchanged for a range of advantages. They may be enabled to attend a prestigious, fee-paying school or to travel widely while young. Their parents may be able to send them on skiing holidays, or to ensure they join a rather exclusive tennis club. The possession of such economic capital enables children to acquire 'social capital'. For example, children attending exclusive private schools may make friends and social contacts that last well into adult life. Such friends themselves often become successful, and hence children find themselves as members of highly successful social networks, which become very useful in advancing their careers in later life. Social capital thus consists of children having access to a complex network of affluent, successful, high-performing people, including not only their peers but also the parents and relatives of their school friends.

In the case of children – probably the majority of young people – who do not possess this level of economic capital, they will generally be unable to acquire the same range of social capital, which benefits their more affluent peers. They may well be *as* intelligent and *even more* academically able than those with more economic capital, but may well find it very difficult to progress as far in life. For some rare individuals, a combination of intellectual and strong personal qualities may result in them excelling in their careers. They may, in effect, be able to acquire social capital despite their family background.

Key idea: Social capital

'Social capital' consists of the range of contacts, networks and acquaintances that are useful in helping people to advance their careers and economic position in society.

Bourdieu went on to point out that for some children economic and social capital are usually transformed into 'cultural capital'. This embraces all the abilities, knowledge and understandings that derive from social capital, and which contribute to success in their lives and careers. For example, a young person who speaks one or two foreign languages fluently, perhaps because they have spent time living abroad, will be at a great advantage in many jobs. In international finance or business, for instance, fluency in a foreign language can give someone an enormous advantage over competitors.

Qualifications are an important source of cultural capital, and a person who has gained a postgraduate qualification from a leading university in their field, will gain an important form of capital. The experience of working for a major international organization is another form of cultural capital, whether that organization be an investment bank, a leading university, or an important industrial research institute. Opportunities to move around the world from one leading organization to another are often the result of the networking opportunities derived from social capital.

For Bourdieu, however, educational success does not depend solely upon achievement in examinations and academic assignments. Aspects of cultural capital such as style of speech, self-presentation, and ability to discuss what we might term 'high culture', such as art, literature and classical music, can all contribute to success at university and later within a career.

Did you know?

Pierre Bourdieu was raised in a working-class family in a very small village called Denguin located in south-western France. The village is situated in the Aquitaine region of Pyrénées-Atlantiques.

Bourdieu's father had a smallholding but left it to work for the Post Office. At home, the family spoke a local dialect that was a variant of the Gascon language. Bourdieu did not therefore have the advantage of being reared in a literary, academic environment. However, he had two advantages. His father, despite his own limited education, encouraged his son to pursue his studies; and, in addition, Bourdieu himself was highly intelligent. From the local lycée he progressed to the famous Lycée Louis-le-Grand at Paris, and after that he went on to gain a worldwide reputation. The interesting and slightly ironic aspect of his life was that he never benefited from the economic and social capital about which he wrote. Nevertheless, through his sheer brilliance he rose to the very heights of the French university system.

Bourdieu appeared to have considerable empathy with the disadvantaged groups in society, and much of his research seemed to have the implicit purpose of improving their life chances. However, there would seem to be two logical ways in which one might approach the phenomenon of disadvantage in society. First, one could try to give working-class pupils access to the types of cultural capital enjoyed by upper-class children. Second, one could encourage a redefinition of what should count as 'high' culture. The latter is a relativistic argument, based on the assumption that all culture is different but of equal value. On this argument the culture of the upper classes is seen as superior, simply because they have the power and influence to define it as such.

Key idea: Cultural capital

Cultural capital consists of the range of skills, knowledge and attributes that help people to succeed in life. This may include academic qualifications and skills, experience of foreign travel, and an understanding of the arts.

The scope of the social sciences

Sociology as a discipline is part of a wide range of subjects grouped under the term 'social sciences'. The social sciences are normally considered to include psychology, politics, economics, and subjects such as 'education' when it is thought of as an area of study in its own right. All of these subjects share the characteristic that they include the study of human beings and their interrelationships within a broader society. In addition, most of these subjects also include elements of study that are close in approach to the 'harder', objective, natural sciences. Of all the social sciences, sociology is arguably the key discipline since it employs a range of quantitative and qualitative research methods that have been used to varying degrees in the other social science subjects.

The subject of psychology is an interesting example. Psychologists may investigate the ways in which individuals interact in small group situations in the workplace, in schools or in social situations. In order to carry out these investigations they may interview people, or ask them to keep personal diaries. These methods will involve qualitative, fairly subjective approaches to research. Other types of psychological research might involve an analysis of cognitive processes, or of mental development. Such research could involve laboratory tests or experiments, and may require the collection of quantitative data. This more objective type of research may aspire to be close to the kinds of methods used in the natural sciences. In other words, psychological research could involve very different approaches depending upon the nature of the research.

Qualitative research often involves the collection of data, and the subsequent generation of scientific theories from that data. This process is known as 'induction'. The theory developed in this way is not regarded as eternally valid, but as a basis for further investigation and testing of the provisional theory. In the case of quantitative research, a set of initial data is used to generate a hypothesis or provisional statement about the world. Further data is then collected in order to try to test the validity of the hypothesis. If the data seems to support the hypothesis, then a theory is constructed. The latter process is known as 'deduction', and is typical of traditional scientific method.

This combination of approaches is typical of social science subjects in general, in that they adopt a research method that seems appropriate for the research topic under consideration.

Social science subjects are empirical in that they collect and analyse data using the senses. They are also scientific in the broad sense outlined above, yet do not necessarily employ a single approach to the scientific method, adapting their approach to the problem under consideration.

Another social science subject is that of education studies. Researchers in education are interested in such questions as why students enjoy certain subjects, which methods help them to learn most effectively, what kinds of teaching strategy are most interesting for them, and what methods of self-study do they employ. Such questions could be investigated using qualitative methods, for example by asking students about the ways in which they go about studying. On the other hand, the learning process can also be researched by using quantitative approaches. We can teach students a topic using different strategies, and then test them on what they have learned. We can thus form a judgement about which learning method is the most effective, and can attach a quantitative measure to that judgement.

Economics is a social science which, like education studies, employs both quantitative and qualitative methods. If we consider a topic such as unemployment, governments monitor the level of this carefully, for example as a proportion of the working population. Equally, governments may be interested in a wide range of statistical data, including the gender balance of the unemployment totals and the mean period of time for which people have been unemployed. This is the kind of data that is often appropriate to analyse statistically. It is less usual that social scientists conduct the type of scientific experiments that are typical of the natural sciences. However, as in education studies, it is possible to employ qualitative research methods in appropriate situations. Interview methods could be used for example, to explore the reactions of people to a period of unemployment.

The social basis of knowledge

One of the most important insights of sociology consists of the process whereby knowledge is created in a social setting. According to the perspective of some sociologists, what is accepted as knowledge in society derives from a process of discussion, evaluation and analysis between groups of human beings. To put it another way, human beings 'negotiate' viewpoints which will become accepted as legitimate knowledge.

For example, if a change is being considered in the motorway speed limit in a country, there is no absolute, objective way in which the most appropriate limit can be determined. Ultimately, the legislature will form a judgement based on a wide number of factors. Importantly, prior to that decision, there will be extensive discussion on the merits and otherwise of various proposals. That discussion will ultimately lead to a consensus, or at least a majority opinion about the most appropriate speed limit. During that process individuals will learn from each other, and perhaps revise their initial opinion. This process of interaction is a major element in what sociologists often refer to as the 'social construction of knowledge'. To give it a slightly more technical name it is sometimes termed 'social constructionism'.

During this process people consider their own opinions about an issue, and relate these to the opinions of others. Individuals then synthesize these different viewpoints, and emerging from this is a sense of understanding and meaning. The medium for this process to take place is human language. Significantly, the process is continuous, and the meaning that we attribute to an issue often evolves and changes over time. The manner in which we understand something today may not be the way in which we understand the same thing in a month's time. Michel Foucault (1926–84), for example, analysed our changing conceptions of madness and insanity.

Did you know?

Foucault pointed out that in medieval times people who were 'insane', or perhaps demonstrating rather eccentric behaviour, were not seen as a particular threat to society. They might be seen as amusing or the object of fun, for example, but not needing to be excluded from society. However, from the 17th century onwards there was a tendency to treat the 'insane' as requiring incarceration. Later still, 'insanity' became viewed as a medical condition that required scientific analysis and treatment.

The analysis of a concept such as insanity is not merely of historical or philosophical interest. In considering the culpability of someone in relation to a crime, the question of whether the accused person is deemed sane or insane is of great importance in evaluating their guilt.

Key idea: Social constructionism

Social constructionism is the theory that our understanding of the world around us is principally created through interactions between people, and the sharing of knowledge and viewpoints.

Like Marx, Foucault was also interested in the nature of power in society. Whereas Marx focused his arguments on the power of the capital-owning class, Foucault addressed the devolved aspects of power in society. He was interested in the way in which both the institutions of the state, and also private sector organizations, exercised power to influence the lives of ordinary people.

'He (Foucault) believed that no such institutions were neutral or independent, and argued that it was an important political task to examine how they were tied to the complex operations of power in our society.'

Ward, Glenn (2010), *Understand Postmodernism* (p. 181).

Sociology has thus opened to public discussion and reflection the processes whereby meaning and understanding are created. In so doing the subject has been a force for liberalism and moderation in society, in that it has pointed to the numerous influences that combine to determine our views about issues. Moreover, it has emphasized that these views are not fixed and rigid, but that they can evolve and develop over time.

Dig deeper

Bulmer, M. (1984), *The Chicago School of Sociology: Institutionalization, Diversity, and the Rise of Sociological Research*. Chicago: University of Chicago Press.

Gane, M. (2006), *Auguste Comte*. Abingdon, Oxon: Routledge.

Miller, J. (2000), *The Passion of Michel Foucault*. Cambridge, MA: Harvard University Press.

Perry, J. A. & Perry, E. K. (2011), *Contemporary Society: An Introduction to Social Science* (13th ed.). Boston: Pearson.

Sperber, J. (2013), *Karl Marx: A Nineteenth Century Life*. New York: Liveright.

Swartz, D. (1998), *Culture and Power: The Sociology of Pierre Bourdieu*. Chicago: The University of Chicago Press.

Test your knowledge

1 Auguste Comte favoured an analysis of society which was...?
   a religious
   b scientific
   c humanistic
   d liberal

2 Sociological research is...?
   a empirical
   b philosophical
   c statistical
   d mathematical

3 In the late 19th century which university established a Department of Sociology devoted to empirical research on local communities?
   a Rome
   b London
   c Chicago
   d Los Angeles

4 One of the earliest scientific studies in sociology was Durkheim's research on...?
   a gender differences
   b unemployment
   c birth rates
   d suicide

5 Marx termed the capital-owning class the...?
   a proletariat
   b middle class
   c aristocracy
   d bourgeoisie

6 The transmission of the features of a social class to the next generation is known as...?
   a social reproduction
   b social coordination
   c social integration
   d social introduction

7 Social capital involves...?

    a   having extensive bank savings

    b   making good investments

    c   being part of an interpersonal network of successful people

    d   having a wide range of friends

8 Social science subjects are typically...?

    a   empirical

    b   statistical

    c   quantitative

    d   deductive

9 Michel Foucault analysed our changing views of...?

    a   the humanities

    b   insanity

    c   progress

    d   philosophy

10 The way in which knowledge is created through human interaction is known as?

    a   social relationism

    b   social acceptance

    c   social constructionism

    d   social absolutism

The role of theory in sociology

This chapter will examine the nature of social theory, and the process of theory falsification and amendment. It will examine the conceptual issue of whether 'social facts' can be said to exist, and hence the debate about the role of positivistic and anti-positivistic epistemologies within sociology. It will explore the range of theories based upon the interpretation of social meaning, and the range of enquiry methods that evolve from that perspective. Among the theories discussed will be 'critical theory', 'feminist theory', 'phenomenology' and 'symbolic interactionism'.

The nature of a theory

When we collect empirical data on the interaction of people in society, one of the difficulties is that we will probably have lots of individual instances of human behaviour. If the data remains as it is, it will be interesting, but we may find it difficult to identify trends and patterns in the data, or to condense the data into general statements. Without this ability to generalize we may not be able to make the most of our observations.

Before we start collecting data it is often best if we have a purpose or aim, which will inform the way we make our observations. For example, we might wish to explore the behaviour of people in a dentist's waiting room. We might guess that parents try to occupy their children in various ways, so that they will not be nervous. This is an example of a hypothesis – a prediction that we will try to test by collecting data. When we have collected some data, we can judge whether or not it seems to support our hypothesis. If we do not find evidence of such parental behaviour then we can discard the hypothesis. If, however, we do observe such behaviour, then we might develop a social theory that suggests that parents try to distract their children in any comparable situation. Such a theory would involve generalization, in that it would apply to a range of situations, and it would also include an element of explanation in that perhaps parents want the treatment to proceed smoothly. In addition, a social theory normally enables the sociologist to predict what might occur in similar situations in the future.

In social sciences, a theory is never the final word on an issue. A sociologist should whenever possible attempt to disprove or falsify a theory by collecting further data. If the data supports the theory, then the theory does not need to change. If the new data appears to contradict the theory, then it will require amendment.

Did you know?

You might think we should set out to prove a theory rather than to disprove or falsify it. However, if we did so, we might be biased because we might assume that the theory is actually 'true'. Therefore if we set out to disprove it, we are likely to be more rigorous in our approach!

A social theory should not be expected to remain the same for ever. As soon as it fails to adequately explain a phenomenon it should be amended, and retested.

Theories, perspectives and paradigms

Some social theories are developed by individual sociologists, and apart from being proposed in academic journal articles, may receive relatively little attention. On the other hand, a theory may be of such broad generality and applicability that it achieves worldwide recognition. There are a number of terms that seem quite closely related to the concept of 'theory', including paradigm, perspective, world view and ideology. Some of these terms are used almost synonymously. For example, a writer may say that someone 'seems committed to Marxist theory', while another may speak of a person as 'adhering to a Marxist perspective'. To take another example, an economist may suggest that the theory of the free market is the best perspective to employ when analysing a contemporary economic system. A different economist may argue that the philosophy of liberal, free trade is the best world view for distributing scarce world resources. Sociologists are a little to blame here, since they sometimes use these terms interchangeably, without a clear definition. Let us therefore explore briefly the nature of these concepts.

A 'paradigm' can be thought of as a way of approaching research and the creation of new knowledge during a particular period. During the medieval period in Europe, the predominant paradigm was that of Catholic Christianity, and the principal epistemological approach was that of Biblical exegesis and the analysis of other Christian texts regarded as legitimate. During the 18th and 19th centuries, however, this paradigm was gradually replaced by a scientific paradigm, which sought to create new knowledge by using the hypothetico-deductive method of 'reasoning'. We are still today employing this basic paradigm, although within the scientific methodology have arisen some variants such as a qualitative paradigm not typical of the original scientific approach. It is worth remembering that the transition from a religious paradigm to a scientific paradigm was very difficult, indeed painful. This is partly because when people are deeply immersed in one paradigm, it is difficult to envisage the possibility of thinking within a different paradigm.

Paradigms also influence the manner in which we enquire into the world, and question our fellow human beings. As Kuhn commented when speaking of scientific revolutions or paradigm changes:

'Each produced a consequent shift in the problems available for scientific scrutiny and in the standards by which the profession determined what should count as an admissible problem or as a legitimate problem-solution.'

Kuhn, Thomas (2012), *The Structure of Scientific Revolutions* (p. 6).

In medieval times heresy was considered an extremely serious offence, and religious authorities would on occasion question whether a person was adhering to accepted theological doctrine.

Key idea: Heresy

If a person believes in, or advocates, ideas that are contrary to the received wisdom of a religion, then they may be said to hold heretical beliefs.

However, within a scientific paradigm it is considered normal, and indeed desirable, to question received wisdom. A scientific theory is considered more widely accepted and legitimate, when it has withstood the test of trenchant criticism.

Did you know?

We are so deeply committed to the scientific paradigm, and to the material progress brought about by scientific knowledge, that it is scarcely possible to imagine moving to a different paradigm. However, although we are so familiar with electronic communication, perhaps in the future we might use other methods such as telepathy! In the future there may be yet undiscovered methods for passing on ideas and thoughts!

Paradigms become dominant and influential when they gain the support of leading governments, and of world organizations, particularly economic and educational institutions. Schools and universities are of especial significance, as they pass on the values and knowledge base of the paradigm to subsequent generations.

A theory, in the sense that we use the term nowadays, arises through a process of scientific reasoning and is continually subject to scientific scrutiny, and attempts to falsify or disprove it. The same is not necessarily true of a paradigm, which may develop through a much more complex process, often involving the support of political authorities.

Some ways of looking at the world are not necessarily widespread, dominant or influential. Indeed they may only be held by a minority of people. For example, the belief that the Earth is flat is not really a theory because it does not derive from accepted scientific methodology, nor does it have the broad scope to be considered a paradigm. The terms 'belief system' or world view are also probably not appropriate since these imply a range of interconnected beliefs. The belief in a flat Earth is probably simply that – a belief.

The term 'world view' is employed within the social sciences, usually to refer to a range of values, ideas, ways of thinking and beliefs that constitute an integrated system for living in the world. Humanism, for example, may be considered a world view. Humanism generally assumes a commitment to rational, logical decision-making, a rejection of religious or spiritual explanations of the world, and an ethical approach which aims at the welfare of human beings and other living organisms. This range of beliefs constitutes a world view, even if we do not attach to it the term humanism. A world view is often chosen by people to represent the general principles by which they wish to live their lives. People may believe that their chosen world view is the best and most appropriate approach to life, but there is no implication in the concept that one world view is objectively better than any other world view.

Much the same is true of the term 'perspective', the use of which is common within sociology. When a sociologist employs a particular theoretical framework or integrated range of concepts to analyse the world or to conduct social research, then that frame of reference is often described as a perspective. A researcher may, for example, speak of themselves as operating within a feminist perspective or conducting research within a phenomenological perspective. We will discuss examples of such perspectives later in the chapter.

Some sociologists may become very committed to a perspective, and may normally conduct all of their research within this particular framework. There is certainly nothing wrong with this, as long as the researcher is clear that this is what they are doing. For example, if they write a research article for a journal it is important that they refer to the perspective that they are using. The reader can then interpret the article and the researcher's findings within that particular frame of reference. There is also no implication within the concept of a perspective, that one perspective is objectively preferable to another. It is possible, however, that a perspective may be more suitable to investigate a particular research question than another. That would be a matter of academic judgement and for the researcher to justify.

A sociologist should not however become so committed to a single perspective that they fail to consider the possibility of using other approaches. This would negate the idea of having an open-minded approach to analysing the world, which is characteristic of the social sciences. Sometimes people do become so strongly affected by a belief system that they may not recognize the influence that they are under. Imagine, for example, children being reared in a totalitarian society where there is a single world view, or political system, to which all citizens are expected to adhere. Such children will never be exposed to other viewpoints and may, in effect, think that the culture of their society is the only possible way of envisaging the world.

Key idea: Totalitarianism

A totalitarian society is one in which the power elite controls all aspects of the belief system within the society.

We might speak of such children as having been exposed to an ideological system, or constrained within a particular ideology.

Did you know?

It could be argued that one of the most valuable things in the world is capacity and willingness to consider the viewpoints of others. Many of the most serious conflicts in history have and do arise because some people are intolerant of the views of others. Once we accept that there are multiple viewpoints in the world, we become more tolerant. However, we do not have to think that all viewpoints are equally correct; merely to respect the rights of others to hold them.

An ideology may not necessarily always be part of a totalitarian political system, nor represent a completely inflexible view of the world, but the use of the concept is very often nuanced to suggest that those who subscribe to an ideology are not as autonomous as they might be. Heywood writes that:

'Ideology is thus equated with dogmatism: fixed or doctrinaire beliefs that are divorced from the complexities of the real world.'
Heywood, Andrew (2007) *Political Ideologies: An Introduction* (p. 10).

In the social sciences it is important for students, researchers and lecturers to be as open-minded and sceptical as possible, and to be self-reflective about their own analytic processes. This means that we should try wherever we can to place our thought processes in the public domain, so that others may appreciate the ways in which we try to make sense of the world. If we can speak and write about sociology in this way, then we are operating within the traditions of social science.

Sociological perspectives

The term 'perspective' is widely employed in sociology, although some writers use it interchangeably with the term 'paradigm'. The concept of 'perspective' is often used where the writer wishes to demarcate an integrated theoretical framework, which can be employed to analyse a sociological question. For example, if we collect sociological data, and wish to regard them as 'facts', in much the same way as laboratory data might be treated in the physical sciences, then we might say that we are operating within a positivist perspective. On the other hand, if we do not wish to treat data as 'social facts', but as partly involving the personal, subjective creativity of human beings, with all its implicit relativity, then we may say that we are operating within an 'antipositivist' or 'interpretative perspective'. The positivist perspective would employ quantitative data, while the antipositivist perspective would use qualitative data.

There are a number of different perspectives that are usually grouped under the broad description of antipositivist. They typically, although not exclusively, employ qualitative data. Examples include 'critical theory', 'symbolic interactionism', 'feminist theory' and 'phenomenology'.

Critical theory is a perspective that on the one hand tries to analyse, understand and systematize social events, but at the same time is interested in trying to improve society. It is interested in an analysis that proposes ways in which society can be changed. Critical theory particularly focuses upon situations where people are disadvantaged, and tries to identify ways in which their lives can be improved. Critical theory has been particularly associated with the so-called Frankfurt School, and some of its leading thinkers, notably Herbert Marcuse (1898–1979), Max Horkheimer(1895–1973) and Theodor Adorno (1903–69).

Key idea: Critical theory

Critical theorists attempt to analyse society and then to try to change it for the better, rather than simply to understand and explain societal mechanisms.

Key idea: The Frankfurt School

The Frankfurt School rose to prominence during the 1930s, but its liberal, radical approach to society placed it at odds with the growing influence of Nazism. Many of the leading thinkers of the Frankfurt School left Germany to work in the United States before the outbreak of the Second World War, but were able to return once the war had ended.

Critical theory demonstrated a liberal, open-minded approach to sociology, which was sceptical concerning a positivist approach to social science, since it argued that all sociological research was inevitably linked to, and affected by, the particular world views of the researchers. Critical theory suggests to researchers that they should analyse their own thought processes during research, and should be wary of any claims on the part of other sociologists that there are views of the world that are true in any absolute sense.

Of course, there is a potential self-contradiction with a perspective such as critical theory. If one rejects positivism on the grounds that it is an ideology committed to the existence of what we may call social facts, while supporting a qualitative perspective in a variety of forms, then critical theorists may be accused of being ideologues of simply a different type. To claim that others are ideologues, while only we ourselves have a balanced and rational approach to the world, could be a dangerous intellectual road to travel.

Key idea: Academic tolerance

Sociologists have to be continually vigilant that they do not assume that their favoured perspective gives them unique insights into an issue. If so, they would be in danger of failing to appreciate the insights of others.

The other perspectives that we shall examine in this chapter have a number of aspects in common with critical theory, such as an awareness of human subjectivity, and hence a tendency to adopt qualitative approaches to research. Symbolic interactionism emphasizes the way in which each and every one of us develops a concept of our 'self' in order to make sense of the world. In addition, we develop a sense of the way in which other members of society think about the world, including us. As Blumer argues:

'The first premise is that human beings act toward things on the basis of the meanings that the things have for them.'
Blumer, Herbert (1986), *Symbolic Interactionism: Perspective and Method* (p.2).

Interactionists are thus continually aware of this dialogue between the self and others who make up their immediate society. This interaction takes place through the use of symbols, which although principally linguistic, may consist of other ciphers such as gestures or facial expressions. The outcome of this continual interaction is a mutual understanding of the nature and meaning of the social world.

Key idea: Symbolic interactionism

Symbolic interactionists study the process whereby human beings communicate and thereby create new ideas about the way society functions.

Since this perspective stresses the investigation of small-scale interactions between different social actors, it is generally assumed that qualitative methods such as interviews and participant observation approaches are much more suitable than quantitative methods. Interactionism does not try to analyse large scale developments in society, and hence survey research would not be appropriate. Importantly, symbolic interactionists stress that there is no world 'out there' that is objectifiable. The social world is, according to them, a human construction, which is continually changing and adapting as different human beings contribute to that construction.

One of the key contributors to social interactionist thought, George Herbert Mead (1863–1931), argued that the process of human interaction helped us to formulate our comprehension of the social world and, in addition, contributed to the way in which our social contemporaries also understand the world. There is thus an intellectually symbiotic process in operation here.

There is within symbolic interactionism a strong philosophical element, in that one chooses, for example, to prioritize subjective elements in understanding society, rather than seeking objective explanations. While feminist theory retains philosophical elements, much of its basis rests upon empirical evidence. Women are underrepresented in positions of authority and responsibility in the workplace; they are typically associated with work in the home rather than in senior positions in industry or the professions; they are not remunerated equally in comparison with men; and they are underrepresented within the political system, having as a gender much less social and political influence compared to men.

Such structural elements in society can be substantiated empirically, although some men appear to be insensitive to the need to transform society, and render it more equal in terms of gender. For feminist theory, the central questions in relation to these issues are first of all to explain how the inequalities come about, and second, having produced explanations of the mechanisms, to attempt to eradicate the inequalities.

For many women a key element in feminist theory is that of the exercise of male oppression and indeed violence, whether of a psychological or physical nature. Such oppression derives ultimately from the differential power in society, with men being able to exercise economic, political and institutional power to a much greater extent than women.

Feminists have noted that the institution of marriage does not in many respects offer an opportunity to improve gender inequality. Women have in many cases to assume responsibility for the home and children, while also seeking to retain a role, however marginal, in the world of work. In the latter case, women often find themselves in underpaid roles with little responsibility, far below their intellectual and skill capacity. Some feminists have argued that the capitalist system encourages this differentiation in gender work roles, since married women provide, through the necessity of their other responsibilities, a source of labour for often unskilled and underpaid jobs. A combination of the demands of marriage, and a working husband, in effect prevents women from exercising their rights to further training and education, which would enable them to assume positions of authority and responsibility in the workplace.

Simone de Beauvoir (1908–86)

Simone de Beauvoir was a celebrated French philosopher, novelist and feminist who became particularly famous during the period after the Second World War. She has always been linked, both intellectually and emotionally, with the philosopher and political activist, Jean-Paul Sartre (1905–80). They met while students at the University of Paris, and famously agreed to a lifelong relationship, but one that would not necessarily exclude their forming other attachments. De Beauvoir was firmly opposed to the institution of marriage. When, as young teachers, Sartre proposed marriage in order that they could obtain teaching posts close to each other, de Beauvoir refused. She always felt that formal marriage, with all its responsibilities would stifle her ambition to be a writer.

Simone de Beauvoir had an illustrious career as an intellectual and writer. In 1954 she won the Prix Goncourt literary prize for her novel *The Mandarins*. She also founded, along with Sartre and others, the influential journal *Les Temps Modernes* (Modern Times). She was an activist for a number of political causes, meeting Fidel

Castro and Che Guevara in Cuba, and arguing against some of the actions of the French army during the war in Algeria. As a feminist she wrote the seminal work *Le deuxième sexe* (*The Second Sex*), which became a bestseller. An advocate for many feminist causes, she argued strongly, for example, for the right of women to choose an abortion.

Simone de Beauvoir and Jean-Paul Sartre were both leading figures in the post-war existentialist movement, which argued, among other things, that individuals are autonomous and should try to create their lives in the form that they would prefer. In a feminist sense, she pointed out that women do not have to adopt the lifestyle that society imposes upon them, but should try to mould their own lives, rejecting if necessary the socialization process. De Beauvoir has had a considerable influence on successive generations of feminists. She is buried in Montparnasse Cemetery, in central Paris, alongside Sartre.

Feminist theorists are not only interested in explaining gender inequalities, but in improving society in this regard. They point out that the marginalization and under-utilization of half of the population is enormously dysfunctional, and that many well-educated women who are trying to contribute at a high level in society are prevented through the operation of institutions such as marriage. Feminists also argue that women possess distinctive qualities as women, which can have a positive role in society, providing women are able to exercise them. For example, one might argue that a sense of conciliation and opposition to aggression and violence are qualities more represented in women, and which would be valuable across the political and economic arenas.

Feminist research has been typically committed to investigating the mechanisms whereby women have been unable to achieve their potential in society. To that extent feminism is a very practical approach to research, and to the acquisition of new social knowledge.

Phenomenology, on the other hand, is a more abstract and philosophical approach to research, which sets out general principles for investigating the social world. Its historical development is associated with the German philosopher Edmund Husserl (1859–1938). Arguably the principal concept of phenomenology is consciousness, and the manner in which this enables people to understand their own experiences of the world. Social research that employs the phenomenological approach is committed to detailed self-reflection upon our experiences. It is thus a subjective approach in the tradition of qualitative perspectives on research.

One distinctive aspect of phenomenological research is that it tries to set to one side the previous knowledge we possess about phenomena, whether theoretical or practical, and to concentrate on understanding our immediate reactions to phenomena. It is in that sense a very spontaneous approach to research, which tries to capture our reactions to the world just as they arise.

Dig deeper

Butler, J. (2006), *Gender Trouble: Feminism and the Subversion of Identity*. New York: Routledge.

Cochrane, K. (Ed.) (2010), *Women of the Revolution: Forty Years of Feminism*. London: Guardian Books.

De Beauvoir, S. (1997) (trans. H. M. Parshley), *The Second Sex*. London: Vintage.

Flynn, T. (2006), *Existentialism: A Very Short Introduction*. Oxford: Oxford University Press.

Gallagher, S. (2012), *Phenomenology*. Basingstoke: Palgrave Macmillan.

Test your knowledge

1 The process of applying a theory to a range of different situations is known as...?
  a application
  b generalization
  c situationalism
  d differentiation

2 The attempt to disprove a theory is known as...?
  a falsification
  b testing
  c data verification
  d validation

3 People committed to an ideology believe in it...?
  a partially
  b rarely
  c when it fits the evidence
  d unshakeably

4 Critical theory is associated with the...?
  a Berlin School
  b Heidelberg School
  c Frankfurt School
  d Paris School

5 Which of the following was *not* a member of the Critical Theory group?
  a Sartre
  b Horkheimer
  c Marcuse
  d Adorno

6 Symbolic interactionists argue that the social world is...?
  a permanent
  b scientific
  c objectifiable
  d a human construction

7 George Herbert Mead was a leading contributor to...?
- **a** Marxism
- **b** symbolic interactionism
- **c** objectivism
- **d** positivism

8 Husserl was a...?
- **a** functionalist
- **b** phenomenologist
- **c** social worker
- **d** psychiatrist

9 Antipositivism is a similar perspective to...?
- **a** solipsism
- **b** empiricism
- **c** functionalism
- **d** interpretivism

10 A dominant paradigm in society usually has the support of...?
- **a** a university professor
- **b** the political elite
- **c** students
- **d** the banks

3

Sociological research methods

A great deal of sociological research is conducted in order to both understand the nature of society and to have a platform upon which social policy decisions can be based. Some researchers favour the approaches of the physical sciences in that they try to measure social phenomena using precise data that can be subjected to statistical analysis. Other researchers adopt a different approach. They interview people, ask their opinions, and collect observational data. This more person-centred approach results in a great deal of written or recorded data that is interpreted by the researcher. With both approaches it is important to collect the data in an ethical way. This chapter will explore the two main approaches, and show you how you can use them in your own research.

Using the methods of the physical sciences within sociology

Sociology is an empirical subject. For it to grow and expand, it requires researchers to collect data and to then analyse that data. The resulting understanding of society adds to the sum total of sociological knowledge. The data collected by social researchers may derive from interviews, measurements, rating scales, observations and autobiographical accounts. In the early 19th century, when sociology was first developing as a subject, there was a feeling that the most appropriate research method to use was that employed in the physical sciences such as chemistry and physics. This philosophical position was known as 'positivism', and was developed by the French philosopher Auguste Comte (1798–1857).

The central claim of positivism was that the methods of the science laboratory could be used to advantage in investigating society. Thus in science, one researcher can measure the temperature of a liquid, or the electrical resistance of a wire, and the measurements can then be replicated by another scientist. The scientific method is seen as being objective and balanced. Émile Durkheim (1858–1917), a French sociologist who was much influenced by Comte's work, felt that society could be investigated in much the same precise, objective fashion.

Durkheim's view of society

Émile Durkheim was born in eastern France in the small town of Épinal in the region of the Vosges mountains. Épinal is probably best known for mass-produced pictures, which were first produced at printworks in the town in the 18th century. They showed often rural or traditional scenes using sharply defined printing inks. In French today, if something is spoken of as an 'image d'Épinal' then it refers to it as reflecting positive, traditional values. The printworks was founded in 1796, and Durkheim, born in 1858, would have been familiar with the prints.

Coincidental perhaps, but Durkheim was himself concerned throughout his life with the mechanisms by which traditional society could be held together. He saw the norms, values, habits and customs of people as welded together in a collective consciousness that would assure the cohesion of society. For Durkheim nothing was more important than maintaining this social solidarity. It is perhaps understandable that he took this position, given the uncertainty of his early life. In 1870, with the fall of the French Second Republic, Prussia annexed Alsace-Lorraine in eastern France. Durkheim was 13 years old when he lived through this traumatic event.

As he looked at society, Durkheim saw many examples of sweeping transformations in institutions and social customs. He was concerned with how stability could be maintained in the face of the dramatic changes resulting from the mass industrialization of Europe. Yet even in the final years of his life, he would not see the stability in society that he craved. In 1914 the First World War broke out, and the following year his son was killed in action. He was unable to overcome this personal loss and died two years later.

In Durkheim's view, society could be seen as being made up of a range of 'social facts', much as science employs a range of concepts such as temperature, electrical resistance, mass and volume. For Durkheim it would be possible to measure a social fact, such as social status, in a comparable way to a physicist measuring temperature. Of course we could not insert a measuring instrument into someone's mouth in order to measure their social status! However, there would be other methods at our disposal, such as interviewing the person, asking about their friends, discussing their job and pastimes, and visiting them in their home. Data collected in these ways could yield information on their social status.

For the positivists, the important issue was that social status as a concept was real, and existed as a measurable social fact. It could be investigated much as we investigate concepts such as mass and acceleration in physics. Within this sociological perspective, it was possible to state that one person's social status was higher than another person's, and even to attribute numerical values to the data. Thus one might claim that one person's status was twice or three times that of another person.

Key idea: Positivism

Positivism is the philosophical position that the methods of the physical or 'natural' sciences can be used to investigate society.

There are a number of advantages to this approach to sociological research. There is an apparent precision about the way in which data is collected and analysed. The numerical form in which analysed data is often presented makes it easy to construct comparisons. For example, organizations can be compared on the basis of their numerical evaluations. If we know that a score of 5 is excellent and 1 is poor, then we can very quickly appreciate that an organization with an overall evaluation of 4 is judged to be better than one with an evaluation of 3.

However, there can be a seductive simplicity about this kind of quantitative research. In a comparison between two organizations it can be easy to overemphasize the value of the quantitative data, and to attribute too much significance to the results. The factors influencing the performance of an organization may be very complex, and yet the performance is represented by a single number, which is used for comparisons with other organizations. Such a process is known as 'reductionism', since it reduces a complex set of features to a single number.

There remains the interesting issue of whether 'social facts' can truly be said to exist in the same way as 'facts' in the physical sciences. When we feel uncertain about the veracity or validity of a piece of information, we sometimes say it is conceptually or sociologically problematic. This means that the information or idea is so complex, and contains so many different nuances, that we feel uncertain about trying to measure it in a straightforward way.

The concept 'social status' is an example of this subtlety. The more we think about the concept, the more complex it seems to become. Some people may have high social status because they were born into a family that owned a lot of land, and possessed a large country house. They may even have had a title. Other people may have high social status because they have achieved a great deal in a particular field, and have become celebrated. Yet others may have performed a particularly courageous deed that has brought fame and status. The examples could go on... Not only do people acquire their social status in different ways but, once gained, that status may be demonstrated in very different ways. Some individuals may be regularly asked to appear on talk shows, while others may not be in the public eye.

The complexity of the concept of social status therefore makes it difficult to research, as if it were a concept like temperature. To collect quantitative data on social status as if the term were simple and straightforward would not do justice to the complexity of social life. One solution would be to define very carefully the precise type of social status we wished to investigate, and then collect quantitative data using a questionnaire or a rating scale. These would give us numerical data which could be analysed statistically.

The alternative would be to accept the problematic nature of the term 'social status', and to collect qualitative, verbal data that acknowledged this complexity. The data would be detailed and quite lengthy, but it would at least accept that the term is complex and that this complexity requires detailed analysis and discussion. This type of approach is discussed in the next section.

Using interpretive approaches within sociology

If we reject the idea that there exist precise and measurable social 'facts', then we have to concede the enormous complexity of the social world, and try to find new ways of investigating it. Under this social paradigm, we do not think of the world as consisting of 'facts' that are independent of human beings, but rather that human beings themselves make sense of the world in their own way. This approach is often known as 'interpretivism' because individuals interpret the world around them and decide for themselves how it appears to operate. The German sociologist Max Weber (1864–1920) was influential in describing the nature of interpretivism. He employed the term *verstehen* or 'understanding' to signify that the approach relied upon the understanding of individual people to make sense of human society.

The approach of interpretivism is sometimes termed 'antipositivism' because it relies not on social facts, but on the meanings that people attribute to the things that they observe around them. Most interpretive research concentrates on the collection of qualitative data – that is, data that is in the form of words rather than numbers. Such data may consist of interviews that have been tape-recorded and then written out as a manuscript; observations of groups of people that have been written up from a notebook; and life history or autobiographical accounts that have been constructed by an individual.

Key idea: Interpretivism

Interpretivism argues that if we are to understand society, then we must try to make sense of the way in which our fellow human beings look at the world.

An important aspect of interpretive research is that pre-eminence is given to the opinions of the respondents who are providing the data. If we interview someone about their understanding of social status, then it is their understanding which is important, not ours. We, as researchers, do not attempt to steer the respondent or interviewee in a particular direction. We simply ask them their opinion, and then record and analyse what they say. The interviewee is not the object of our research. The interviewee is the subject of the research, and it is their views that are of interest.

There is sometimes a confusion about the use of the terms 'empirical' and 'scientific'. 'Empirical data' is data that is gathered through the use of our senses. For everyday purposes this includes the data likely to be collected and used in both positivistic and interpretive research. Therefore the use of the term is not generally out of place when discussing either category of research.

The use of the term 'scientific' may be slightly more problematic. Some purist positivist researchers may feel that only positivism is truly scientific. Others will argue that positivism is involved in testing hypotheses in order to validate theories, whereas interpretivism is used primarily to generate theories. On this model, both positivism and interpretivism are 'scientific', but in a slightly different sense.

The positivist approach to collecting data

In positivistic research the commonest type of data collection instrument is the questionnaire. Other types include rating scales and psychometric tests. There are many different kinds of question that can be used in a questionnaire. The multiple choice question is a common type. An example is as follows:

Please rate the study facilities in the university library, by ticking one alternative only:

1 Excellent

2 Good

3 Satisfactory

4 Inadequate

If this question were given to a sample of students, then the number of ticks given to each option could be used as part of a statistical analysis. On a basic level, we could count the number of students who ticked 'Excellent', the number who ticked 'Good' and so on. If we had also asked a question about gender, then we could compute the number of males and females separately who ticked 'Satisfactory' and the number of males and females who ticked 'Inadequate'. This would not tell us anything very definite about gender differences in attitudes to the library, but it might give us initial clues.

There are both advantages and disadvantages of this type of question. On the positive side, the question could be given to a large number of respondents if necessary and it is relatively easy to add up all the responses. Once all the questionnaires have been analysed the researcher is left with some clear numerical data as a basis for drawing conclusions.

However, this precision can be a little deceptive. When they are responding to the question, one student may think that the range of books is 'excellent', but that the range of audio-visual material is 'inadequate'. Another student may think that the range of academic journals is 'good', but that the number of computers in the library is only 'satisfactory'. It will be difficult for such students to decide how to respond.

The problem is that in drawing up the questionnaire, the researcher has summarized the library facilities into four categories, when really the issue is more complex. When a researcher summarizes an issue in this way, it is sometimes called 'reductionism', since it reduces or oversimplifies the nature of the issue. However, in many research situations this kind of simplification can be advantageous.

One of the concerns about positivist research is that the research process, including the way the data is collected, can easily reflect the ideology of the researcher. This can reduce the impartiality of the research. As Gray writes:

'Questionnaires reflect the designer's view of the world, no matter how objective a researcher tries to be. This is true not only for the design of individual questions, but often about the very choice of research subject.'
Gray, David (2004), *Doing Research in the Real World* (p. 189).

If we are interested in the broad trends in society, it may be helpful to employ this kind of positivist approach, in order to be able to summarize an issue for general consumption. On the other hand, if we want to understand the deeper feelings people have about an issue, or the complexities of their thinking about something, then we need to employ an interpretive approach.

Interpretive techniques for collecting data

The most common interpretive approach to collecting data is probably the interview. An interview can consist of a series of highly structured questions, but this is tending towards a positivistic approach. In interpretive research, the interview tends to be rather 'open' and unstructured. The researcher simply raises an issue with the respondent, and leaves them to discuss it as they see fit. The researcher or interviewer may prompt the respondent here and there, but does not normally try to direct them very much. The researcher tries to encourage the respondent to reveal their feelings, and to talk freely. The interview is usually tape-recorded, if the respondent is in agreement, and then transcribed into text later.

The amount of data produced in this way can be quite considerable. Even a ten-minute interview can generate a large amount of transcribed data. This is in contrast to ticks in boxes for positivist research. Interview transcripts can be time-consuming to analyse, and we will deal with this issue later in the chapter. Other types of interpretive data collection include participant observation and life history research.

If you are interested in studying a distinct group of people or a community, then participant observation may be appropriate. In this approach the researcher will first need to be accepted as a member of the group, or as a 'participant'.

Did you know?

When ethnographers are studying social groups that are 'deviant' in some way, for example operating outside the law, this can pose particular problems. When using participant observation to study a criminal gang or subculture, the sociologists could easily find themselves drawn into illegal activities! Moreover, it may not be easy to extricate themselves from the research field when they have finished collecting data. Careful thought should be given to this before the research starts.

The researcher will also need to obtain permission to collect the type of data that they want. This process can raise a number of ethical issues, which we will discuss later. Having obtained the relevant permission, the researcher would then take notes or maintain an audio or video record as appropriate. As with interviews, the analysis of the data can be time-consuming. Obtaining introductions to people who will help the researcher become familiar with the research context is sometimes not easy. As Flick points out:

> 'Another problem is how to access the field or the studied subculture. In order to solve this, key persons are sometimes used who introduce the researchers and make contacts for them.'
> Flick, Uwe (2006), *An Introduction to Qualitative Research* (p. 222).

Life history research, as the term suggests, involves encouraging an individual respondent to relate key elements of their life, so that this can be used as research data. The data may take the form of informal interviews, documentary data and photographs. Once again, the data analysis process can be complicated and time-consuming.

One of the commonest interpretive research approaches is ethnography. To some extent this approach developed from anthropology and its tradition of studying communities and societies in other countries.

Did you know?

In order to study overseas cultures early anthropologists used to rely upon artefacts such as carvings, weapons or utensils that had been removed to Europe. They often had not visited the society or country itself. However, they gradually realized that as researchers they needed to have an intimate contact with a society in order to understand it.

Anthropologists learned the importance of living in close proximity with the community being studied, and where possible learning the language. Anthropologists developed research techniques that were similar to what we now recognize as 'participant observation'. It was realized by sociologists that these methods could be used to investigate communities nearer home, such as a cultural group, an ethnic group, a school community or the people who worked in a department of a large organization. This approach became known as 'ethnography' or 'ethnographic research'. It adopted a range of methods including interviews and life history research. Importantly, though, all ethnographic research is characterized by attaching primary importance to the viewpoint of the respondents.

> **Key idea:** Ethnography
>
> Ethnography is a research approach used to study distinct communities or social groups, and to try to understand the meanings people attach to the social world.

Questions of sampling

When you are conducting research it is rarely possible to collect data from absolutely everyone in the group you are studying, i.e. the 'research population'. In a few cases it may be possible. For example, if you wanted to collect data from all primary school headteachers in England, it would be theoretically possible to obtain their addresses and send each a questionnaire. In many cases, however, the population might be very large, and you may not be able to contact them all. In such a case you would have to limit your data collection to a proportion or sample of the population. How you draw that sample is very important, because the process could introduce bias into the research. The ultimate purpose of the sampling process is to be able to form a judgement about the nature of the entire population, based only upon the sample.

In positivist research this estimate is made using the analytic processes of statistics, and for the process to have any validity the sample has to be obtained using a 'probability sample'. This is a sample in which each item in the population has a known chance of being included in the sample. The basic type of probability sample is a simple random sample. An example of a random sampling process would be to have, say, 100 numbered balls and to decide that you want a sample of 20. Computerized random number generators are available that would produce 20 numbers at random between 1 and 100. These would then constitute your sample.

In qualitative or interpretive research statistical analysis is not employed, and hence a probability sample is not needed. Most interpretive research manages with much smaller samples than quantitative research. This is partly a practical matter as it would be too time-consuming to conduct large numbers of interviews. In addition however, qualitative research sets out to explore the deeper, more detailed thoughts of respondents, and this takes considerable time. Such research is difficult to achieve with larger samples.

It is very often the case that interpretive research requires respondents with certain characteristics. For example, in a study of the issues that arise for employees when starting a new job it would clearly be useful to have in the sample individuals who have started a new job recently. Therefore a special attempt would be made to locate people in this category. Such a sample is known as a 'purposive sample'. It is usually composed of individuals selected according to previously determined criteria.

It would probably not be too difficult to identify people who had changed job recently or started a new career, but sometimes sociologists are faced with a research study where it is very difficult to identify respondents. For example, suppose you wanted to do an interpretive study of body builders who used steroids, in order to examine the reasons for taking them. Body builders who take steroids may not be willing to admit that they do so, and hence identifying a sample of respondents to interview could be difficult. When researchers are confronted by such a problem, they often use a technique known as 'snowball sampling'. They would first identify one person who uses steroids, and then ask that person to put them into contact with someone else who does the same. As each person was interviewed, they would then ask for a further contact, and so on. Hopefully this would enable the researcher to contact a sample of sufficient size.

Did you know?

Sociological research can sometimes raise complex moral and legal problems. For example, if research is being conducted on any kind of illegal drug taking, then the issue may arise of whether the police should be informed. Before such research commences it would be necessary to discuss it with colleagues or an ethics committee, in order to determine the most appropriate course of action.

The analysis of data

Quantitative data obtained from questionnaires or from another form of numerical data is usually analysed statistically. A 'descriptive analysis' is where the data is summarized in some way to make it easier to understand. For example, the researcher might draw a histogram, from which it would be easier to understand the general trend of the data.

An 'inferential analysis' is where the researcher has data from a sample of, say, university students and wants to generalize to all university students in the country. Both types of analysis can be performed using a computer program such as the Statistical Package for the Social Sciences (SPSS). However, with such a program it is important to input the data correctly, and to be able to understand the results that are generated. In other words, the results from such software need to be interpreted, and this requires an understanding of statistical methods.

Key idea: Inferential statistics

Inferential statistics do not tell us 'facts' about the world. They only give us the probability that certain variables are connected.

Data obtained from interpretive research requires a different analytic approach. One of the commonest approaches is known as grounded theory analysis (Glaser and Strauss, 1967). The purpose of this method is to seek patterns in the qualitative data, and integrate these patterns into a theory. This theory can then be subsequently tested for validity, by collecting and analysing more data.

On this model even data on the most apparently mundane of research topics can generate social theory. For example, supposing researchers collect observational and interview data on the way street cleaners appear to structure their working day. The cleaners explain in interview that they each have a greater allocation of streets to clean than is possible in a single day. They thus have to make choices about which streets to clean and which to leave. Observations by the researchers suggest that other things being equal, the cleaners will give priority to the dirtiest streets, and also to the residential streets rather than those with factories or large office blocks. When interviewed about this the cleaners pointed out that if their managers observed one dirty street made completely clean, this conveyed a much more favourable impression than cleaning several streets by picking up isolated pieces of litter. Second, if they cleaned residential streets really well, then they often received positive feedback from the residents at the city cleansing department. The researchers thus developed a theory that the cleaners were prioritizing in their work those jobs that were likely to elicit positive comments from either the public or their supervisors.

The researchers sought supporting evidence for their theory with cleaners in a different part of the city, and obtained similar results. They then tested their theory with horticulture workers from the city parks and gardens department, and found that they generally cut lawns and weeded flowerbeds wherever they felt this would have the greatest impact and solicit the most praise from managers and the public. The researchers continued to test their theory with other groups of city workers to explore aspects of their motivation.

We can thus see that this theory is 'grounded' in the data that was collected, and has emerged by careful observation, analysis and testing. On the grounded theory model, a theory is never 'proven' in any absolute sense. It is only provisionally accepted as valid as long as any new data collected appears to fit it. If the theory fails to explain new data, then the theory must be adapted and re-phrased. In short then, no social science theory can be said to be 'true'. It can only be said to reflect existing data, until it is 'falsified' by some new contrary data.

> **Key idea:** Grounded theory
>
> Grounded theory is a process of generating theory from qualitative data. Such a theory should not be accepted absolutely, but should be tested against new emerging data.

Social research ethics

When people offer to help with a research study, and to act as respondents or interviewees, they may sometimes later regret taking part. They may feel they have spoken too freely about a sensitive issue; they may worry that they have been too outspoken about someone they know; or they may later worry about how the results of the research will be disseminated, and whether they themselves will be named in the research report.

It is very important that those who help with research are treated fairly, and that they know the exact nature of the research before they become involved. This entire issue about the way in which respondents are treated is generally known as 'research ethics'. One of the most important principles in social research is that the respondents should not be harmed either psychologically or physically through their participation in the research study. One of the ways in which this is assured is by researchers adhering to the principle of 'informed consent'.

This is an important ethical principle, and asserts that before someone agrees to take part in a research study they should be provided with all the relevant information to help them decide whether they wish to participate. They should be informed about the nature and purpose of the study in terms they can understand; the data collection process should be explained along with their role; it should be made clear that a respondent can opt to leave the study at any time; the total time commitment should be explained, along with the means of dissemination of the research study findings. In other words, absolutely everything that the respondent needs to understand, in order to make an informed decision, should be explained before they commit to the research. In addition, as Aldridge and Levine argue:

'We should make it easy for respondents to raise any queries they may have. In some cases it may be desirable to give the name of a responsible person whom they can contact if they want to verify who we are and the nature of our research.'

Aldridge, Alan & Levine, Ken (2001), *Surveying the Social World: Principles and Practice in Survey Research* (p. 22).

The potential participant should definitely be told who will have access to the data collected. It should also be made clear where, and for how long, the data will be stored. This is the principle of confidentiality. The research team should not make any promises in this regard unless they are sure they can keep them. Finally, the research team should make clear to the prospective respondent whether his or her real name will appear in the research data or final research report. The normal convention is that the names of respondents are anonymized in some way to protect their identity. In any case, the process for assuring anonymity should be explained to all prospective participants as part of the informed consent procedure.

Procedures for research ethics are taken very seriously by social science researchers, and nowadays research studies by reputable organizations are not normally approved unless they address ethical issues adequately.

The methods used by sociologists to explore the social world constitute an important and interesting branch of the subject, and it has become so important that it is almost now a separate academic discipline in itself.

Dig deeper

Bryman, A. (2012), *Social Research Methods* (4th ed.). Oxford: Oxford University Press.

Corbin, J. & Strauss, A. (2008), *Basics of Qualitative Research* (3rd ed.). London: Sage.

Gorard, S. (2013), *Research Design: Creating Robust Approaches for the Social Sciences*. London: Sage.

Jupp, V. (Ed.) (2006), *The SAGE Dictionary of Social Research Methods*. London: Sage.

Matthews, B. & Ross, L. (2010), *Research Methods: A practical guide for the social sciences*. Harlow: Pearson.

Oliver, P. (2010), *The Student's Guide to Research Ethics* (2nd ed.). Maidenhead: Open University Press.

Test your knowledge

1 Positivism is the research approach which argues that...?
   a ...researchers need to be enthusiastic about their subject.
   b ...the methods of the physical sciences can be used in sociological research.
   c ...researchers do not like negative mathematical values.
   d ...the use of three + signs helps to solve algebraic equations.

2 Quantitative research aims to...?
   a ...collect data in the form of numerical measurements.
   b ...collect large quantities of data.
   c ...carry out a survey on a very small sample.
   d ...collect small quantities of data.

3 Interpretive research involves...?
   a ...interpreting research using statistical tests.
   b ...analysing future trends in research.
   c ...judging the best sociological theory to employ.
   d ...analysing the meanings that people attach to the social world.

4 Empirical data is data which is...?
   a ...statistical in nature.
   b ...generated in a science laboratory.
   c ...collected through the use of our senses.
   d ...produced through mental reflection.

5 Name two data collection methods commonly used in ethnography.
   a participant observation and interviews
   b statistics and interviews
   c life history research and large-scale surveys
   d surveys and statistics

6 A simple random sample is an example of...?
   a a probability sample
   b a purposive sample
   c a non-probability sample
   d a snowball sample

7 Grounded theory analysis is used to...?

    a ...analyse statistical data.

    b ...analyse social science hypotheses.

    c ...analyse scientific arguments.

    d ...analyse interpretive data.

8 Informed consent is...?

    a ...a principle in research ethics.

    b ...being told how to take measurements.

    c ...using computer statistics packages.

    d ...agreeing to a research method.

9 What does SPSS stand for?

    a Social Previews in a Sociological Survey

    b Statistical Package for the Social Sciences

    c Statistics and Progression in a Sociological Survey

    d Statistics Professionals in Social Sciences

10 A snowball sample is used when...?

    a ...the sample is quantitative.

    b ...the sample is very large.

    c ...respondents for a sample are difficult to identify.

    d ...the sample is larger than the population.

Part Two

The Social Environment

4

Urban and rural contexts

Chapter 4 will explore some of the differences between urban and rural environments, and the historical factors that have led to industrial urbanization and a commensurate movement of population from the countryside. In urban contexts such issues as poverty, unemployment and the interface between different ethnic and cultural groups will be analysed. In addition, the gentrification of inner-city areas, and the consequences will be evaluated. An examination of the rural context will involve an analysis of the level of cohesion of rural communities, and of opportunities especially for young people.

The Industrial Revolution

Prior to the early to mid-18th century, Europe and America consisted of largely agrarian societies. People lived in villages or small towns, and were employed in occupations directly or indirectly related to agriculture. Such technology as existed generally consisted of cottage industries. Such activities as spinning, weaving and small-scale iron smelting took place in workshops attached to the home, or in the home itself. Entrepreneurs who could obtain contracts for, say, the production of cloth, would distribute the work on a sub-contracting process. This system of employment enabled home workers to maintain their agricultural work, while fitting in manufacturing work when the opportunity allowed.

Key idea: The Industrial Revolution

The Industrial Revolution consisted of a series of technological advances from the mid-18th century onwards, which resulted in the mechanization of manufacturing industry in Europe and America.

However, the pay was very poor, and the nature of the manufacturing process such that it was difficult for workers to increase their productivity. The income of a typical working family was low. Rural cottages were damp and cramped, and malnutrition widespread. Cottage industries relied upon water-wheels as a source of energy for such activities as the grinding of corn. Where heat was required for the manufacture of farm tools, then charcoal was employed. Rural life expectancy was low, rarely exceeding about 35 years.

In the early 18th century, however, a number of technological advances and inventions combined to change this rural lifestyle. The first industry to experience widespread changes in working practices was the production of textiles. Richard Arkwright (1732–92) patented a spinning frame that enabled raw cotton to be spun into cotton thread through a mechanized process. More significantly, however, Arkwright realized the advantages of centralizing the location of his spinning machines, and importing workers to live close to the new factories. Workers were attracted by the prospect of regular work, and it was normal for all members of a family, including children, to be employed in the factories. Hours of work were very long, and the work hard. In the early stages of industrialization, the transition from rural to urban life did not result in an improved quality of life. Children were required to do very dangerous work, such as crawling under fast-moving machinery to collect cotton waste. In the northern areas of England, the growth of the urban infrastructure could not keep pace with the influx of population.

Most of the early factories were powered by water wheels, which limited the location of manufacturing to places where there were fast-flowing streams. Rivers tended to reduce in volume during the summer, and hence although water power was inexpensive, it was unreliable. The invention in 1712 by Thomas Newcomen (1664–1729) of an effective steam engine transformed the energy requirements of the new factories.

By 1778, Newcomen's steam engine had been brought to further levels of sophistication by James Watt (1736–1819). The steam engine ensured that factories could function throughout the year, and they also generated more power. Significantly, in terms of energy requirements at least, there was no longer the necessity to locate factories near a river. Entrepreneurs could build factories near to a ready supply of labour, which further encouraged the rapidly expanding urbanization. Coal was needed to power steam engines, which were useful in operating the pumps needed to keep deep coal mines clear of water. There was thus a symbiotic relationship between the key developments which characterized the growing industrialization.

In England most of the coal deposits were located in the north of the country, which tended to encourage the development of heavy industry in those areas. This difference in employment patterns between the north and the south of the country, created a range of social and economic differentiation which has persisted in various forms to this day.

There has always been the fear that different forms of energy would either prove unreliable, or too expensive. This has been true of newer developments in energy production since the Second World War. As Yearley argues:

'In the 1950s and 1960s it was hoped that nuclear power generated from uranium would replace that from fossil fuels; however, as it turned out, nuclear power was also very expensive once the costs of waste disposal and decommissioning were taken into account.'

Yearley, Steven (1992), 'Environmental Challenges' (p. 129).

Key idea: Urbanization

Urbanization is the movement of people from the countryside to large metropolitan areas. It is associated with a transition from agrarian employment to work in manufacturing industry.

Another major industrial development was the ability to manufacture steel that could be used for the construction of railways, bridges and weaponry. In 1855 Henry Bessemer (1813–98) took out a patent for the so-called 'Bessemer Converter', which was able to manufacture steel from pig iron by passing pressurized air through the molten metal in order to oxidize and hence remove the impurities in the iron.

As cities expanded in England in the early 19th century, conditions worsened considerably for the working classes. Child labour was a widespread phenomenon, and the pollution caused by the new industrial processes was extensive. Living conditions for workers were very bad, giving rise to the spread of infectious diseases such as smallpox and typhoid. These conditions were documented through the research of a young German social philosopher Friedrich Engels (1820–95), who had been sent by his father to work at a cotton mill he owned in Manchester.

During this period Manchester epitomized the typical social problems created by the Industrial Revolution in an urban context. Engels wrote up his research and published it in 1845 as *The Condition of the Working Class in England*. For most of his life, Engels was a close colleague of Karl Marx, and at times supported Marx financially. The researches of Engels suggested to him that the living conditions of working people were significantly worse during the period of early capitalism than they had been prior to the Industrial Revolution.

Did you know?

Engels moved to Manchester at the age of 22, but he was already familiar with some of the consequences of factory work and the industrial revolution in Germany. Nevertheless, he was appalled at the conditions under which working people existed in Manchester. Engels had become a committed socialist while in Germany, and shortly after arriving in Manchester he met a young lady named Mary Burns who felt as he did about social issues. They remained a couple until her death, but they never married as they felt that marriage was a bourgeois institution. Mary showed Engels around the working-class areas of Manchester so that he could gather data for his research on working conditions. In Manchester, Engels led two separate lives. On the one hand he lived the life of a rich young industrialist from a well-to-do family; on the other, he was existing as a socialist radical, writing for left-wing publications and challenging the capitalist system.

The development of urbanization

There were clear distinctions to be made between the social existence of people in a rural environment prior to industrialization, and that of an industrial urban context. In a rural context, although there were often shortages of food and material goods, this was compensated by a strong sense of community in which people would offer mutual support wherever possible. When people moved to the cities this sense of community was quickly lost. People lived in very close proximity, often with those from different areas and traditional occupational groupings. The welfare of the individual person or individual family became paramount, and the social and ethical bonds that had tied people together in the rural lifestyle were largely broken.

The German sociologist Ferdinand Tönnies (1855–1936) provided a theoretical basis to such developments. He described two fundamentally different types of social structure, which reflected to a degree the pre-industrial rural society and the post-industrial society of Europe. The two types of society described by Tönnies were *Gemeinschaft* and *Gesellschaft*.

Gemeinschaft referred to a society that had a high degree of social cohesion and was characterized by communities in which people collaborated, helped each other where necessary and had a sense of empathy for each other's problems and difficulties. In such a community there would typically be a strong sense of shared ethics and values, and an appreciation of how people should typically behave in such a community. The norms and values of the community were learned, often in childhood, through a process of socialization. People understood these values and tried to adhere to them on the understanding that they were important for the cohesion of society. Such norms were often unspoken, and yet well understood. This theoretical construct of Tönnies is typical of the rural, pre-industrial communities of Europe.

Gesellschaft, on the other hand, is the type of community typified by an industrial society in which each individual is working for themselves, and the relationships between people are a function largely of pragmatic connections that mutually benefit each person's economic success. In a society such as this, relationships are not controlled by moral values and norms as in a typical rural society, but by legal-bureaucratic rules that are enforceable by law and the judiciary.

Key idea: *Gesellschaft*

Gesellschaft is a type of society described by Tönnies that is typical of urban life, and in which each individual tends to be preoccupied with their own employment and economic progress within the society.

The different types of community can exist, however, within the same city environment. When rural workers migrated to the city they would very often try to obtain accommodation in the same area, in order to sustain their sense of community. These areas were often in the inner area of the city, where inexpensive housing was available, and which was very often located close to the factories providing work. Wealthier, professional families would frequently relocate to the outer suburbs, where they tended to live more individualistic lives, without the sense of community and cohesion manifested by the industrial workers of the inner city.

Such a pattern of life in large cities was first described by the Chicago sociologist Ernest Burgess (1886–1966). His theoretical framework was described as the Concentric Zone Model, and postulated a series of concentric areas within large cities, each with a different pattern of settlement and employment. His model did not apply to all cities, but it proposed a general framework that was of general applicability.

He argued that the central zone of a typical large city was given over to the offices of large business corporations such as banks, insurance companies and the head offices of major companies. Residents of the outer suburbs had the financial resources to commute into this zone for work. Moving outwards from the centre the next zone consisted of shops, factories and a range of inexpensive accommodation for working people who liked to live very close to their place of work. In this zone there would be large factories and manufacturing centres, infrastructural centres such as bus terminals, and grand but decaying houses that formerly belonged to those people who had since migrated to the outer suburbs.

Moving outwards again would be a large zone occupied primarily by large-scale working-class housing such as terrace houses, or in more recent times, tower blocks of apartments. This accommodation was sufficiently close to the factories in the inner area of the city. Moving outwards again would be the suburban housing in leafy suburbs, typically consisting of semi-detached houses on estates, and with sufficient transport networks to enable people to commute to the central city area. Finally, the extreme outer zone would be occupied by very wealthy families, whose members were employed in the large corporations in the city centre.

Key idea: Concentric Zone Model

The Concentric Zone Model is a theoretical perspective of the structure of a large city, which sees the offices and factories located nearer the centre of a city with various types of housing arranged in concentric circles around the exterior.

Of course, large cities are very flexible entities that evolve and change according to economic and social pressures. In some cities, middle-class families from the suburbs have moved back into inner city areas, and sought to renovate older properties. Such social movement has been termed 'gentrification'. It has led sometimes to working-class families moving outwards to the suburbs, and slowly relinquishing the inner city. The gentrified areas are typically characterized by the opening of small chic boutiques, coffee shops, specialized food shops, fashionable bars and the conversion of former factories and dilapidated housing into contemporary apartments and renovated houses. People who move into such gentrified areas are often attracted by the vibrant atmosphere and excitement of the inner city.

Key idea: Gentrification

Gentrification is the gradual restoration of inner-city, working-class housing by middle-class residents, accompanied by an often parallel movement of former working-class residents to suburban areas.

Did you know?

Once the Second World War had ended, some of those who had survived six years of danger and austerity wanted an exciting life. They wanted access to cinemas, theatres, jazz clubs, concerts, art galleries, and every conceivable type of cultural experience. These were available in the centres of large cities, but not in the suburbs. Therefore those who could afford it moved nearer to city centres and renovated houses and apartments. In some cases this forced up housing prices and prevented traditional residents from buying a property in these 'gentrified' areas.

A different distinction between pre- and post-industrial societies was outlined by Émile Durkheim, who focused upon the way in which employment was structured in the two societies, and the manner in which employment patterns led to forms of social cohesion.

Durkheim described a rural, pre-industrial society as manifesting 'mechanical solidarity'. By this he meant that in such a society many people worked in a similar type of employment, and hence had shared values. For example, when people are working in agriculture they share a sense of working in harmony with the seasons, and of carrying out certain activities such as planting and harvesting at specific times of the year. They appreciate the importance of weather patterns, and of taking this into account when determining work priorities. This shared understanding of the cyclical nature of agriculture helps to develop a set of norms that encourage cohesion in society.

'Organic solidarity' on the other hand, argued Durkheim, is the type of cohesion typified by an industrial society. In such a society there is considerable differentiation in the type of work conducted by people. Yet all these different types of work are functionally related, in the sense that a person in one type of work cannot function effectively without the support of workers in other types of work. The textile worker, for example, needs the coal provided by the miner in order to provide energy for the power looms. Equally, the textile worker provides cloth for the clothes of the steel worker, who in turn provides steel for the railways, which help transport some textiles for export. In other words, all of these different roles are interdependent, helping to generate a sense of cooperation between these different types of employment.

Many of the features of urban life outlined by Tönnies, Burgess and Durkheim can be recognized in modern and indeed postmodern urban environments. Modern cities are typically characterized by differentiation and diversity with regard to many aspects of their society. Migration to the cities has created multi-ethnic, multi-faith and multi-national groupings that may range from being introspective to being well integrated with other social groups. Some social groups may work in distinctive forms of employment, while others may, through their educational attainment, have moved into a range of professional roles. Indeed, urban environments are typified by the availability of educational opportunities, which open the possibility of society becoming meritocratic, and of young people having the possibility of rapid upward social mobility.

Cities are also typified by the latest developments in computing and electronic communication, which can give employment opportunities to young people. Indeed, the leading developments in contemporary cities arguably derive less from the manipulation of labour and capital, than from the manipulation of knowledge and its applications. As Allen has argued:

'On this account, the principal opposition between social classes does not stem from the ownership and control of private property, but from access to information and its uses.'
Allen, John (1992), 'Post-industrialism and Post-Fordism' (p. 175).

Equally, these developments help to create diverse types of employment, which open up career opportunities.

The wide variety of employment prospects in a city environment has a number of consequences for social life. People can establish employment-based networks that are constructed around the career patterns of individuals. These networks can create communities with a sense of belonging, not unlike the traditional kind of community found in rural settings. It can be argued that relationships within the city are often transitory and formal, although within such work-based networks this need not necessarily be so.

A diversity of career prospects also increases the possibility of physical mobility either within a single city, or between cities. There are far more opportunities for changing jobs, diversifying careers, or totally changing employment trajectory. It has also been argued that within the city environment people may act in a more individual manner, being preoccupied with their own interests and needs, although the existence of the types of networks outlined above may ameliorate this tendency.

One of the leading sociologists of urban social development was the American Louis Wirth (1897–1952). Wirth was originally from Germany, but migrated to live with relatives in the United States. He was of Jewish ethnicity and much of his early research involved analysing how rural German-Jewish emigrants to the United States succeeded in settling in dense urban areas such as Chicago.

The professional life of Louis Wirth

Many professional sociologists seek to progress their careers by researching in their chosen branch of the discipline, and then writing and publishing their findings in academic journals. While Louis Wirth did this, and indeed did it very well, he also had a broader ambition for himself and for the academic sociologist in general. He was very keen that the sociologist should not be exclusively a scholar, but should employ sociological knowledge for the benefit of humanity. This belief drew him into a wide range of different fields, including social work, housing provision, ethnic relations and the planning of cities. He also tried to contribute as much as possible to the administration and leadership of the profession of sociology, achieving among other roles that of the presidency of the American Sociological Association. He viewed the city as arguably the most significant facet of contemporary life, and as indicated in the quotation below, viewed it as a great influence over the nature of modern existence.

Wirth argued that:

> 'The influences which cities exert upon the social life of man are greater than the ratio of the urban population would indicate, for the city is not only in ever greater degrees the dwelling-place and the workshop of modern man, but it is the initiating and controlling centre of economic, political, and cultural life that has drawn the most remote parts of the world into its orbit and woven diverse areas, peoples, and activities into a cosmos.'
>
> Wirth, Louis (1938), 'Urbanism as a way of life' (p. 2).

He took a balanced perspective in respect of the modern city, and its advantages and disadvantages. In terms of negative features he was concerned about the way in which family relationships were brought under pressure by modern city life. He also noted the existence of racial discrimination, particularly in relation to immigrant groups.

On the more positive side, Wirth was aware that the sheer diversity of city life often encouraged freedom, creativity and many other facets of life that are loosely referred to as part of 'civilization'. He thus saw urbanization as an almost inevitable part of modern industrial and commercial life, and one that created a culture generally supportive of human development.

Dig deeper

Crump, T. (2010), *A Brief History of How the Industrial Revolution Changed the World*. London: Constable & Robinson.

Griffin, E. (2010), *A Short History of the British Industrial Revolution*. Basingstoke: Palgrave Macmillan.

King, S. & Timmins, G. (2001), *Making Sense of the Industrial Revolution*. Manchester: Manchester University Press.

Lees, L., Slater, T. & Wyly, E. (2008), *Gentrification*. Abingdon, Oxon: Routledge.

Tönnies, F. (ed. and trans. Loomis, C. P.) (2002), *Community and Society*. Mineola, NY: Dover.

Test your knowledge

1 The Industrial Revolution started in the...?
  a 20th century
  b 18th century
  c 17th century
  d Middle Ages

2 Thomas Newcomen was associated with harnessing...?
  a steam power
  b wind power
  c water power
  d wave power

3 Henry Bessemer developed a process for manufacturing...?
  a pig iron
  b alloys
  c aluminium
  d steel

4 The concepts of *Gemeinschaft* and *Gesellschaft* were developed by...?
  a Engels
  b Durkheim
  c Tönnies
  d Marx

5 Ernest Burgess articulated a model of urban development known as...?
  a the Industrial Model
  b the Suburban Model
  c the Social Development Model
  d the Concentric Zone Model

6 The renovation of working-class urban areas by the influx of capital is termed...?
  a gentrification
  b affluence
  c restitution
  d urban empathy

7 Louis Wirth carried out research on?
   a German-Jewish migration
   b industry in San Francisco
   c the Detroit car industry
   d the oil industry in Alaska

8 The concepts of mechanical and organic solidarity were developed by...?
   a Marx
   b Engels
   c Weber
   d Durkheim

9 In his early life Engels carried out research on the working class in which city?
   a Luton
   b Manchester
   c Bristol
   d Munich

10 Richard Arkwright developed a more efficient method of...?
   a generating electricity
   b smelting copper
   c spinning cotton
   d coal mining

5

Social and work organizations

This chapter will examine the nature of organizations in society, and particularly the nature of employment in organizations. There will be an analysis of the nature of hierarchies, and of the mechanisms and processes by which individuals can exercise mobility within them. The chapter will compare formally structured organizations with the informal organizations that evolve within them. The nature and purpose of such informal organizations will be analysed, along with a discussion of the autonomy and freedom that can exist for individuals within bureaucratic structures.

Organizations and society

An organization consists of a number of people who interact because of shared interests or for the achievement of clearly defined goals. Most organizations are connected in some way with the broader society in which they exist. Such a connection may be relatively minor and unstructured, or it may consist of strictly defined interactions that are regulated by a range of rules and conditions. A local sports club, for example, may have relatively modest aims and only a small number of officials, yet may be connected with the national or international body of that sport. On the other hand, a large multinational business conglomerate will have a complex hierarchy of job roles, and precisely defined aims. Such a company will have a range of relationships with the wider society, including the procurement of resources and the marketing and sale of the products it manufactures.

One of the interesting features of organizations is that almost irrespective of the changes in membership or personnel they largely seem able to continue their key roles and functions. There may be some changes when a key person leaves or retires, but generally things do not normally fall apart. Part of the reason for this general optimism is that organizations are usually perceived as consisting of a number of integrated systems and role functions, often linked in a hierarchical model. If one or two people leave, even if they are very important, the majority of the organizational system can continue in its normal functioning. Not only is this true internally to the organization, but usually also between the organization and the structures of the broader society. Thus if a company which supplies raw materials to a corporation becomes bankrupt, then the relevant employee in the corporation will usually be able to locate a different supplier.

An analogy is often proposed here between an organization and a living organism that exists within its own environment or ecosystem. Just as living organisms exist in equilibrium with their particular microclimate, so organizations are seen to have evolved as part of the society in which they exist. Some organizational systems are described as 'closed' in that they are relatively independent of the surrounding society; while those that are well integrated with society are often described as 'open'.

Key idea: Closed system

A closed system or organization is one that has relatively little interaction with the surrounding society, or with other organizations.

It is probably inaccurate to make a rigid distinction between an 'open' and a 'closed' system or organization. It is more appropriate to think of them existing on a continuum, where an organization is *more* open or *more* closed in relation to another organization.

One of the leading advocates of an open system perspective in relation to organizations was the Harvard sociologist Talcott Parsons (1902–79). Parsons analysed a number of ways in which an organization may be related to the broader society. He pointed out, for example, that organizations will very often reflect the norms, values and ethics of society. In the case of a capitalist society, for instance, relatively few organizations will challenge the prevailing value system of the profit motive. However, from time to time some organizations, such as religious bodies, do draw attention to the effects of capitalism on the less-fortunate members of society. It is also worth noting that organizations that espouse and support the values of society will, very often, receive economic support from other institutions commensurate with the level of their initial support. For example, a university which is at the forefront of research in new technology, particularly technology that has high economic value, may well receive grants that enable it to carry out further research in this area.

Parsons, like Durkheim, was an advocate of the functionalist perspective, which saw individuals as contributing to the essential stability of society. This is not to say that society is continually stable. Events such as wars or natural disasters often conspire to destabilize society, but human beings tend to work to recreate the former stability. One of the principal methods for achieving stability is the socialization of human beings. The socialization process tends to encourage individuals towards the type of behaviour which will encourage societal stability. For example, we encourage our children to be honest and to tell the truth, a behaviour pattern that encourages a sense of cohesion in society. If the contrary occurred, and children were reared to lie regularly, then this would be dysfunctional to stability in society.

The same functionalist principle could be argued to exist in organizations, where employees or organizational members are socialized into the values of that organization. For instance, an organization may espouse a set of ethical principles when conducting business, and new employees may be inducted into these principles when joining the organization. The human resources or training departments of an organization may reinforce these moral principles by putting on staff development programmes that explain the company's approach to business dealing. The staff annual appraisal system conducted by managers may also reinforce these values. Hence, the different departments of an organization can be seen as functional in supporting the company's philosophy. Within a functionalist perspective, the different divisions of an organization are perceived as working in an integrated way, in this example to combine an ethical approach to business with successful economic performance.

Robert K. Merton (1910–2003), an American sociologist at Columbia University, provided a different insight into functionalism with his concepts of 'manifest' and 'latent' functions.

The manifest function or functions of an organization are those functions that are clear and evident to both organizational members and members of the public. The latent functions, however, are those functions that exist but are unstated or not internally or externally obvious. A motor-racing team, for example, may have a manifest function of winning motor races. On the other hand, in preparing its cars for races it may try to develop technological innovations that will be useful for production cars, and this will remain a significant latent function. A television production company may have a manifest function of making and selling new television programmes. On the other hand, it may have a latent function of introducing the general public to new ideas on a topical issue.

Formal organizations are often established with a clear hierarchy, management system, set of goals, and a means of analysing the effectiveness and efficiency of the organization. Nevertheless, for the organizational systems to function effectively they require the committed work of the employees. Unless the employees are working in the interests of organizational goals, then the successful running of the organization may not be achieved. The relevance for society of the actions of individual people is enshrined in what can be termed 'social action theory', which was first articulated by Max Weber (1864–1920) and was later developed by other sociologists.

The central concept of the action perspective is that we all interpret the events that take place around us in society, and allocate different degrees of significance to those events. The meaning that people attribute to events then affects the actions they take. For example, suppose that the management of an organization starts to discuss the possibility of making redundancies. The meaning attached to this event may differ between members of staff. Some may become very demotivated and reduce their work output, on the grounds that they may be on the verge of losing their jobs anyway. Other workers may feel that it would be better to make a special effort to work hard in order not to be selected for redundancy.

Key idea: Social action perspective

The social action perspective reflects the idea that we interpret events around us, and then attach a certain degree of significance to them. On the basis of this we then choose to act in a particular way.

Social action and organizations

The action perspective does not assume that the social significance of events derives entirely from individual interpretation. It also acknowledges the influence of socialization. For example, in the case of a person brought up on the ethic of diligent, hard work, it may be very difficult for them to start to make only a minimum effort in the workplace. In the redundancy situation described above, such a person may continue to work diligently whatever the threat of losing their job.

Through the process of socialization, society provides a range of meanings and interpretations for human beings. Some people accept and acquire meanings in this way, while others reject some of these interpretations in constructing their lives. Equally, human beings have an effect upon organizations and upon society. For instance, when an organization is confronted by a conflictual situation, such as the potential for redundancies, then employees discuss the situation among themselves, and give voice to their various opinions. This exchange of views helps to create the prevailing viewpoint within the organization. Thus individuals are helping to create the prevalent perspective among the workers of the organization.

Action theory owes much of its development to the philosophical and sociological perspective of 'phenomenology'. The origin of this approach is normally credited to Edmund Husserl (1859–1938).

Did you know?

Edmund Husserl was Jewish by birth. From 1933 onwards, with the rising power of the Nazi Party, Husserl was not permitted to publish any of his academic articles. In addition, he lost his post at the University of Freiburg, and could not maintain any of his previous academic links with the university. However much of his scholarly writing was secretly transported to Leuven in Belgium, where an archive of his work was founded. He died in 1938 of a lung infection.

Husserl defined phenomenology as research into the nature of human consciousness, and the way in which the consciousnesses of different people interrelate with each other. Husserl's phenomenology proved to be a very influential philosophical position, which had a strong impact upon a number of different sociologists.

Key idea: Phenomenology

Phenomenology is the study of the way people view phenomena within their conscious experience, and from a subjective viewpoint.

One of these sociologists was Alfred Schütz (1899–1959), an Austrian who for much of his academic career worked at the New School for Social Research in New York.

The New School (formerly the New School for Social Research)

The New School is an internationally known university located towards the south of Manhattan island, and originally founded in 1919. The reasons for its establishment can be traced back to 1917 during the period of the First World War. At this time jingoistic attitudes were quite prevalent in the United States, and at Columbia University in New York there was some conflict between the university authorities and the lecturing staff. Some lecturers thought that the United States should not have involved itself in the war. After the resignation of some of the faculty from Columbia, a group of professors decided to start a new college that would operate on liberal lines. Those who contributed to the New School in its infancy included Thorstein Veblen, John Dewey, Bertrand Russell and Harold Laski.

The New School was open to a wide range of academic approaches and perspectives, and enabled adults to study there without the need to have prior qualifications. The School had many connections with European intellectuals, and became aware in the early 1930s of the rise of Nazism in Germany, and the associated dangers for those working in higher education. The director of the New School, Alvin Johnson, obtained funding to sponsor a large number of professors (many Jewish) from Germany to come and work at the New School, and to bring their families to the United States. This influx of intellectuals to New York became known at the New School, as The University in Exile, and it was formally established in 1933. A year later the New School was created a university. Today the New School is located in the Union Square area of Manhattan, around 14th St and 5th Avenue. It retains its commitment to a liberal, student-centred approach to education.

Schütz considered that the main subject for phenomenological research should be the everyday world, or 'life-world' as he termed it, in which people work, live, develop relationships, study and bring up children. Schütz argued that we learn ways of coping with this life-world simply by living within it. He often referred to such ways of coping as 'typifications' and noted that very often these have existed for a long time.

As an example we might consider the case of formal meetings that take place in organizations. There is a fairly predictable pattern to such meetings, involving a call for agenda items, a formal agenda, minutes taken in the meeting, followed by the approval of the minutes at the next meeting. However, in addition, people who have attended a number of such meetings will be familiar with the general way in which attendees conduct themselves. People are generally cautious in what they say; they avoid making sweeping, unsubstantiated statements; they try to say what they think, but in a manner that avoids confrontation; and they try to adduce evidence for the claims they make.

We learn these strategies or typifications through the actual process of attending a lot of meetings. If, for example, a senior member of staff happens to be at a meeting, most people would probably avoid challenging his or her viewpoint. However, this strategy may not be universal, and we do sometimes come across people who 'rock the boat' in meetings! Typifications, therefore, do not exist to be unquestioningly accepted and learned, but sometimes may be rejected as people seek to develop their own strategies to exist in the life-world.

Did you know?

Alfred Schütz was Austrian by birth. Although a leading and very influential philosopher and social scientist, he also worked in the legal department of a bank. He apparently did this in order to earn money for his family. Much of the time it appears that his legal work took precedence over his sociological studies. With the rise of the Nazi party in Germany, he left Austria to live in Paris with his family and in 1938 managed to emigrate to New York.

Here he both taught and continued his banking work. Some of his extensive philosophical writings are kept in an archive at Yale University.

Schütz influenced a number of sociologists including the American Harold Garfinkel (1917–2011). Garfinkel, like many other sociologists, was interested in the issue of how society managed to remain relatively stable in spite of the numerous recurring threats to that stability. Many sociologists, including Garfinkel, felt that scientific reasoning or rationality was important in maintaining the stability of society. The interesting question for Garfinkel, however, was the way in which this rational thinking developed among human beings. Previous sociologists such as Durkheim and Parsons considered that so-called social facts were very important in encouraging rational discussion about society. Garfinkel, on the other hand, argued that rationality developed through the medium of human talk.

As Matthewman et al argued:

'Human interaction in social situations is amazingly complex and diverse and the collective social arrangements that we construct and within which we live our individual lives are the result of choices among multiple possibilities.'
Matthewman, Steve, Lane West-Newman, Catherine & Curtis, Bruce (eds.) (2007), *Being Sociological* (p.6).

In other words, in their everyday discussions, people interact and persuade each other of the value of having reasons and evidence for what they believe. Garfinkel termed this type of study, 'ethnomethodology'.

Key idea: Ethnomethodology

Ethnomethodology is the analysis of the means by which everyday social life generally maintains a measure of stability. In particular, it studies the linguistic strategies employed by people to achieve this stability.

Consider the following two methods by which managers might introduce a systems change to members of staff:

1 We have decided to change system A to system B because we think it will free more staff time for other duties, and will also maximize profits.

2 We have decided to consider changing system A to system B because evidence suggests it will be easier for staff to operate and more convenient for customers. In principle, it should therefore increase profits, which will benefit the company as a whole. We have put a summary of the changes on the company website, and hope you will let us have your views within the next three weeks. If staff have significant reservations about the proposed changes then we will reconsider the idea.

The first option tends to reflect much more the personal will of the management, whereas in the second option there is a mention of the use of evidence, of consultation and of the possibility of changing the strategy in the light of opinion. Hence the second option reflects much more Garfinkel's notion that rationality is created within the ordinary everyday conversation of people.

The American sociologist Aaron Cicourel (1928–) has argued that while human talk is significant in helping human beings make sense of the social world, other means of communication are also of importance.

As Bilton et al argue:

'Language is the most important source of symbolic meaning in human social life, though other symbols – such as dress, demeanour, expression, even smell – are important too. Social encounters therefore necessarily involve other people interpreting what we are like.'

Bilton, Tony et al (2002), *Introductory Sociology* (p. 502).

We should not forget the wide range of non-verbal communication which exists, and the way this helps us to understand the feelings, thoughts and emotions of other human beings. In meetings, for instance, the facial expressions and body language of those sitting across the table from us can be informative.

Erving Goffman (1922–82), in his celebrated book *The Presentation of Self in Everyday Life,* explored the strategies employed by human beings in order to present a particular view of themselves to another person or to the world in general. When two people are talking they are simultaneously learning about the image projected by the other, and also trying to present a particular view of themselves.

As Goffman wrote:

> 'Information about the individual helps to define the situation, enabling others to know in advance what he will expect of them and what they may expect of him. Informed in these ways, the others will know how best to act in order to call forth a desired response from him.'
>
> Goffman, Erving (1956), *The Presentation of Self in Everyday Life* (p. 1).

The way in which we present ourselves may differ depending upon the features of the immediate situation. Goffman introduced the analogy of a theatrical performance to explain this phenomenon. He argued that people often behaved in a similar way to actors on the stage, trying to present a particular view of themselves which they considered appropriate to the time and occasion. In other situations, they might not be so concerned to present a particular image, and might be more relaxed, offering deeper insights into their 'real' self or personality. The extent to which we do this might depend upon the other people present, and the nature of the social context.

Did you know?

Besides his extremely noteworthy academic career Erving Goffman was very successful in investing in the stock market. He also enjoyed playing cards and gambling, and for a while actually worked part-time as a croupier.

We are familiar, of course, with the kind of image of ourselves that we try to portray in a work or formal organizational context. We often try to appear professional, and this may reflect itself in the kind of clothes that we wear, and the form of calm, balanced language that we use. We may, for example, try to avoid too much emotive language. In general, we may try to support the accepted company or organizational policy on things, only speaking contrary to this in a carefully considered, reflective manner. Behind the scenes though, in a staff room, or in an informal meeting with friends, we may speak very differently. We may speak in a very informal register, making it eminently clear what we think about company policy, and indeed some of the decision-makers in the company. Expressing shared dissatisfaction may also be a means of consolidating relationships between workers in an organization.

The construction of knowledge

Continuing in this broadly phenomenological tradition, the work of the sociologists Peter Berger (1929–) and Thomas Luckmann (1927–) has been very influential, particularly in terms of their 1966 book, *The Social Construction of Reality*. The title of the book quite accurately describes the general thesis of the authors, which is that a great deal of our knowledge of the way in which society functions is created by human beings. In addition this sum total of social knowledge is continually changing, adapting and indeed being created.

Key idea: Constructionism

Constructionism is a theory concerning the way knowledge is created, which assumes that knowledge is largely created through human beings sharing their sense of what is significant in the world.

We can illustrate this from an imaginary example within an educational organization. Suppose that a student walks into a college and says that she was a psychology student there 12 years ago, and would like a transcript of her results from her degree programme. She is sent to the course director, who has changed from the person who taught her 12 years previously. The course director does not have any results from his predecessor, and suggests she goes to the registry department. They say that unfortunately the college computer system was changed ten years ago, and no computerized records are available from before that date. There may, however, be some paper records, but it will be a time-consuming process to locate these – even if they exist. The student is advised to telephone again in two weeks' time to see if there has been any progress.

In the meantime, there are discussions between registry and the psychology department about whose responsibility it is to maintain long-term historical records of module and course results. It is discovered that there is no existing system to define responsibilities, and hence new protocols are gradually developed that allocate duties to named roles. In this way, a small but important set of procedures is added to the body of knowledge in the college that describes the 'way things are done'. This body of knowledge is subsequently acquired by new members of staff joining the college. Importantly, this knowledge is not rigid or fixed, but as in this example, is being augmented and altered as part of a continual process that is produced by human beings.

Similar processes may take place in informal organizations. In a weekend sports club, for example, the stock of knowledge may include the type of person whom the club is trying to recruit as a member. Playing competence and experience may be important criteria, but the club may also be looking for commitment to attend training sessions, and to help with coaching young players. None of this may be written down, but it will undoubtedly be part of the sometimes unspoken stock of knowledge of the club.

Dig deeper

Gallagher, S. (2012), *Phenomenology*. Basingstoke: Palgrave Macmillan.

Garfinkel, H. (1984), *Studies in Ethnomethodology*. Cambridge: Polity.

Godwyn, M. & Gittell, J. H. (Eds.) (2012), *Sociology of Organizations: Structures and Relationships*. Thousand Oaks, CA: Pine Forge.

Lewis, M. & Staehler, T. (2010), *Phenomenology: an Introduction*. London: Continuum.

Moustakas, C. (1994), *Phenomenological Research Methods*. London: Sage.

Smith, J. A., Flowers, P. & Larkin, M. (2009), *Interpretative Phenomenological Analysis: Theory, Method and Research*. London: Sage.

Test your knowledge

1 An open system is an entity or organization that...?
   a is easy to join
   b has no entry fee
   c is well integrated with the external society
   d is ready to accept new ideas

2 Talcott Parsons was born in the...?
   a 20th century
   b 19th century
   c 18th century
   d 17th century

3 Functionalists tend to be interested in...?
   a revolution
   b the decline of the Church
   c the stability of society
   d moral virtue

4 The manifest functions of an organization are...?
   a handed freely to members
   b considered as part of decision-making
   c functions that are clear and evident to most people
   d part of general fiscal planning

5 The action perspective involves...?
   a prompt academic decision-making
   b separating out key ideas
   c careful statistical analysis
   d interpretation of the meaning of social events

6 The New School for Social Research is located in...?
   a Rome
   b San Francisco
   c New York
   d Amsterdam

7 Husserl defined phenomenology as the study of...?
   a consciousness
   b predispositions
   c integration
   d abstract ideas

8 Berger and Luckmann's seminal work was called?
   a *Reality and its Forms*
   b *The Social Construction of Reality*
   c *The Nature of Reality*
   d *Existence and Reality*

9 ...And it was published in...?
   a 2001
   b 1951
   c 1990
   d 1966

10 The latent functions of an organization are...?
   a not immediately obvious
   b the key management aims
   c a source of conflict
   d mentioned in all marketing information

6

The political control of social existence

This chapter examines the ways in which political power is exercised in society, and the ways in which different groups can challenge that power. It will analyse the mechanisms by which different social groups typically manage to attain and sustain political power, including post-structuralist assessments of the exercise of political power. The chapter will not only analyse this in relation to established political parties, but also in connection with other major social movements. There will be a discussion of the relationship between social class and the exercise of power, and the consequences that this has for differential opportunity in society. The chapter will also evaluate the manner in which organizations, such as the media, can affect the exercise of power.

The sociology of politics – concepts and theories

The sociology of politics is concerned primarily with the interaction between those who hold political power, and the nature of the society in which that power is exercised. There are other important questions which arise from this basic area of study. These include, for example, the mechanisms by which citizens are able to gain political power, and the procedures by which they can exercise that power.

The concept of 'power' is central to the sociology of politics, and there is frequent discussion of the links between those who gain political power, and certain interest or cultural groups in the wider society. It is often asserted, for example, that people with a certain educational or cultural background have an advantage when it comes to gaining political power.

A major area of interest in political sociology is the interplay between interest groups in society and the political class. In a liberal democracy, society should in principle be able to exercise a number of checks and balances over the political system, in order that the system does not accrue excessive power. In many cases interest groups are in a state of conflict as they compete to exercise most influence over political decision-making. It is a feature of many contemporary societies that a range of different interest groups in civil society, and also political groupings, compete for political power and influence. There is thus not one predetermined locus of power, but a range of influential groups who may exercise more or less political power depending upon the fluctuating political and social environment. The political nature of society is thus seen as pluralist, which contrasts with the view of society as being controlled largely by elites.

An elite is a group which by virtue of certain characteristics – say inherited wealth, or educational, social or cultural capital – is able to exercise political power out of all proportion to the group's numbers. Finally, one can argue that political power is often related to social class. Within this perspective, the bourgeois class with the capacity to control capital may be able to use that to exercise political power. Equally, although in the earlier stages of the Industrial Revolution the proletariat was relatively impotent in exerting political influence, the class gradually began to understand the power of such actions as the withdrawal of labour.

Pluralism and political power

As a political philosophy 'pluralism' rests firstly upon the assumption that human beings generally hold many different beliefs. Rather than structuring society around just one, or perhaps two, of these approaches, it is better to try to encourage people from different groups to work together. This avoids a situation where one group becomes extremely powerful, and also where one particular philosophy becomes too influential throughout society. For pluralism to succeed and to be workable, it is important that the different interest groups are willing to engage in pragmatic discussion, and in principle try to reach a compromise on issues. It is also supportive of pluralism if different groups appreciate the value of diversity in society. One distinct advantage is that a range of different views is maintained in society, without one view becoming too dominant.

Key idea: Political pluralism

Political pluralism argues that as people hold a diversity of views, the most effective policies involve compromise and the integration of ideas.

In a plural society an interest or pressure group will have its own beliefs, ethics, values, attitudes and priorities. When a number of different pressure groups are all trying to influence government, it becomes difficult for the latter to formulate a policy that will appeal to the generality of society. Government therefore may be hampered in its decision-making. The opposite may also apply in a situation where the government has a clearly defined policy, and pressure groups find it very difficult to challenge and change that policy. Overall, pluralism as a philosophy of society tends to be associated with a liberal democracy, committed to the ideas of free debate and discourse, and a respect for alternative viewpoints.

The concept of elites

In sociological terms an elite is a group of people who are small compared to the size of the general population, and yet are able to influence society politically and in other ways. In medieval times those who possessed military power were also often able to exert political power. In addition, as the maintenance of armed forces usually required considerable financial resources, economic and military power were often a prerequisite for the possession of political power.

At the time, the Church also exerted considerable political power. It possessed wealth and was able to give official support to the commencement of a war, as in the Crusades, against those who stood opposed to its interests. The clergy was also extremely well educated in comparison with other social groups, and hence was able to function very effectively in carrying out legal and bureaucratic roles in society. The possession of a high level of education was important in the promulgation of legislation, and in the exercise of power through bureaucratic processes.

Key idea: Elites

An elite is a relatively small group of people who exercise considerable influence and political power out of all proportion to their numbers.

Many of these characteristics of elites appear to have continued into modern society. The American sociologist C. Wright Mills (1916–62) argued in his book *The Power Elite* (1956) that certain groups of people, notably those in senior positions in the armed forces, or in large business or industrial organizations, held a great deal of political influence. There are three important questions that arise from this proposition. The first is whether there is truth in the assertion that elites actually exist.

The second is whether they do exert greater political and other influence when compared with the rest of society; and third whether it is legitimate that small groups of people should exert such influence.

It can certainly be argued that elite groups in society do exist. These would include senior members of the legal profession, of the traditional universities, of banks and large industrial conglomerates, of the civil service and of the armed forces. Some of these people may have come from traditionally wealthy backgrounds, although not necessarily. It can be argued that many have risen through a meritocratic system, notably by means of educational achievement, to reach high status positions. Although some will have attended famous private schools and then gone on to study at long-established universities, others will have gained entry to the same universities via the state school system. Once in these high-status universities, they make friends and contacts, which will often last a lifetime. Many of these friends will eventually rise to high positions in their chosen career, giving rise to networks that may well become mutual-aid networks in later life. Some of these young people may work in politics from leaving university, while others will have an initial career, and later seek political office. As such people will be in relatively senior jobs, it seems inevitable that they will exert greater political and other influence when compared with the general population.

Key idea: Meritocracy

A meritocracy is a society or organization in which the most able people rise to the senior posts, irrespective of other factors such as personal wealth or the influence of family or friends.

As to the third proposition above, this raises very complex practical and moral questions. Let us first consider the negative factors in relation to elites exercising political power. Although they may have started from different social classes as children, they will have progressed to a similar level of higher education, probably acquiring at least some similar values along the way. The exercise of power by a highly educated, scholarly minority may be open to accusations of bias. Members of the electorate may prefer to be represented in government by more members of the working class, who although possessing less formal education may be considered closer to the realities of everyday life. There is also the implicit assumption by some sectors of the electorate that government elites tend to work towards their own best interests rather than for the welfare of the majority of the electorate. Whether justified or not, this belief tends to support the view that working people are often unable to change or influence government policy so that it becomes fairer to the disadvantaged members of society.

Did you know?

C. Wright Mills suffered from high blood pressure and the risk of heart attacks. There was a continual possibility that he might die at a young age. He was known to his friends and colleagues as an energetic academic with a large output of scholarly work. His intense work schedule may have been explained by his knowledge of his precarious health. Sadly, he died of a heart attack on March 20, 1962 at the age of 45. Throughout his relatively short life, Mills was also widely known as a free-thinking and challenging scholar, as Sterne shows in the following extract.

'... Mills both inspired students to move beyond their political apathy and offered a model of humanist radicalism that was neither doctrinaire Marxism nor bland liberalism. For other writers, he was a daring figure who helped keep alive a critical and engaged sociological spirit in an age where the field was becoming more technocratic.'

Sterne, Jonathan (2005), 'C. Wright Mills, the Bureau for Applied Social Research, and the Meaning of Critical Scholarship' (p. 67).

On the other hand, members of elites would probably argue that by virtue of their level of education and professional experience they are the best people to be governing the country. They would point out that they have reached a responsible position in society through protracted hard work and discipline, qualities that fit them well to exercise political power. They might also suggest that it is not necessary to have experienced different types of disadvantage in order to want to make society fairer and more just for people who are less fortunate than others. Elites would probably argue that they possess the administrative, managerial and analytic skills to help change society for the better and ensure wider opportunities for all citizens. Of course, even assuming the influence of elites in government, how one could reduce that influence and render government more egalitarian and democratic is a separate question.

The Italian sociologist Vilfredo Pareto (1848–1923) felt that there was a certain inevitability about societies being ruled by elites. Even when a society strove to be democratic in its political structures, Pareto felt that ultimately an elite or elites would gain political control. Elites would typically possess a variety of qualities that fitted them to rule, including intellectual and organizational abilities. Busino, referring to Pareto's views of elites, writes that:

> 'The groups and classes are in conflict but there is also a struggle within these groups and classes. The part of the group or class which tries to ensure hegemony over its own group or its own class, or also over all groups and all classes, is called the élite.'
>
> Busino, Giovanni (2000), 'The signification of Vilfredo Pareto's sociology' (para 30).

He felt that the remainder of society was either too apathetic to want to obtain political power, or was inferior in terms of the qualities needed to rule. The end result was, according to Pareto, that the mass of society could be relatively easily controlled by the elite in power. Pareto was also opposed to the theory of Marx that eventually the proletariat would rise and replace the bourgeoisie. According to Pareto, even if the original elite was removed from power, it would simply be replaced by a different elite. In other words, evidence suggested, according to Pareto, that there was frequently a rotation of elites in society.

Gaetano Mosca (1858–1941), an Italian political thinker and contemporary of Pareto, was largely in agreement with Pareto's thinking on elites, although he felt that elites owed much of their ability to hold political power to their organizational skills. Robert Michels (1876–1936), a German sociologist, argued that there was an inevitability in society that gradually a small elite of politicians would assume power and would rule in an authoritarian manner.

Social class and politics

Social class analyses of politics are usually related to the prevalent economic system. The economic system tends to exert a strong influence upon the social class system that has evolved. In the context of a traditional capitalist society, those who own substantial amounts of capital, and normally also the means of production, control the lives of the majority of the workers who sell their labour to the owners of production. Within a Marxist conception of society this is a distinctly exploitative relationship. This can be described as a 'structuralist' perspective in that the life of the individual person is affected primarily by the economic structure of society. Thus, where there are two distinct social classes of the bourgeoisie and of the proletariat, this leaves little freedom for average workers to control or amend the direction of their lives. Within this model, the life chances of people are related intimately to the economic system.

From a classical Marxist point of view such an economic system is fundamentally unfair and unethical. Marxists consider it to be so unstable that ultimately the working classes will rise up in revolt, and a new society, a socialist society, will result. However, there is recent evidence that political systems, such as the former Soviet Union and East Germany with highly centralized socialist economies, have not been able to sustain such a system.

A variety of factors have undermined the socialist system in favour of a form of capitalism. The economy of the Industrial Revolution was founded upon a fairly rigid system of heavy manufacturing, which offered little variety and flexibility in terms of employment opportunities for the majority of workers. However, as newer forms of technology developed, and particularly with the information technology revolution, there were important consequences for the social class system. A much more affluent working class evolved, along with various strata of well-educated middle classes. The latter had much wider opportunities in terms of their life chances, and were typically employed in such occupations as teachers, social workers or civil servants. Political affiliations no longer related precisely to social class divisions. Indeed, new threats to capitalism appeared. The decline in manufacturing industry led to a reduction in traditional employment, and an increase in work in the service industries. Service industry work was not necessarily well-paid, and did not always prove sufficient for young people to progress in their lives. It was thus more difficult for a political party to offer hard work and ambition as a route to self-advancement.

Post-structuralism and political power

The structuralist view of political power is that the major systems of society – for example, the economic, military and industrial systems – affect the way that people can exercise dominion over their own lives, can exercise a degree of autonomy and can participate in the political life of their country. A Marxian structuralist view held that the proletariat had very little influence over their individual lives, and certainly very little political power. Marx held that the proletariat was generally constrained by the bourgeoisie and left with few choices in life.

The French philosopher Jean-Paul Sartre (1905–80) was not a structuralist in the sense that he believed in overarching societal systems that affected everyone, but he did believe in the fundamental principles of living, which left human beings with obligations as to how they should live their lives. Sartre advocated a philosophy he termed 'existentialism', which argued that from birth onwards people were confronted with choices concerning how they would live their lives. People had a responsibility to think carefully about the choices available, and to consider the kind of person they wanted to be.

Sartre was also an advocate of being politically 'engaged'. In other words, people should not simply drift through life, permitting others to determine what would happen in the world, but should make their own choices concerning the kind of world in which they wanted to live. For Sartre, people should consider carefully how they wanted society to be politically organized, and should participate in the process of making the type of society they wanted.

Key idea: Political engagement

Jean-Paul Sartre argued that people had a moral responsibility to be politically engaged, and to reflect upon and articulate the type of society in which they wanted to live.

Sartre and Marx each had a view of society that they considered affected all people. Marx's view related to the way in which economic forces affected the lives of individuals, and Sartre's view involved the way in which he thought human beings should determine the nature of their own existence.

Michel Foucault (1926–84), a philosopher and sociologist who to some extent succeeded Sartre as a leading intellectual in France, felt somewhat differently about the scope and distribution of power. Foucault believed that there was no single ideology, philosophy of life or theory of social existence that could be employed to explain the lives of all people. He himself did not wish to be associated with any particular school of thought, since he felt that social life was too complex to be reduced to a single perspective. This was especially so in connection with power, and its distribution in society. He felt that there was no single locus of power in society, but that many people and groups exerted power in different ways.

The political thought of Jean-François Lyotard (1924–98)

Lyotard was a French philosopher and sociologist who is often seen as the leading spokesperson of postmodernist thought. He knew Michel Foucault and taught at the same university. After graduating from the Sorbonne, he taught in a lycée in

Algeria from 1950 onwards. This was during the period of French colonialism in Algeria. At the time, Lyotard was in favour of a left-wing revolution in Algeria to overthrow the colonial administration. During this period he became a member of the left-wing group 'Socialism or Barbarism'. However, by the mid-1960s he had become disillusioned with Marxism. He began to feel, rather like Foucault, that human society and political interaction were too convoluted to be summarized within a single all-encompassing theory such as Marxism.

During the 1970s and 1980s Lyotard was a professor at the University of Vincennes, and upon retirement became a visiting professor at numerous universities around the world. He died in Paris in 1998.

As Sweetman points out in the following extract:

> 'Jean-François Lyotard has described the postmodern condition as one characterized by an "incredulity towards metanarratives", and perhaps this is the best definition we get of the term from within the ranks of leading postmodernist thinkers (which, in addition to Lyotard, would include Foucault, Derrida and Barthes).'
>
> Sweetman, Brendan (2005), 'Lyotard, Postmodernism, and Religion' (p. 142).

Lyotard expounded upon this idea in his famous book *The Postmodern Condition: A Report on Knowledge* (originally published in French in 1979). Lyotard is a pluralist who feels that political events are so varied that no one political perspective or party can provide a basis for understanding them.

If we think of power as the ability to influence events in society, then apart from political parties, many groups such as the judiciary, the police, the armed forces, trades unions, financial institutions and major commercial organizations all have the ability to affect events. No single organization can assume that it has exclusive access to power. Even though Foucault did not think of himself as belonging to a particular social perspective, many people have classified him as a post-structuralist in the sense that he did not accept the overriding influence of societal structures.

Did you know?

After the May 1968 riots by students in Paris, the French government attempted to reform the higher education system. It established new universities, such as the Experimental University of Vincennes. Foucault was made the head of the department of philosophy. When the university opened in January 1969 there were continuing student occupations and interventions by the police.

Foucault saw the exercise of power as operating in a very dispersed manner, and frequently deriving from the way in which human beings interacted with each other in social situations. Thus even very powerful politicians do not necessarily wish to exercise power in a totally arbitrary way, but often want to seek the approval of different pressure groups in society for the policies that they are advocating.

Key idea: Foucault's ideas

Foucault did not wish to be associated with any single school of thought, partly at least because he did not feel one particular perspective could explain the complexity of society.

The media and political control

The relationship between those who work in the media and politicians is to some extent a symbiotic one. Politicians need journalists and editors in order to have their ideas disseminated, while media workers need to understand the ideas and policies of politicians in order to discuss political trends. The media in general have an essential role to play in ensuring that the electorate is well informed about political trends, and ultimately in elections individuals are able to cast their vote from a basis of knowledge and understanding of political policy. In this sense the media have an important function in a democratic society.

The media are also important in identifying and investigating any occasions where politicians fall short of the high standards expected of them. The exercise of this function can often be the cause of embarrassment and irritation to politicians but is again a necessary check and balance in a democratic society. There can also be situations where politicians reveal issues that may be less than positive for the media. For example, those associated with companies that operate in the field of mass communications may be shown to have been biased in the way stories are presented. As different organs of the media are frequently in competition with one other, there may also be issues about the way in which information is collected and processed in order to create a newsworthy story.

Sometimes the media prove to be very powerful in terms of indirectly helping one political candidate rather than another. For example, when political leaders are involved in television debates, some prove more adept than others at working in a visual medium, and hence influencing the electorate. This raises the question of whether performance on television is a necessary criterion for, say, running a government. A candidate may be good at one, but not necessarily good at the other. The new types of social media have also had a great effect in the political arena.

Did you know?

The smartphone is changing the way in which people receive political information. This new type of dissemination crosses social boundaries of all types. Significantly, politicians are unable to influence or control the new types of information flow via social media. They are often finding themselves reacting to public opinion on social media rather than controlling it.

Various forms of social media enable political leaders and parties to disseminate their policies and ideas much more rapidly, and also to judge the extent of their support. They have also proved very effective in political fundraising campaigns. Politicians need to learn to utilize social media to their advantage, but also being aware that there are inherent pitfalls if they do not use them with the same degree of fairness and honesty that they would employ in other contexts.

Dig deeper

Foucault, M. (trans. Sheridan, A.) (1995), *Discipline and Punish: The Birth of the Prison* (2nd ed.). New York: Vintage.

Hayden, T. (2006), *Radical Nomad: C. Wright Mills and his Times*. Boulder, Colorado: Paradigm.

Lyotard, J.-F. (1984), *The Postmodern Condition: A Report on Knowledge*. Manchester: Manchester University Press.

Malpas, S. (2003), *Jean-François Lyotard*. London: Routledge.

Mills, C. Wright (1956), *The Power Elite*. New York: Oxford University Press.

Wolfsfeld, G. (2011), *Making Sense of Media and Politics: Five Principles in Political Communication*. Abingdon, Oxon: Routledge.

Test your knowledge

1 Pluralism assumes that...?
- **a** ...human beings hold a range of different beliefs.
- **b** ...two or more human beings hold the same belief.
- **c** ...a majority of human beings hold the same belief.
- **d** ...a majority of the electorate supports the government's view.

2 An elite is...?
- **a** ...a large group of powerful people.
- **b** ...a group of people who want to gain power.
- **c** ...a relatively small group of people who can exert an undue amount of influence.
- **d** ...a small group of people with little power.

3 C. Wright Mills wrote a book entitled...?
- **a** *The Source of Power*
- **b** *The Power Elite*
- **c** *Influence and Power*
- **d** *Elites and the Exercise of Power*

4 In a meritocracy the people who rise to the most influential positions are...?
- **a** the richest
- **b** the ones who support the leading political party
- **c** the ones who live in the capital city
- **d** the most able

5 Pareto felt that...?
- **a** ...it was inevitable an elite group would govern society.
- **b** ...elites could not govern in a democracy.
- **c** ...elites were intrinsically unstable.
- **d** ...elites would ultimately fail.

6 Mosca felt that elites were successful because of their...?
- **a** money
- **b** organizational skills
- **c** social contacts
- **d** education

7 Sartre argued that people should be...?

   a politically neutral

   b politically conservative

   c politically astute

   d politically 'engaged'

8 Foucault argued that...?

   a ...no single organization could exclusively control power in society.

   b ...the army controlled power in society.

   c ...the government controlled power in society.

   d ...the banks controlled power in society.

9 The media...?

   a ...assist the government in the exercise of power.

   b ...obstruct the government in the exercise of power.

   c ...act as a check and balance in the exercise of power.

   d ...encourage the electorate to challenge the government.

10 Michels thought that, eventually, an elite would...?

   a ...rule society in an authoritarian manner.

   b ...decline in influence.

   c ...expand its influence to neighbouring countries.

   d ...form a government.

7

Religion and secularization

This chapter examines the transition in some countries from a largely religious society to one that is largely secular. The chapter will also analyse the ways in which political power can be linked to religious influence, the mechanisms by which religiously inspired value systems can exert influence within a country. There will also be a discussion of the ways in which some religions apparently disseminate their value and belief systems in some countries, whereas in others they do not do so.

The sociological study of religion

When sociologists study a religion, it is not necessary for them to be a member of that faith. Neither is it necessary for them to believe any of the main tenets of that religion. The main reason for this is that the sociologist tries to stand outside the religious belief system in question, and to examine it in an objective, dispassionate way. The sociologist examines and analyses the rituals, beliefs, places of worship, organizational hierarchy, prayers and scriptures of the religion, without becoming personally involved. It is still possible for sociologists to be members of the religion they are studying, but it may sometimes be harder for them to take a balanced and objective view. As members of the faith they may become so close to the religious customs and beliefs that it becomes very difficult to see them in a clear light. It is important to remember that sociology is a social science, and hence sociologists should use the same kind of enquiry methods that are employed in the other social sciences.

The full range of sociological research methods are used to study religion, but the method selected should be related to the issue being investigated. If you want to investigate the number of adherents of a particular faith, then you would need to employ quantitative or statistical methods. If you were interested in the personal beliefs of individual members then you would probably employ phenomenological or interview methods. On the other hand, if you were wanting to gather data on religious ceremonies and practices, then you might employ observational methods.

There are many aspects of religions that interest sociologists. A great many religions have a complex social and hierarchical organization, and sociologists are interested in how these social structures developed. A hierarchy usually involves a power structure, with influential people at the top who are very often charged with maintaining the traditions of the religion. Those with power and influence are usually involved with, among other duties, the selection of members of the clergy, the interpretation of religious texts, the conduct of sacraments and ceremonies, and the care of the financial and other assets of the religion.

Sociologists are interested in the evolution of religious hierarchies and the way in which they sustain themselves against the various challenges to their authority. Religions can sometimes find themselves in conflict with a secular society and its changing values. As Keysar points out:

> 'Generally, participation in religious activities requires both economic and social commitments, payment of donations or fees, and conformance to the policy, schedule and set of rules of the congregation and its leaders.'
>
> Keysar, Ariela (2014), 'Shifts along the American Religious-Secular Spectrum' (p. 2).

Many religions have been traditionally male dominated, and as secular society has increasingly been committed to gender equality, this has led to tensions between religious and secular values. Other areas of tension include differences in the values of late capitalism with, for example, Christian values. Some Christian leaders have pointed out the difference between the search for ever-increasing profits and the Christian values of concern for the poor and dispossessed.

Most religions have been interested in the educational process, not least since the latter has been a training ground for future members of the clergy. In addition, the education system of a state has been seen as a means of disseminating religious values. Some schools, which were originally religious foundations, have continued to have a close association with a particular faith. The way in which these issues interact with concepts such as power, authority, status and social class has been of continued interest to sociologists.

Secularism and religion

The conflict between a religious organization and a secular state is often so profound that it is part of a revolutionary situation. A paradigmatic instance of this was during the French Revolution of 1789, when one of the key aims of the revolutionaries was to reduce the power of the Catholic Church.

Ultimately, in 1905, there was a so-called Concordat that affirmed a clear separation between the Church and the State. As a result of this, citizens were guaranteed on the one hand freedom of worship and no political interference in religious matters, while on the other there was to be no intrusion of religious belief into government or state functions.

In recent years this principle has been challenged by the desire of young French women of Muslim faith who wish to wear traditional Islamic headscarves within state educational institutions. The French government saw this as a challenge to the principle of secularism in schools, and in 2004 under the presidency of Jacques Chirac there was a ban on the wearing of any religious symbols in French schools. As a further statement of this principle, in 2013 the minister of education, Vincent Peillon, prepared a Secularism Charter to be on display in every French school to emphasize the key arguments for the separation of religion and the state.

The practical implementation of the Charter may, however, pose some difficulties. It may be difficult to define precisely the characteristics of a headscarf in order to define whether or not a student is behaving contrary to the Charter. It also raises questions such as whether commonplace objects, say Christmas trees, are in fact religious symbols. The French secularist model tries to make a clear-cut distinction between religious and political issues, and yet contemporary society is becoming increasingly complex and plural. It may be that in a postmodern multicultural society, it will become very difficult to sustain absolute divisions of the type advocated in French secularism.

Key idea: Church vs. State

The separation of religion from the State, as in the French constitution, is sometimes difficult to operationalize, for example when deciding whether a decorated Christmas tree should be erected in the town hall, since some may argue it is a religious symbol.

In the Iranian Revolution of 1979, a largely secular government was replaced by an Islamic republic. In the early 1970s Iran was ruled by the American-supported regime of Reza Shah Pahlavi, who presided over a westernized regime. In a complex political situation most opposition groups demanded a variety of social reforms and wanted a return to traditional Islamic values. The key focus of reform was the ayatollah Ruhollah Khomeini, who was in exile in Paris. Following widespread demonstrations and strikes Shah Pahlavi left Tehran in January 1979. One month later the ayatollah returned from Paris, and subsequently the creation of an Islamic Republic received majority support.

There are a variety of hypotheses for the collective social movement against the regime of the shah, but one could plausibly argue that it was at least partially about a rebellion against the introduction of a foreign (i.e. Western) culture. It seems possible that the Iranian population had become weary of westernized economic and social policies, and wished to revert to traditional religious values.

Classical perspectives on the sociology of religion

In one of the earliest studies of sociology and religion, Émile Durkheim (1858–1917) analysed data on suicide, and attempted to relate this data to the religion of the individual. He argued that Roman Catholics appeared to have a lower suicide rate when compared with the Protestant community. He hypothesized that Catholic society had a greater degree of social integration, and that individuals were more closely connected to the values and norms associated with Catholic culture. This provided people with a degree of support that helped them through periods of difficulty when they might be inclined to commit suicide. Protestants, on the other hand, with a lower degree of social integration appeared to be more prone to suicide.

Key idea: Durkheim on suicide

Durkheim's research on suicide suggested that different degrees of social integration, which themselves derived from religious belief, were a factor in people taking their own lives.

This study was of particular sociological interest since it appeared to show a connection between an individual act and the nature of the broader society. In other words, features of the society in which an individual lived (in this case, religion) could have consequences for a person's individual behaviour (in this case, suicide). Durkheim's research was published in 1897 in his book *Le Suicide*.

Karl Marx (1818–83) shared some similarities with Durkheim in terms of his methodological approach. He was systematic and scientific in analysing his data on society and economics. For Marx, religion was a distraction from the central issues of life in a capitalist society. It gave false hope to members of the proletariat that their lives could improve under the existing capitalist system. Rather than the distorted view of reality provided by religious belief, Marx wanted working people to adopt a more scientific view of society, and to realize that their lives could be improved only when the capitalist society was replaced by a socialist system.

The approach of Max Weber (1864–1920) to the study of religion was somewhat different to the more quantitative techniques of Durkheim and Marx. He sought, where possible, to place himself in the position of the adherent of a religion, in order to understand the faith from the 'inside'. This approach represented the beginnings of 'interpretative sociology'. As a general principle, Weber was interested in exploring the relationship between religious belief, and the social, cultural and economic development of different countries.

Weber hypothesized that as a country developed a more and more sophisticated political and economic system, then the predominant religious system changed. He argued that as society became more complex, then there was a tendency for the religious system to change from a form of mysticism to variants of polytheism, and finally to a form of monotheism. In his studies of Hinduism he noted that the caste system appeared to reduce the possibility of social mobility.

Key idea: Weber's approach

Weber's approach to the study of a religion was to try to see the belief system from the point of view of the adherent. This involved trying to develop an empathy with the rites and rituals of the faith.

Weber's most celebrated thesis connecting religion with the economic and political development of a country was his argument concerning the Calvinist branch of Protestantism and the rise of capitalism. Calvinism tended to argue that not all members of the faith would necessarily gain salvation. It was necessary for the aspirant to demonstrate holy works, and Calvinism made the connection between spirituality and work that was economically successful. Weber thus argued that Protestantism had the effect of supporting the development of capitalism, by defining entrepreneurially successful work as being of spiritual value and esteemed in the eyes of God. Weber never argued that Calvinism was the only variable responsible for the development of capitalism, but that it was probably one factor. Weber discussed his hypothesis in his celebrated book *The Protestant Ethic and the Spirit of Capitalism*.

Female leaders of religious organizations

Although religions have traditionally been male dominated, there are examples of female spiritual leaders who have made a significant and lasting contribution to the world's religious life. Two examples are Helena Blavatsky (1831–91) and one of her disciples Annie Besant (1847–1933).

Helena Blavatsky was born in Russia and became a celebrated spiritual philosopher and religious mystic. As a young woman she travelled to many parts of the world, extensively visiting North and South America, Egypt and Greece. However, it was the religious traditions of India, Nepal and Tibet that had the greatest influence upon her. In 1873 she visited the United States, and in 1875 along with H. S. Olcott and W. Q. Judge she established the organization for which she would become famous – the Theosophical Society.

The Society was committed to the idea that there existed a spirituality which underpinned and linked the main religious traditions of the world, and thereby served to provide a unifying dimension for all of humanity. It was committed to the study of the different world religions, but with an emphasis upon the religions of the Indian subcontinent. It also believed that human beings possessed a great potential in terms of spirituality, and that this could be revealed with the correct study and religious practice. The Society opened its headquarters at Adyar near Chennai. In more recent times it has become one of the major influences on the New Age movement.

Besant had many interests besides religion, and was among other things a campaigner for human rights. In 1888 she publicized the dangerous working conditions of the women who worked in match factories in London. She became a member of the Theosophical Society in 1889, and in 1907 its president. A lifelong promoter of Indian culture, Besant supported Indian independence, and was also instrumental in the establishment of Benaras (now Banaras) Hindu University, to this day a leading seat of Hindu and Sanskrit studies.

The sociology of new religious movements

One of the features of contemporary society has been the development of new religions. Some of these are entirely separate from long-established mainstream faiths, while others have fragmented from existing religions, often through doctrinal disputes or under the influence of a new, charismatic leader. It is difficult to establish clear criteria for defining an organization as a new religious movement. Even the apparently straightforward issue of defining 'new' is problematic. A number of sociological issues have been raised about new religious movements, many concerning the process by which new members are recruited and then inducted into the movement.

Did you know?

The new religious movement called Heaven's Gate believed that the Earth was going to be cleaned and re-formed. The movement was established around 1970 in California by Marshall Applewhite and Bonnie Nettles. They proposed that the only strategy to survive the cleansing of the Earth was to join an alien space ship, which was said to be flying near the Hale-Bopp comet. Once aboard the UFO the members of Heaven's Gate would be transported to a higher spiritual and psychological level, which would enable them to survive the coming transformation of the world. The members of the group had very few material possessions and led a simple, limited existence.

The group was convinced by Applewhite that the only way to join the UFO was to commit mass suicide. The 39 members of the group, including Applewhite, did this over a three-day period in March 1997. The bodies of all members were found in the same positions, and wearing the same clothes. It is difficult to know whether this indicated a consensus concerning Applewhite's teaching, or whether he was a dominating leader who was able to impose his will.

Much of the criticism of new religious movements has centred around suggestions that potential members are brainwashed during the induction process. As Gallagher has suggested:

> 'Some family members troubled by their loved ones' involvement with innovative groups began to look closely at the communities and their leaders, and they often concluded that their offspring were somehow being exploited.'
>
> Gallagher, Eugene (2004), *The New Religious Movements Experience in America* (p. 3).

It has been asserted that potential recruits are often young and impressionable, eagerly seeking a sense of meaning in life, and may not have a secure background. It has also been suggested that new religious movements frequently use unethical psychological processes to encourage people to join.

While some of these assertions may contain elements of truth in some instances, there is research evidence that this is only part of the truth.

Key idea: New religious movements

Some criticisms of new religious movements have asserted that they attempt to recruit younger and perhaps more vulnerable young people to their organization who are not equipped psychologically to challenge the recruitment strategies.

Eileen Barker (1938–) carried out seminal research on the recruitment process employed by the Unification Church, or 'Moonies', as they were more commonly known. She documented her research in a 1984 book *The Making of a Moonie: Choice or Brainwashing?* Her research dispelled several myths about the recruitment process. During the period of the research there were far fewer members of the Church than was commonly supposed. The recruitment process was not very effective, with around 90 per cent of each cohort not joining the Church. In addition there was a high proportion of new recruits who, after a relatively short period of membership, decided to leave the Church. There is thus some evidence, that at least in this case, potential members were not significantly swayed by group pressure or other factors in becoming members of the Unification Church.

Did you know?

The New Age Movement, which developed in the 1960s and 1970s, espoused many of the principles associated with the 'counterculture'. It argued for a plural society, a holistic approach to the world including an emphasis upon ecology and the environment, and an ability to draw upon a wide range of spiritual traditions. The New Age movement has been influenced by many groups and practices including Theosophists, neopagans, yoga, meditation, and Hindu and Buddhist traditions. It believes that the world can be steered towards a 'new age', characterized by a sense of unity, cooperation and non-violence. In this 'new age' for the planet Earth, it is argued that not only will individuals be transformed spiritually, but society itself will take on a new and positive form.

The process of investigating new religious movements is complicated by the range of terminology that is employed for smaller religious groups, or for those that break away from larger, well-established religions. The best-known conceptual model, which was influenced originally by the work of Max Weber, is known as the Church-Sect Continuum. It seeks to link together the concepts of church, denomination and sect, and also to indicate the way in which a cult or a new religious movement can be seen to develop from these. In this typology, the word 'church' is employed to indicate a well-established religion which, within those societies in which it is established, represents the dominant and exclusive world view. Such a religious organization will normally have acquired considerable economic power and, with that, political power. Such is its degree of influence that it will usually seek to operate what is in effect a religious monopoly. Although this type of church will normally seek to oppose any dissent, at the same time it usually brings with it a degree of stability to the society.

A denomination arises when a subgroup decides to no longer accept the orthodox teaching and practice of a church. This may happen gradually, or it may occur as the result of a sudden rift with the established church. The term is normally used to designate a fairly major grouping, with its own clearly formulated theology, forms of worship, creed and scriptures. While a denomination would not usually wish to be reabsorbed into the original church, it normally sustains amicable relationships with it, and indeed with any other denominations of the same church. A denomination would normally be accepting of a multi-faith society, while at the same time retaining the core beliefs that distinguish it from other churches and denominations. A denomination will often have its own body of priests, who will have specifically defined functions within the organization. Anglicanism is an example of a denomination within the Christian Church; while Shaivism is a denomination within Hinduism.

Sometimes groups will break away from denominations, often on doctrinal grounds. Such groups are frequently known as 'sects' and can subsequently grow into relatively large organizations. Indeed they can develop complex institutional infrastructures and in effect become denominations. Cults differ from sects in that they are not as closely based upon existing religious traditions or theologies. They tend to be more innovative and radical, and are often led by a person with charismatic qualities. Perhaps partly because of the often extreme and unusual aspects of their belief system and practice, cults do not always grow very large in terms of membership. Some cults have developed adverse reputations because of extreme behaviour. One example was the Peoples Temple led by Jim Jones, which while established as a commune in Guyana, was the scene of a mass suicide or murder of members in November 1978. The word 'cult' has thus come to have pejorative connotations, and hence cults are often referred to as 'new religious movements'.

Did you know?

The Branch Davidians was a new religious movement that developed in the mid-1950s. At the end of the 1980s it was headed by David Koresh at headquarters near Waco, Texas. From time to time there were reports by people of hearing gunfire from within the headquarters, and there was other evidence that the Branch Davidians were collecting weapons. A court warrant was obtained to search the premises on 28 February 1993. Police officers and officials of the Bureau of Alcohol, Tobacco and Firearms tried to carry out the search. Gunfire broke out and four government officers were killed, along with some members of the Branch Davidians. There followed an FBI siege of the premises that lasted 51 days. Eventually, the premises were overrun on 19 April, and an intense conflagration followed. Koresh and 75 other Branch Davidians were killed. With hindsight it seems evident that the members of the group were deeply committed to the teachings of Koresh. As Tabor and Gallagher have suggested:

What the authorities apparently never perceived is that Koresh's preaching was to him and to his followers, the only matter of

Constructionism and religion

'Social constructionism' is a philosophical approach particularly associated with the sociologist Peter Berger (1929–) that has been applied by him to the study of religion. The basic premise of constructionism is that society itself creates the elements that we recognize as being a significant part of society. In the case of religion, constructionism proposes that certain aspects of the world are defined as sacred or mystical, and that these are a product of society. These objects may take a number of different forms, and have their own particular significance. Examples include caves or trees associated with a historical religious figure; relics of religious teachers such as bones or spiritual artefacts; and constructions such as crosses or statues.

Key idea: Social constructionism

Social constructionism in religion places an emphasis upon the role of society in creating objects and processes that have spiritual content and significance.

These sacred objects may be the subject of prayer or meditation, and hence contribute to the spiritual life of the individual. Within the parameters of social constructionism, objects in the world do not have any intrinsic spiritual or religious qualities, but only those given to them by people.

Dig deeper

Barker, E. (1984), *The Making of a Moonie: Choice or Brainwashing?* Oxford: Blackwell.

Blavatsky, H. P. (de Zirkoff, B. Ed.) (1978), *The Secret Doctrine*. Wheaton, IL: Theosophical Publishing House.

Calhoun, C., Juergensmeyer, M. & VanAntwerpen, J. (Eds.) (2011), *Rethinking Secularism*. Oxford: Oxford University Press.

Heelas, P. (1996), *The New Age Movement*. Oxford: Blackwell.

January, B. (2008), *The Iranian Revolution*. Minneapolis: Twenty-First Century.

Test your knowledge

1 In France the Concordat of 1905 affirmed...?
   a ...the power of the Church.
   b ...the separation of Church and State.
   c ...the governance of the Church.
   d ...the continuation of a male priesthood.

2 The Iranian Revolution and creation of an Islamic Republic took place in...?
   a 1973
   b 1975
   c 1977
   d 1979

3 Who wrote *The Protestant Ethic and the Spirit of Capitalism*?
   a Durkheim
   b Berger
   c Luckmann
   d Weber

4 Helena Blavatsky was connected primarily with which religious tradition?
   a Church of England
   b Buddhist Society
   c Theosophical Society
   d Jainism

5 Heaven's Gate was a...?
   a UFO tradition
   b Christian tradition
   c Sikh tradition
   d Pagan tradition

6 Members of the Unification Church are sometimes known as...?
   a Roman Catholics
   b Protestants
   c Taoists
   d Moonies

7 A group that breaks away from a denomination is often termed a...?

    a sect

    b cult

    c faith

    d tradition

8 The headquarters of the Branch Davidians was in...?

    a Washington

    b San Diego

    c Waco

    d Los Angeles

9 Who was the leader of the Peoples Temple?

    a Jim Smith

    b Jim Jones

    c John Jones

    d John Smith

10 Annie Besant was associated with the founding of?

    a Delhi University

    b Punjab University

    c Benaras (Banaras) Hindu University

    d Mumbai University

8

Society, the mass media and the Internet

This chapter contrasts the perspective of the media as on the one hand principally reflecting and reporting on society as it currently exists, while on the other viewing it as analysing and recreating society using whatever subjective analyses it wishes to employ. Within the latter perspective the media and journalists are seen as defining that which is important in society, and placing differential emphasis upon social and political events. In the modern age, knowledge was generally only available to powerful elites, who were able to purchase a sophisticated education for their children. In the postmodern world, the Internet has, on one view, democratized knowledge, so that all individuals can potentially become 'experts' and challenge received wisdom. Social media appears to encourage participants to submit their life trajectories for public consumption. The chapter will analyse these issues, although it is difficult yet to predict the full consequences for society.

The nature of the mass media

In the early days of the mass media, when there were very few radio and television channels, there was little basis of comparison in terms of the way news stories were reported. There was an implicit assumption that 'the news' was a more or less objective account of the reality of world events. However, as a greater variety of media outlets became available the general public was able to compare newspaper accounts with audio and visual reporting. The result was a growing awareness that a news event could be presented from a variety of different perspectives, each of which had its own sense of legitimacy.

There is now a general acceptance that there is no objective truth or reality in society waiting to be reported and disseminated. We look to journalists to try to make sense of economic, political and cultural events, knowing full well that their analysis will inevitably be affected by their own background, education, interests and personal value system. We are also increasingly aware of the important role of photojournalists in reporting events. Different impressions may be given by a photograph depending upon the time of the day, direction, whether it is close or long range and the number of people in the shot. The advent of mobile phone photography also means that members of the public, who by chance are present at significant events, can take and distribute their own images. To that extent, in an electronic age, we are all part of the mass media.

Thus, whether accounts, articles or photos emanate from either professional journalists or from members of the public, there is an element of selectivity in determining the events to report. In some cases events, be they earthquakes, elections, wars and so on, are sufficiently significant to demand reporting; but in many instances it is a matter of choosing one smaller event rather than another. This process of selection enables the mass media to record, analyse and distribute what are seen as important elements in society. Thus the mass media reflect what they see as the nature of society but, in addition, they also help to create the essence of society. For example, at any one time there may be numerous conflicts taking place around the world, but perhaps only one is discussed on the national news. This conflict may have been chosen because of its potential political implications, or because it is located in an area of economic and industrial importance. The act of selecting it, however, not only records a societal event, but brings this to the forefront of public attention, thus attempting to define what is significant in the world.

Theoretical perspectives on sociology and the media

The argument that the mass media are closely involved in determining the issues that the public considers important is known as 'agenda-setting'. Assuming that a certain degree of intentional agenda-setting is a reality, then it begs the question as to whose or which agenda is being addressed. Some argue that editorial decisions are almost inevitably influenced by the people and organizations that own the media outlets. In other cases, there may be long-standing political or ideological affiliations that exert influence.

When people in the media select a particular subject for emphasis, or perhaps run a series of articles on the same theme, they are through that selective process in effect setting an agenda. As Lanson & Stephens put it:

> 'In fact, news judgement is an indispensable skill at all levels of journalism. Editors need this skill to decide which of the flood of press releases and tips they get every day are worth pursuing, and which stories in each day's paper deserve the most prominence.'
>
> Lanson, Gerald & Stephens, Mitchell (1994),
> *Writing and Reporting the News* (p. 10).

Key idea: Determining news issues

It is often argued that the mass media are instrumental in determining the news issues that the public regard as significant.

Continually bringing a topic into the public consciousness encourages people to reflect on that subject, but it does not tell them what to think. The 'framing' process links to the subject of the agenda by encouraging people to think about the subject in a particular way. This is done by suggesting a range of concepts that might be employed in the analysis of the subject, or by suggesting other topics with which the subject might be connected.

Key idea: News analysis

One role of the mass media is to analyse news events. This often has the effect of encouraging the public to think about news items in a particular way. Some may argue that this can have positive or negative consequences depending upon the circumstances.

For example, a tsunami might be presented as an unfortunate natural event that occurs from time to time. On the other hand, it might be presented as being linked to global warming and the consequences of climate change. Finally, it might be framed as a result of climate change, which is linked to a lack of political will to reduce carbon dioxide emissions. The way in which the mass media frame the tsunami encourages the public to take a particular stance on the related societal, political or economic issues.

We are all dependent upon the mass media to a greater or lesser extent, usually because we simply do not have the time to assemble all the knowledge and analysis needed to understand the world. The degree to which we need this knowledge depends upon a number of societal factors. This theory, often known as 'Dependency Theory', argues that when society is going through major changes such as wars, conflicts, political upheaval, changes in energy production or economic uncertainty, we rely much more on the mass media for information. In these circumstances we want to understand society so that we can position ourselves more effectively in order to respond to the changes. However, during periods when society is relatively stable, we may have less dependence upon the media, since there are fewer social changes to understand.

Although as a society we place great reliance on the mass media for information and analysis, we are also increasingly autonomous when it comes to reflecting on issues and events in society. This is partly because we have access to a great deal of information on the Internet, which enables us to evaluate articles we read or hear about in the media.

Key idea: The power of the Internet

Widespread access to the Internet has revolutionized the capacity of people to interpret and attribute meaning to news events. People can now form authoritative judgements through a ready access to expert knowledge.

For example, suppose that we read about a new potential treatment for a serious illness. We can relatively easily verify some of the claims made by checking information on the Internet, or by consulting the original research on which the claims are made. This type of verification was not a practical possibility before the advent of the Internet. This perspective on the mass media, that people are able to form their own judgements about issues reported in the newspapers or television, is known as 'culturalist theory'. Moreover, the capacity of people to interpret the mass media has also been enhanced by the increasing spread of higher education.

Despite the increasing independence of people in interpreting events, some sociologists such as Stuart Hall (1932–2014) have reminded us that the media often tend to present a distorted picture of black people, and that we are sometimes slow to recognize this inherent bias. Black people are mentioned in debates on sport, immigration, race or crime, but are more rarely included in discussions of other issues. One may ask whether there is a self-fulfilling prophecy operating here, where black people are, for example, less frequently presented as academics or intellectuals, economists, bankers or government ministers, and hence younger black people do not tend to have role models to follow.

Did you know?

Stuart Hall was one of the key founders of the discipline of Cultural Studies. This area of study examines cultures and sub-cultures, and their relationship with those in a position of power and authority. For example, it could consider the educational performance of young black people, examined within the context of their history, their music, family background and ethnicity. Importantly, the cultural studies approach would typically examine the attitudes of the traditional educational system to these issues.

Key idea: News reporting

It is important to remember that the 'news' is ultimately created by people, and hence there is always the potential for bias and distortion. Professional journalists try to avoid this, but there is always the possibility that subjectivity will encroach into news reporting.

The power of the media in exerting influence on the public had been highlighted by Harold Innis (1894–1952) of the University of Toronto. As a young man he had fought in the First World War, and had noted the power of the mass media in encouraging men to volunteer to fight. Throughout his academic career he remained opposed to media monopolies, which he saw as moulding public views on issues.

Did you know?

At the age of 22 in 1916 Harold Innis volunteered as a member of the Canadian Expeditionary Force to fight in the First World War. He took part in the Battle of Vimy Ridge in April 1917. Vimy is situated on the Douai Plains in the Pas-de-Calais region of northern France. Today it is a low ridge covered in trees, yet it provides the only high ground on a surrounding flat plain. For this reason it had great tactical significance during the war, and was

Innis was also a great influence on his younger colleague at
the University of Toronto, Marshall McLuhan (1911–80).
McLuhan became arguably the most famous and celebrated
writer on issues concerning the mass media. Although he wrote
extensively on the media, he probably became most famous
through the aphorisms that caught the imagination of the
public. In saying that 'the medium is the message' (McLuhan
1964, p. 7) Marshall McLuhan pointed to the importance of the
way in which images and ideas were transmitted, as opposed to
the significance of the ideas themselves. Thus to stand looking
up at the large advertising screens in Las Vegas or Times Square,
New York is to be affected as much by the glittering colours and
movement of the images, as by the presumed ideas that they are
seeking to transmit.

Key idea: The significance of the medium

McLuhan pointed out the importance of the way in which ideas
were disseminated around the globe, suggesting that the medium
of transmission was sometimes more significant than the ideas
themselves.

McLuhan was also several decades ahead of his time by
pointing out the way in which electronic media could link
human beings around the world, thus pre-dating the Internet.
He used the term 'global village' to encapsulate this idea
(McLuhan & Powers, 1989).

Some sociologists, notably Herbert J. Gans (1927–) of
Columbia University have set out to examine empirically
the process of news creation. Gans was well known for his
research involving participant observation, and he employed

this approach on a lengthy study of the newsrooms of major news organizations (Gans, 2005). He noted that the traditional approach to news gathering involved approaches to leading 'authorities' in a particular field, or to leading politicians. He felt that this approach was rather biased in that it examined the news from the perspective of the wealthier social classes and of major business and finance organizations. His view was that the interests and concerns of the working classes were significantly underrepresented in news production, and that this could be corrected by drawing upon a wider cross-section of people when collecting news stories. In relation to representation by ordinary people, Gans wrote:

'The news media continue to reinforce the idea, particularly through their continuous and detailed coverage of election campaign events (and non-events), almost as if the never-ending coverage could prove that the citizenry still holds the ultimate power.'

Gans, Herbert (2003), *Democracy and the News* (p. 2).

This idea of a much more eclectic news-gathering process was termed 'multiperspectival journalism' by Gans. It was to be characterized by employing a broader cross-section of journalists than was traditionally the case, and in particular by using ordinary members of the public as journalists, when appropriate.

German sociologist Jürgen Habermas (1929–) was also democratic in his approach, in the sense that he supported what he called the 'public sphere' (Habermas, 1989). According to Habermas, the public sphere was more of a principle, than necessarily an actual forum in which debate took place. Nevertheless, he conceived of the public sphere as a range of different media within which ordinary people could debate topics and issues, and hence make their opinions known to government. These media could include the printed press, radio, email, and in more contemporary times, electronic social media. The key characteristics of the public sphere were, according to Habermas, the possibility of all citizens participating in debate, and that discussions should be conducted in the spirit of a critique of society based upon rational principles of sociological enquiry. As Habermas asserts:

> 'Alone among the disciplines of social science, sociology has retained its relations to problems of society as a whole. Whatever else it has become, it has always remained a theory of society as well.'
>
> Habermas, Jürgen (1984), *The Theory of Communicative Action, Vol. 1: Reason and the Rationalization of Society* (p. 5).

Did you know?

Born in June 1929, by the closing months of the Second World War in early 1945, Habermas was drafted – at only 15 years of age – into the German Army to help in the final defence of Germany. At the end of the war in May 1945, and with the emerging revelations of Nazi atrocities, Habermas was appalled at the true nature of National Socialism in Germany. This awareness remained with him throughout his life, influencing his academic work.

Habermas always harboured certain suspicions concerning the press since he felt that they were agents of corporate business, and would thus ultimately undermine the key principles of the public sphere. Not dissimilar views were held by Marcuse (1968), who was critical of the values of corporate and industrial society.

Herbert Marcuse (1898–1979)

Marcuse was very critical of corporate, capitalist society because he felt that it created a value system that was constructed around the greater and greater consumption of material goods. As consumption increased then industrial production had to keep pace. There was often no real need for many of these consumer goods, but people were persuaded that they needed them. Widespread advertising, normally using the mass media as a vehicle for dissemination, was central to the act of persuading people to extend their consumption of goods. Once people became committed to a consumer society, the ever-increasing need for material possessions became a form of social control. The desire for consumer goods could be used to persuade people to commit to increased levels of industrial work. Marcuse was concerned that within such a scenario people would cease to think critically about society, as they devoted themselves to a materialistic lifestyle.

Originally the mass media, and notably the written press, was needed to provide expert interpretation of events for members of the public. The advent of the Internet and sophisticated mobile phones has now provided almost unlimited knowledge to all, with the result that individuals can analyse events for themselves. This will no doubt result in a transformation of the media, yet in ways that are difficult to predict.

Dig deeper

Barker, C. (2012), *Cultural Studies – Theory and Practice* (4th ed.). London: Sage.

Campbell, R., Martin, C. R. & Fabos, B. (2012), *Media & Culture: An Introduction to Mass Communication* (8th ed.). Boston: Bedford/St Martin's.

McLuhan, M. & Fiore, Q. (1967), *The Medium is the Massage: An Inventory of Effects.* Harmondsworth: Penguin.

Ryan, M. (2010), *Cultural Studies – A Practical Introduction.* Chichester, West Sussex: Wiley-Blackwell.

Street, J. (2011), *Mass Media, Politics and Democracy* (2nd ed.). Basingstoke, Hants: Palgrave Macmillan.

Test your knowledge

1 In relation to the mass media 'agenda-setting' is...?
  a ...organizing a meeting efficiently.
  b ...passing the agenda to the meeting secretary in plenty of time.
  c ...letting everyone have a say in the agenda.
  d ...influencing the way in which the public consider certain issues as important.

2 In the mass media the concept of 'framing' relates to...?
  a ...the way in which people are encouraged to think about an issue.
  b ...the way a photo is presented in a newspaper.
  c ...the cover of a news magazine.
  d ...photographs of journalists.

3 Dependency theory argues that we need the mass media more...?
  a ...at the weekends.
  b ...when society is going through a period of rapid change.
  c ...when society is fairly stable.
  d ...when a major new film is released.

4 Culturalist theory suggests that...?
  a ...people want to understand other cultures.
  b ...people want to learn foreign languages.
  c ...people can form their own judgements about issues in the media.
  d ...people prefer accounts of literature and the arts in the media.

5 Harold Innis was known for his opposition to...?
  a tabloid newspapers
  b the power of the media
  c news magazines
  d TV news channels

6 Marshall McLuhan was famous for his slogan...?

    a the message is the medium

    b the medium is the message

    c the media make up the message

    d the massage of the message

7 Herbert Gans carried out an empirical study of newsrooms using...?

    a a positivist approach

    b participant observation

    c a phenomenological approach

    d statistical surveys

8 The principle of drawing upon a wider cross-section of people when collecting news stories is known as?

    a multiperspectival journalism

    b trade reporting

    c varied reporting

    d systematic approach journalism

9 Habermas felt it important to have a forum within which a rational critique of society could take place. He called this?

    a the forum

    b the public society

    c the society of debate

    d the public sphere

10 McLuhan's term 'global village' anticipated the development of...?

    a the garden city

    b skyscrapers

    c the Internet

    d modern architecture

9

Health and social policy

The provision of health care in society raises a number of
important sociological issues. The starting point of discussion
of health care is arguably the philosophical thesis that everyone
is entitled to the same level of care by society in order to help
them maintain a good state of health and to prolong their
lives. The question then becomes, how do we achieve this in
a world of increasingly limited resources? The chapter will
discuss the consequences of an increasingly ageing population
and the quality of health care. Questions of economics overlap
with sociology here, where the citizen has higher and higher
expectations in terms of treatment. The chapter will also discuss
the issues of the social control of people's behaviour, in terms
of, say, tobacco and alcohol consumption, in order to minimize
their health needs.

The sociology of health

If someone is healthy, then this can be considered as a matter of luck or of a fortunate genetic inheritance. On the other hand, it can be thought of as a result of a number of different social or environmental factors. A person who comes from a wealthy family may have the opportunity to live in a healthy, unpolluted environment, and to have the facilities to play sport and take a lot of exercise. Such a person may have had a sound education and appreciate the benefits of a balanced diet. As a result of their education he or she may also understand the adverse consequences of an excessive consumption of alcohol. They will also know that smoking or taking drugs will be likely harmful to health. Some people therefore are fortunate by virtue of their birth, and perhaps also in terms of their lifestyle choices, to improve their chances of being healthy. Others may not have the same advantages. Even if they are aware of the nature of a healthy diet, they may not be able to adopt one for financial reasons.

These latter issues involve a range of social factors that have an impact upon the origin of illness. If someone suffers from a form of congestion of the lungs, for example, then the immediate cause may be that the person worked in a dusty industrial environment. However, one can extend the analysis by reflecting whether the person had the opportunity to take a different kind of job, in which there was less atmospheric pollution. Flexibility in terms of career is often a function of the degree of education and training undertaken by an individual, and this in turn may be related to social class. In other words, when evaluating the cause of an illness, there may be a complex network of social factors that are operating. Every one of us is born into a subculture of one sort or another, which has certain characteristics in terms of, say, alcohol consumption or of eating. It is not always easy to resist the social pressures emanating from these subcultures, and to different degrees we bear the consequences of our adhering to such norms and values. These ultimately have an impact on our health.

In short then, we can argue that illnesses have a number of different causes, some of which are indeed clinical, but others may well be social. If we are to fully understand the nature of health and illness, then we need to fully understand the complexity of the social background to these phenomena.

> **Key idea:** Social pressures
>
> Social pressures inherent in a particular subculture may encourage patterns of behaviour that are harmful to health.

A Marxist perspective on health

For a Marxist, the relationship between the owners of the means of production and those who work for them leads to a situation where the latter are disadvantaged in terms of health. An example would be in the case of industrial accidents, where workers may be injured sometimes because of a lack of due diligence on the part of employers in ensuring the safety of the work environment. Marxists would also argue that the continuous desire on the part of employers in a capitalist system to generate profit leads to a lack of care with regard to their employees. This, according to Marxists, can lead to employers accepting, for example, a polluted work environment that can have adverse health consequences for their workers. Equally, the desire of employers to limit wage increases reduces the potential for workers to afford a healthy diet and lifestyle.

> **Key idea:** Marxism and the health of workers
>
> A Marxist perspective argues that the pursuit of profit in a capitalist society can lead to the exploitation of workers by their employers.

According to Marxists, there are thus considerable social inequalities in terms of standards of health that are immediately traceable to the basic unfairness of a capitalist system.

A functionalist analysis of health

One of the essentials of the functionalist approach to society is that each human being has a specific function, the fulfilment of which helps to maintain the cohesion of society. More accurately, perhaps, one might say that each human being has several functions that require simultaneous fulfilment. For example, a woman may be a mother, a wife, a writer, a teacher and a tennis player. A typical human being will have a variety of different roles; the successful conduct of each will probably require a reasonable but different level of health. If someone is a member of a sports team, and sprains his or her back, they may not be able to continue in that role. However, if they also work as an accountant, they may be able to continue working.

This kind of situation was analysed by Talcott Parsons in his 1951 book *The Social System*, and he employed the term 'sick role' to describe someone who was unable to conduct their normal functions, to some extent or another, because of their illness. Parsons thought of someone who was ill as being 'deviant', in the sense that they were forced to 'deviate' from their normal role(s) in society.

Such a person substituted some or all of their typical roles for a new role, that of the 'sick role'. According to Parsons this role had a number of characteristics.

Did you know?

In a sociological sense 'deviance' is very often a relative concept. A particular behaviour pattern may be normal in one situation, but definitely not acceptable in another. Hence drinking alcohol to excess may be inadvisable, but still the norm at a student party, while the same consumption of alcohol may be thought of as utterly inappropriate at a church council meeting. Quite apart from deviance being defined by the norms of a particular social group, it can also be at least partly defined by an individual. In a sense, deviance may be a little like beauty, in that its nature exists in the eye of the beholder. Of two members of the same peer group, one may find a behaviour acceptable, while another finds it to deviate much too far from the group norms.

Key idea: 'Sick role'

Talcott Parsons coined the idea of the 'sick role' for the person who through illness was unable to fulfil their normal role in society.

The most important feature of the sick role was that if the person's condition was to be accepted as genuine, then an external authority such as a doctor needed to affirm the nature of the illness. Once this was accomplished, then the person could assume a genuine sick role in society.

For this role to operate effectively in society, Parsons took the view that an individual should not be considered responsible for their illness, and should not be expected to fulfil their previous roles in society. There are, however, some problems with this position. We might consider, for example, the case of someone who has drunk alcohol to excess and developed chronic liver disease. One might argue that such a person is responsible for their own illness, and therefore does not merit being permitted to assume an official sick role. On the other hand, we might accept an argument that the person is genetically susceptible to alcohol addiction, and therefore has been in effect unable to help themselves. In that sense they would not be held responsible for their illness. This distinction is important because the general public is less likely to accept the legitimacy or relevance of the sick role in cases where it is felt that the individual could and should have helped themselves.

Key idea: Lifestyle matters

Some argue that when a person's lifestyle is the cause of their illness, then they do not deserve to be able to adopt the sick role.

An ageing population

The proportion of older people in the populations of most Western countries is increasing dramatically. Better health care, more sophisticated treatments and medication, and a better standard of living have all contributed to this. As the United Nations reports:

> 'Ageing results from the demographic transition, a process whereby reductions in mortality are followed by reductions in fertility. Together, these reductions eventually lead to smaller

proportions of children and larger proportionate shares of older people in the population.'

United Nations (2013), *World Population Ageing 2013*.

ST/ESA/SER.A/348 (p. 3).

Nevertheless, as people grow older they start to suffer from a variety of ailments, which are exacerbated by the fact that many elderly people live on their own, or in less-than-desirable accommodation. The result is that elderly people often make greater resource demands upon the health and social care systems. In addition, the number of people of pensionable age, relative to the size of the working population, should continue to rise, leaving a smaller and smaller workforce to sustain older members of society. In parallel, the overall cost of pension payments will continue to rise. The situation is made more problematic because young couples are not having children at the same age as in previous generations. The reduction in the birth rate results in there being a smaller population of young people to create wealth for the future, and to help support an ageing population.

However, a functionalist may well argue that there are some positive features about the role of elderly people in society. Since they live for longer, they pay income tax for a longer period on their pension income, and in addition have considerable spending power in the economy. Also, the nature of work is changing: it involves less hard, physical work than in previous years, and is increasingly computer-based. This enables older people to continue to work part-time past their formal retirement age, and to make a contribution towards the economy.

In a case where it is accepted that a person should assume the sick role, it is normal that society does not expect them to continue with their usual roles, for example at work. However, some people who have the opportunity to assume the sick role, and to legitimately avoid working, prefer to continue with their job, even in a capacity of reduced duties. Indeed, employers are often keen for employees to do this, and will often invest in infrastructure that enables ill or temporarily disabled people to continue working.

To have to assume the sick role is traumatic for many people, as it prevents their continuing with the normal rhythms of their life. As Gjernes points out:

> 'To become ill or injured is experienced as a new situation by workers who are used to be in good health and able to use their body as a working tool. The new condition has many consequences and it interrupts the habits and routines of the workers' everyday life; it also challenges their identities and embodied individual subjectivities.'
>
> Gjernes, Trude (2013), 'Work, Sickness, Absence, and Identity-work' (p. 176).

As the above quotation indicates, many people relate their own self-concept and sense of identity to a work role, and when they are ill look forward to resuming their employment. It is an assumption of the sick role that the individual will attempt to recover. However, much may depend upon the nature of the illness. Some illnesses are so serious and irreversible that a cure may seem highly unlikely. Yet, in order to legitimate the sick role, the individual is still expected to do his or her best to find a remedy. To that end they should consult medical experts and follow whatever regime is suggested.

Within a functionalist perspective people who occupy the sick role legitimately are still deviant, to the extent that they are not fulfilling their traditional role in society; but it is a role of 'approved' deviance, in that society recognizes the validity of their role.

The social construction of health and illness

The 'Western' conception of health and illness tends to see the human body as a mechanical construction. Under certain circumstances it functions very effectively, but under adverse conditions it may malfunction. The Western medical model tries to identify the organ or organ system that is not functioning properly, and then seeks to make some type of intervention to remedy the problem. This intervention may involve the administration of chemicals, or the conduct of surgery. In other words, the intervention is physical rather than psychological. The overall assumption within this perspective is that there is a precise, and in principle identifiable, problem with the working of the body, and that there exists, in principle, a precise means of remedying this problem. The advantage of this perspective is that it subjects the body to the systematic investigation of hypothetico-deductive science. On the other hand, it fails to acknowledge the interrelated nature of the body, both internally and also with the external environment.

Did you know?

The model of health within Eastern countries and cultures is much more in tune with the relationship between the body and the whole environment. The concept of health within the Hindu and Buddhist traditions involves a sense of harmony between both the physical and psychological elements of the body, but also with the environment within which the body exists. Hence, within Ayurvedic medicine, for example, diet and yoga play a very important part in the therapeutic role, emphasizing the health of the whole person. As Di Stefano argues:

> 'Today, holism has come to signify a philosophical position that acknowledges the essential unity of creation. It carries the synergetic understanding that wholes are greater than the sum of their parts.'
>
> Di Stefano, Vincent (2006), *Holism and Complementary Medicine: Origins and Principles* (p. xviii).

Diet in particular has been recognized in the West as being an important element in maintaining health, and at the same time related to issues such as poverty. It is difficult for a family to maintain a healthy diet when it is living off a low income.

Occupational health

The relationship between personal illness and environmental factors is often clear when we consider the impact of a person's occupation upon their health. Some occupations are simply more dangerous than others, either in terms of fatalities or of the risk of serious illness. The construction and raw material extraction industries, such as mining, have traditionally been considered very dangerous. In construction there is the risk of falling, or of objects falling on the employee. In mining, apart from rock falls, there is the danger of inhaling dust that will have an adverse effect upon the lungs.

Did you know?

The worst mining accident in European history took place in March 1906 in the Pas-de-Calais region of northern France, at the Courrières mine. More than 1,000 miners were killed. It is thought that an accumulation of coal dust ignited, resulting in a very large explosion. Three days after the explosion some of the mine workings were sealed as it was supposed that no one was left alive. Yet 20 days later 13 miners were found alive, and 4 more days after that a further miner was discovered alive. The action of the mining company led to great anger on the part of the mining communities, exacerbated by the poor equipment provided to miners, and also the low wages. After the disaster there was a long and bitter strike, which finally resulted in somewhat improved working conditions. A Marxist analysis of this event would point to the company owning the mine providing less-than-adequate safety equipment in order to facilitate a rescue. In this case, the rescue teams did not have oxygen masks, which were at the time available.

Working in factories where there is cutting, grinding, rolling or drilling machinery can be very dangerous for employees, while driving or working alongside heavy vehicles generates considerable risk. In order to mitigate the occupational risks of these and related areas, employers have traditionally employed one or both of two types of strategy. The first is to analyse the dangers of the occupation, and then make changes in order to reduce the danger. Hence air filters can be installed to absorb dust, and stronger beams to try to prevent rock falls. The second strategy is to provide safety equipment for employees, for example chemical-proof suits to prevent contamination. Employers may also attach safety guards on machinery, or require on-site drivers to adhere to a speed limit.

Key idea: Occupational illnesses

There is often a close relationship between the illnesses that people acquire and the nature of their present or previous employment.

Some of these measures require the industrial employer to adopt certain safeguards, but also require the employee to use these safeguards. Hence, for example, where an air filter is installed, it is important that the employee remembers to switch this on. Second, where the employer provides safety suits, these must clearly be worn appropriately in dangerous environments. In many cases there is thus a shared responsibility between employer and employee.

One of the contentious areas in occupational safety is the tension between the employers trying to maintain as high a profit margin as possible, and workers and trades unions trying to maintain good standards of safety. A Marxist analysis of this tension will suggest that within a capitalist system, employers will generally try to generate the greatest profits, at the expense of worker safety, particularly if the latter involves considerable investment in safety equipment or in procedures which will inevitably slow down production.

Another contentious area, less specifically related to occupational hazards but still related to the health of the population in general, is the role of advertising. It can be argued that the marketing of powerful cars, which will inevitably travel much faster than the legal speed limit, encourages dangerous driving. The advertising of food products that contain added sugar, or products high in fats, is not encouraging healthy eating and is arguably contributing to obesity.

An area of increasing concern in occupational health is that of work-related stress. Some occupations, such as police officer, fire officer or being a member of the armed forces, are inherently stressful because of the personal danger involved. Other occupations, such as a surgeon, are stressful because of the gravitas of the life and death decisions involved. Many jobs, however, are not inherently stressful, and yet they become so because of the manner in which they are organized or administered. Many jobs in banking, insurance, business, commerce and retail may become very stressful because of the imposed need to meet organizational targets. It is often said that we live in a target-driven culture, where the attainment of the target is more important than the general manner in which an employee carries out the work.

The impact of targets is often seen in occupations such as teaching and social work, where the job to a large extent involves helping with the personal development of an individual. The job is so diverse that it is not easy to specify its outcomes in terms of targets. Certainly in teaching, for example, one can specify that students attain certain grades in external examinations, but this may be to overlook the many other ways in which a teacher may help a student. People will certainly have different views about the efficacy of targets in work performance, but there are certainly arguments that they contribute to enhanced levels of work stress.

Dig deeper

Channing, J. (Ed.) (2007), *Safety at Work* (7th ed.). London: Routledge.

Ervik, R. & Linden, T. S. (2013), *The Making of Ageing Policy: Theory and Practice in Europe*. Cheltenham: Edward Elgar.

Gelder, K. (Ed.) (2005), *The Subcultures Reader* (2nd ed.). London: Routledge.

Lad, V. (1985), *Ayurveda: The Science of Self-Healing* (2nd ed.). Twin Lakes, WI: Lotus Press.

Shilling, C. (2002), 'Culture, the "sick role" and the consumption of health'. *The British Journal of Sociology*, Vol. 53 Issue 4 pp. 621–38.

Test your knowledge

1 The causes of illness are partly genetic and partly the result of...?
   a   inheritance
   b   the kind of person we are
   c   external social factors
   d   diseases we catch

2 A Marxist would argue that a desire for profits on the part of employers in a capitalist system can lead to...?
   a   a reduction in standards of health and safety at work
   b   better wages for workers
   c   a wealthier society
   d   an expansion in industrial production

3 That each human being has a particular role in society which helps to sustain cohesion is an argument of...?
   a   Functionalists
   b   Marxists
   c   Symbolic Interactionists
   d   Phenomenologists

4 The concept of 'sick role' was analysed by Talcott Parsons in his book entitled?
   a   *The Sociological System*
   b   *The Functional System*
   c   *The Socialist System*
   d   *The Social System*

5 According to Parsons, someone who was ill was 'deviant' in not being able to...?
   a   work hard
   b   conduct their normal functions in society
   c   do their job
   d   play sport

6 For a person to assume the 'sick role', the person's condition has to be verified by...?
   a   a work colleague
   b   a sociologist
   c   a police officer
   d   a medical professional

7 The Eastern concept of medicine normally takes into account internal clinical factors as well as psychological and environmental factors. It can thus be described as...?

a therapeutic

b holistic

c meditational

d psychosomatic

8 Being born into a particular subculture may result in our adopting patterns of behaviour that affect our...?

a friends

b social welfare

c long-term health

d sleep patterns

9 When a person assumes the 'sick role' it is not normally expected that...?

a ...they are ill

b ...they will continue with their normal work role

c ...they need to see a surgeon

d ...they need medication

10 Parsons took the view that a person assuming the 'sick role' should...?

a ...be held responsible for their illness

b ...not be held responsible for their illness

c ...not see a doctor

d ...not try to recuperate

Part Three

The Global Society

10

Ethnicity, culture and the movement of peoples

Historically, people have migrated for a variety of reasons including availability of pasture and water, a fear of invasion, or indeed the desire to conquer and subjugate other groups. During modernity, they often moved to find work or to escape the relative poverty of a rural environment. In the early years of the 20th century, for example, many black people moved from the southern states of the United States to the rapidly industrializing centres of the north, such as Chicago. Many of the original migrants to North America had also sought to escape persecution in Europe. In the postmodern age, global communication has informed people in developing countries of the material standard of living in the developed world, resulting in often desperate attempts to avail themselves of a more affluent existence. This chapter will analyse the pressures that can result in the global migration of peoples.

The origins and causes of migration

There are many potential factors which lead people to migrate. In the most general terms, the cause usually involves the unsatisfactory nature of their life in their country of origin. This may include a lack of suitable employment, or in a rural context a lack of grazing and water for livestock, poor crop yields, and hence lack of food for the human population. Civil war, invasion or other forms of conflict may provide a pressing need to migrate. Many of the migrants seeking to reach Europe in the second decade of the 21st century have been either escaping from violence and warfare, or have been driven by economic forces. Such factors that cause people to leave their place or country of origin in search of a better life elsewhere are often known as 'push' factors. The factors that draw people to a new destination are known as 'pull' factors. They may include the prospect of a suitable job, a peaceful existence and life in a democratic society.

Not all migration involves a long journey to a new country or society. There are sometimes large-scale movements of people within the same country. In the late 19th and early 20th centuries many black people migrated from the southern states of the United States to the northern states in search of a more racially liberal society, and where greater industrial development offered better employment opportunities. This period of migration also involved a movement from rural to urban environments such as Chicago and Detroit. Migration often tends to involve a process of urbanization since it is normally in large cities where there is a concentration of job opportunities.

Did you know?

Booker T. Washington (1856–1915) was one of the key leaders of the African American community in the period following the abolition of slavery. He emphasized the need for gradually improving educational opportunities for black people. He was able to gain considerable assistance from all sectors of society for the establishment of schools and colleges to help the African American community.

It has often been the case that young male members of families have migrated in order to find better paid employment, and hence be able to send money back to their extended family at home. In a village or small town this can result in some families becoming relatively wealthy compared to others that are not receiving money from overseas. However, in this case such deprivation can be a push factor in encouraging further emigration.

Key idea: Migration terminology

'Emigration' is the process of leaving one's homeland; 'immigration' is the process of entering a new country; while 'migration' is the term used to describe the overall process.

This was probably one of the factors in the 1950s and 1960s encouraging people to migrate to the UK from the Indian subcontinent. As a generality, many migrant workers are employed in jobs that indigenous workers are reluctant to fill. This tended to happen with the previously mentioned Indian and Pakistani immigrants who worked, for example, on the night shifts in textile mills in the north of England. Even given the nature of the work, there was still a large differential between the wages in England and the typical earnings in the Indian subcontinent. Wage differentials between the country of origin and the country of destination remain one of the biggest factors in encouraging emigration.

Multiculturalism

This term is interpreted in a number of different ways, and there does not seem to be a consensus on its meaning and use. As Hartmann and Gerteis argue:

'But perhaps the first and most fundamental problem is the lack of theoretical clarity about what we mean by multiculturalism.'
Hartmann, Douglas & Gerteis, Joseph (2005), 'Dealing with Diversity: Mapping Multiculturalism in Sociological Terms' (p. 219).

Multiculturalism certainly represents a situation of cultural diversity, in which two or more cultural or ethnic groups live in the same country or region. In one understanding of multiculturalism, these different groups maintain their own cultures, while largely sustaining an independent existence. Within this model, the groups are generally tolerant of each other, and yet there may be a limited degree of integration. This model of multiculturalism may or may not be linked to a philosophy of cultural relativism in which there is an assumption of the general equality of different cultures and religions. Relativism assumes that although cultures and religions may have many differences with respect to, say, ethical issues, they do have a deep-seated equality in terms of the contribution that they make to the world. Nevertheless, cultural relativism, like multiculturalism, remains a philosophically problematic term with little consensus on an agreed meaning.

Multiculturalism may also be associated with varying degrees of integration. This, however, raises the issue of which elements of one culture could legitimately be integrated with certain elements of another culture.

Dr W. E. B. Du Bois (1868–1963) one of the first African Americans to hold a university post in sociology, argued that African Americans should affirm their American citizenship through integration, while at the same time retaining and recognizing their African heritage.

Migrants as refugees

Migration is often motivated not merely by economic factors, but by an urgent wish to escape from persecution, political instability, genocide, ethnic cleansing or warfare. These events often involve human misery and death on a large scale. Unfortunately, the examples are so numerous that one can but indicate a few instances.

During the 1930s, as the Nazi policy of anti-Semitism was increasingly enforced, many Jews attempted to emigrate from Germany and find refuge in the UK or the US. Unfortunately, some delayed their attempts to migrate and were exterminated in concentration camps.

The 'ethnic cleansing' that took place in the former Yugoslavia during the early 1990s was not on the same scale as the genocide perpetrated by the Nazis, but nevertheless constituted a terrible series of events. There was systematic murder and rape in an attempt to render certain areas more ethnically homogeneous. This persecution was also characterized by the attempted destruction of the culture of certain ethnic groups, thus making it difficult for them to reconstruct their identities when the fighting finally stopped. The Yugoslav conflicts throughout the 1990s resulted in large-scale emigration from the area, with many thousands of people settling in Germany, Switzerland, Scandinavia and North America.

Not all large-scale migrations are the result of persecution; some take place because of the results of political decisions. An example was the partition of India in 1947. Following the attaining of independence by India, after the long campaign by the Indian Congress Party, there was a large-scale movement of people, largely along religious lines. Muslims living in India travelled northwards to the newly created state of Pakistan; while Hindus and Sikhs migrated southwards to the newly independent India. The entire migration route was marked by murders and large-scale massacres. The number of deaths is difficult to estimate but may well have been in the region of a million.

The end of this migration saw the beginnings of the Indian and Pakistani diaspora to a number of countries, but largely to the United Kingdom.

Key idea: Diaspora

A diaspora is the large-scale dispersal of a religious, ethnic or racial group from one particular location to, usually, a number of destinations. The diaspora may be caused by a number of factors ranging from persecution to economic factors.

One of the largest historical diasporas was that created by the slave trade between West Africa and the Americas during the period approximately from the 16th century to the 19th century.

Cruel in the extreme to the slaves, it generated huge profits for the organizers, as Thomas notes:

> 'The merchants of Lisbon had been hoping for gold from West Africa. They had found some, but slaves were in more ample supply.'
>
> Thomas, Hugh (1997), *The Slave Trade: The Story of the Atlantic Slave Trade 1440–1870* (p. 23).

Another major diaspora was that of Irish men and women who left Ireland in search of better economic conditions; many went to the United States. A major factor in the diaspora was the famine during the mid-19th century, caused largely by the spread of potato blight.

Sometimes, political decisions had a major effect upon the development of a diaspora. The defeat of South Vietnam by North Vietnam in 1975, and the exodus of United States forces at the conclusion of the Vietnam War, had significant consequences for the population of South Vietnam. Those who felt that they could not exist under a communist regime began to try to leave the country by sea, and the sufferings of such 'boat people' became an international cause célèbre during the late 1970s.

In the case of some communities, they appear to have experienced several diasporas spread over a number of generations. A significant example is that of East African Asians, and in particular those who lived in Uganda. In the last years of the 19th century a number of companies recruited workers from India to help build the Uganda Railway. More than 30,000 workers were recruited and taken to East Africa. The work was extremely dangerous, and many lost their lives, either through illness, accidents or man-eating lions. Between 6,000 and 7,000 workers decided to remain in Uganda once the railway was completed, creating the beginnings of an Asian community. Some workers travelled to other East African countries where there were job opportunities in the colonial civil service.

The Asian community in East Africa was economically very successful. They bought houses, started businesses, opened farms and tea estates, and were generally more financially successful than the majority of the indigenous residents. This led to considerable ill-feeling on the part of the African majority. After Idi Amin took control of Uganda in 1971, he spoke in a forthright manner about the lack of integration between the Asian and African communities, and also on the extent to which the Indian community controlled the economic life of the country.

The following year, in August 1972, President Amin ordered the expulsion of all Asians who were not Ugandan citizens. They were given 90 days to leave Uganda. In 1972 there were approximately 80,000 Asians in Uganda, of whom just over one quarter carried Ugandan passports. In theory, the latter had a right to stay, but such was the negative attitude towards Asians that the vast majority of the community decided to leave.

Many had UK passports and moved to Britain. The British government did its best to try to persuade President Amin to abandon his threat, but failed in this endeavour. Flights from Kampala to London commenced in September of 1972. Before they left, Asian families were required to either allocate their businesses and property to an approved Ugandan citizen or to leave it for the Ugandan government to reallocate. In reality, much of the considerable wealth went to supporters of President Amin. The emigrant families could only take minimal possessions with them on the aircraft, and of the order of £50 to help with immediate expenditure. The majority of Asians moved to Britain, but others travelled to Canada and to India. In some cases, families emigrated to India, and having reorganized their lives, moved later to the United Kingdom. Some descendants of those who were expelled in 1972 have subsequently returned to Uganda, rebuilt a life there, and in some cases managed to gain reparations for assets lost prior to leaving.

In looking back upon the history of the expulsion of the Indian community from Uganda, it is worth considering the influence of British colonialism. In the 19th century, during the days of Empire, the British encouraged workers to migrate from one country to another, depending upon the need for labour.

In colonial India there existed groups of English-speaking, well-educated Indians who had worked in the administrative system of the Raj, and who were able to transfer these skills to East Africa. In addition, the British needed to build railway communications in East Africa in just the same way in which they had constructed a rail network in India. Again, India was a resource of qualified Indian engineers who could take their expertise to Uganda.

During the first half of the 20th century, the Indian and Pakistani community in Uganda established itself, gradually becoming wealthier as individuals established businesses and commerce. They tended to live in their own communities, separate from the indigenous Africans. They founded their own schools and other institutions necessary for a separate life. When Uganda gained independence from the British in 1962, there in effect existed two social strata in Uganda: the majority indigenous African population and an economically powerful Asian minority. There was very little integration between the two communities, except for the necessities of business and trade. Ultimately, the economic differential between the Asian and indigenous communities led to growing tensions that were at least partly the cause of the events of 1972.

Did you know?

Assimilation of one culture by another can take place when an immigrant group adapts closely to the culture of the host population. This may be advantageous to the immigrant group in terms of being able to adjust to a new society. On the other hand, there is the risk that the immigrant group will lose its original culture.

European expansion

In many cases around the world, expansion by peoples of European descent has been a significant threat to the cultures of indigenous inhabitants. Notable examples include the westwards expansion in the United States, and the colonization of Australia. In the United States the end of the Civil War in 1865 freed the government to pursue a policy of western expansion into Oklahoma territory, and to encourage settlers to move west.

There was a belief that this strategy would bring 'civilization' to the West, and also increase the prosperity of the United States.

Did you know?

Ethnocentrism is the approach that people take when they view the world from the perspective of their own cultural or ethnic group. Implicitly, they regard their own culture as superior to the others. Eurocentrism is an approach giving primacy to European values and culture, particularly when considering undeveloped or underdeveloped countries. Religiocentrism is the assumption that one's own religion reflects a more accurate view of the divine, faith and belief than other religions.

In 1889, US president Benjamin Harrison permitted a large section of Oklahoma to be made available for settlers. The subsequent 'land run' enabled would-be settlers to claim ownership of an area of farmland. So rapid was the development of Oklahoma that by the end of 1889 the government realized that the majority of the available land had been claimed, and that to all intents and purposes a western limit to expansion no longer existed.

The United States government tried by various means to relocate indigenous inhabitants, leading to numerous 'Indian Wars'. The Battle of Wounded Knee in December 1890 was probably the final significant event of such conflict. By 1924 all indigenous Americans had been formally offered citizenship of the United States. The conflict between the settlers moving west and the indigenous inhabitants had been painful and difficult in the extreme.

Key idea: American Indians

At this time there was little appreciation of the culture of American Indians. They led a nomadic lifestyle and had a very close relationship with the natural environment. Their spiritual beliefs were also linked closely to the living world. Their culture was much more complex and sophisticated than was the common assumption of European settlers.

Native American tribes had frequently been forced through various measures to relocate from their traditional lands, and it is scarcely surprising that under these circumstances their history, culture and languages were in danger of disappearing. By approximately the 1960s, however, there was a growing interest in the culture of ethnic minorities and indigenous peoples. Children who were the descendants of indigenous Americans had been educated in the American high school system, and had progressed to university. Some began to conduct social and historical research on Native American ethnicity, and gradually this evolved into a distinct area of study. Conferences on Native American culture were held, and academic journals founded. This is now a well-established academic area.

Key idea: Indigenous cultures

In universities throughout the world anthropologists and sociologists are increasingly interested in the cultures of indigenous communities. There is an appreciation of how much we can learn from such societies, particularly in terms of their relationship with the natural environment.

The treatment of the indigenous people of Australia followed a broadly similar pattern to that in the United States. When the process of colonization of Australia commenced in the late 18th century, there was immediate conflict with many of the indigenous inhabitants. Infectious diseases brought from Europe had a serious effect upon the Aboriginal Australians, and resulted in the eradication of many communities. In addition, the widespread use of alcohol had a continuing debilitating effect upon indigenous communities.

Just as in the United States, there was a long-term strategy of driving the indigenous inhabitants from their traditional lands and hunting areas. Having to leave their home territory had a serious effect on the indigenous people, both psychologically and physically. Most of the forced migrations were achieved by the use of violent methods, and the treatment of the Aboriginal Australians could legitimately be described as genocide. With the passage of time however, there were some attempts to achieve a form of integration and to make reparations for previous injustices. In 1963, all Aboriginal Australians were given the vote in federal elections, and in 1976 the Aboriginal Land Rights Act returned some land entitlement to indigenous groups. However, as Chesterman and Galligan suggest:

> 'Central to the new Commonwealth's approach to citizenship was the term 'aboriginal native'. People who came within that category were denied, in addition to the franchise, basic benefits such as the maternity allowance and invalid and old-age pensions.'
> Chesterman, John & Galligan, Brian (1997), *Citizens without Rights: Aborigines and Australian Citizenship* (p. 12).

Key idea: Connection to the land

Indigenous Australians have a different attitude to their traditional lands than do European settlers and immigrants. For indigenous people the land is very much connected with their mythology, with their spiritual beliefs, and with the physical aspects of survival in extensive desert areas.

By 2007, the United Nations in New York had recognized the unique position of indigenous peoples around the world, and the parallels in the kind of oppression that they had faced. The United Nations published the Declaration on the Rights of Indigenous Peoples, which laid out a set of ethical principles by which indigenous peoples should be treated.

Dig deeper

Collier, P. (2013), *Exodus: Immigration and Multiculturalism in the 21st Century*. London: Penguin.

Goodhart, D. (2013), *The British Dream: Successes and Failures of Post-War Immigration*. London: Atlantic Books.

McGrath, A. (ed.) (1995), *Contested Ground: Australian Aborigines under the British Crown*. Crows Nest, NSW: Allen and Unwin.

Modood, T. (2013), *Multiculturalism* (2nd ed.). Cambridge: Polity.

Rattansi, A. (2011), *Multiculturalism: A Very Short Introduction*. Oxford: Oxford University Press.

Test your knowledge

1 In migration, 'push' factors are those that cause people...?
   a   to seek a job in their new country
   b   to take their family with them
   c   to leave their homeland
   d   to resist emigration

2 'Pull' factors are those that...?
   a   dissuade people from migrating
   b   draw immigrants to a new destination
   c   draw people to a different culture
   d   persuade people to remain in their homeland

3 Emigration is...?
   a   another name for migration
   b   the process of settling in another country
   c   the process of adjusting to a new culture
   d   the process of leaving one's country of domicile

4 In which year did the Partition of India take place?
   a   1947
   b   1957
   c   1942
   d   1939

5 A diaspora is the large-scale migration of a people from one country to...?
   a   Europe
   b   the Americas
   c   a single destination
   d   a variety of locations

6 Assimilation takes place when an immigrant group...?
   a   adapts to the culture of the host community
   b   rejects the culture of the host community
   c   gains employment in a new country
   d   returns regularly to its original country

7 Ethnocentrism is the perspective of people who...?

    a ...prefer their own way of life.

    b ...want their children to be educated in the same way as themselves.

    c ...believe that their own ethnic group is the most important on Earth.

    d ...look at the world through their own particular world view.

8 The Battle of Wounded Knee was the final major battle of...?

    a the American Civil War

    b the wars between indigenous Americans and western settlers

    c the American War of Independence

    d the conflicts to end racial segregation

9 When Europeans first settled in Australia, the indigenous peoples consequently suffered from...?

    a infectious diseases brought from Europe

    b a nomadic lifestyle

    c a shortage of food

    d a shortage of drinking water

10 The 1976 Aboriginal Land Rights Act...?

    a ...permitted the sale of Aboriginal land.

    b ...allowed indigenous people to farm.

    c ...permitted hunting on Aboriginal land.

    d ...returned the title deeds of some Aboriginal land to indigenous groups.

11

Differential economic opportunity

Sociology is interested in the different levels of opportunity possessed by social groups. Different levels of economic opportunity may result from some groups having better access to education, access to better paid jobs in the area they live, whether or not they live in an urban or a rural environment, and the capacity of some groups to familiarize themselves with new technologies. In southern India, for example, cities such as Cochin have a wealthy middle class, at least partly because of the thriving computer industries in that city. Socioeconomists would at least partly explain this by the policy of successive state governments in Kerala to ensure a high literacy rate in the population. This chapter will thus explore the interface between economic decisions, such as investment in education or the establishment of high technology industries, and how these can have an impact upon social opportunities.

The influence of geography

Differential opportunity, whether in terms of access to education, health, employment or housing, is often a factor of geography: where we are born or where we live. If we happen to be born in a developing country, only if we are extremely intelligent or talented in some field are we likely to escape our humble beginnings. Even then we will probably need help and good fortune. A young able child may be sponsored through education, but again the disadvantages of geography will be difficult to surmount.

Key idea: Good fortune

The fate of where a child happens to be born is a major factor in the life chances experienced by that child.

Even within a developed country there can be significant differences between geographical areas in terms of economic opportunities. This is particularly noticeable between rural and urban areas. A child born to working-class parents in the rural American Midwest would probably have had to relocate to Detroit or Chicago to find a wide range of educational, training or employment opportunities. There are, for example, in the region of 70 higher education colleges or universities in the metropolitan Chicago area. However, not all young people migrating to large urban areas would be able to access high status, highly paid jobs. Major cities such as London and New York are key world financial centres, which employ highly educated people earning very large salaries. However, in terms of the total city workforce, such people are in the minority.

Did you know?

The 'North–South divide' is used to describe the economic differences between London and the South-East of England on the one hand, and the Midlands and North on the other. People certainly tend to *believe* that health facilities and educational provision are superior in southern England to the rest of the country, notwithstanding the empirical reality. House prices are much higher in London, which makes it even more difficult than normal for young people to buy a house. However, if people sell a house in London, and move elsewhere in the country, then they will be at a financial advantage.

The skyscraper offices, hotels, and executive bars and restaurants frequented by elite workers are staffed by much greater numbers of service workers such as cleaners, porters, waiters and bar staff who earn very low salaries, and have few career prospects. Increasingly, people who work in our cities in service industries or construction work are frequently employed on zero hour contracts, within the terms of which they do not know from one day to the next whether they will have any work. This often prevents their becoming established with stable residential and other living arrangements.

Key idea: Worker disparity

In most large international cities there is a stark distinction between rich people working in the finance and business sectors, and a much larger number of very poorly paid workers in the service industries.

Did you know?

A welfare state is a form of democratic organization of society in which a nation tries to ensure a minimum standard of provision for all citizens. In Britain, in 1942, William Beveridge produced a report outlining ways in which this could be achieved. By the end of the Second World War in 1945 steps were being taken to provide free health care and education, good quality housing, and a system of social security to ensure that people received state assistance when they experienced major difficulties in their lives. This entire policy was termed the welfare state.

This situation is being exacerbated by the increasing number of older people in our large cities. One consequence of this is the relatively diminishing pool of younger workers able to sustain the economy of a city, and their reluctance to take on some of the less well paid, or unskilled, work available.

Singapore, for example, has achieved remarkable economic success built upon a sophisticated education system, and a highly educated, highly computer literate workforce. Yet there are insufficient indigenous workers to fulfil the needs of the construction industry and the domestic service sector. The construction sector is staffed largely by immigrant workers from India and Bangladesh, while women from the Philippines are prevalent in the domestic sector. By the standards of many of the indigenous workers of Singapore, many of the immigrant workers earn extremely low salaries. In addition, there are problems of integration between immigrant workers and the indigenous population with, for example, Indian workers living in the area of 'Little India' where there are Hindu temples and Indian cultural shops.

Key idea: Immigrant labour

Many developed economies encourage immigrant labour to work in areas where there is insufficient indigenous labour. There are sometimes consequences for both the donor society and the recipient society.

There are many millions of migrant workers in the Middle East and the Far East. Although in the context of the host economy, they are usually working for low salaries, they are still able to send home sums of money that are very significant to their families in the country of origin. Such transfers of money make a great deal of difference in terms of raising the living standards of poorer families, and in helping child poverty. Nevertheless, even such large-scale patterns of employment can be affected by changes in the global economy, as is pointed out by Abella & Ducanes:

> 'It matters greatly how the economic slowdown will touch different regions of the world because migrant workers are not uniformly distributed across the same countries. South Asian workers are largely concentrated in the Gulf States where public investments are foreseen to remain strong in spite of the severe drop in oil prices.'
>
> Abella, Manolo & Ducanes, Geoffrey (2009), 'The Effect of the Global Economic Crisis on Asian Migrant Workers and Governments' Responses' (p. 144).

Rapidity of change

The revolution in information and communication technology during recent decades has led to enormous social changes in some countries, but arguably this trend has often resulted in greater rather than reduced economic differences between social classes. As an example of such a trend we might take the case of Bangalore (or Bengaluru) in the state of Karnataka in southern India. Bangalore is often known as India's 'silicon valley', or more accurately 'silicon plateau', owing to its location on the Mysore Plateau. Its altitude results in an equable climate with relatively low humidity. This is one of the reasons why in colonial times it became a desirable retirement centre for the professional and middle classes. English was widely spoken, and there were excellent schools in the area. The high-quality educational infrastructure was probably a factor in the selection of Bangalore for the development of an aeronautical and electrical engineering industry in the 1950s and 1960s. The result was an elite, technologically sophisticated workforce, which was ideally placed to support the development of the information technology revolution when it started in the early 1980s.

Many young, well-educated IT engineers travelled to the United States to gain broader experience, and took this back to India as the computer industry grew. The reputation of Bangalore drew many computer engineers from all parts of India to share in the expansion of high technology industries. The population of the city expanded until it now has well over 8 million inhabitants.

Key idea: IT industry

The great expansion in IT industries, particularly in partially developed countries, can tend to produce a differentiation between the poor and the increasingly wealthy.

However, while the city has many contemporary buildings and technology centres, the essential infrastructure has not kept pace with the development of the IT industry. Notably, the water supply facilities and waste disposal measures are inadequate for the many thousands of people who have been unable to participate in the IT dream. Many people in Bangalore still earn a completely inadequate livelihood through such activities as the recycling of waste gathered from the city's many refuse tips. As Benjamin argues:

'Issues of poverty remain submerged by the euphoria over the expansion of the information technology industry and Bangalore is, in many senses, a "divided" city. The glass-walled computer-ready office complexes, exclusive shopping malls and entertainment facilities that rival the best in the country contrast with the dense squatter settlements and their very poor services in central areas of the city.'

Benjamin, Solomon (2000), 'Governance, economic settings and poverty in Bangalore' (p. 38).

This tension between the achievements of a well-educated, technological elite and a working class that finds it very difficult to improve its lot in society raises many questions about the fairness of society. There are many examples around the world of comparable situations to that in Bangalore, where a largely meritocratic elite can continue to grow richer, while a working class that supports that elite stagnates in terms of economic advancement.

The state of Kerala, India

There are many parallels between the economy of Kerala and that of Bangalore, although Kerala also possesses some unique features. The long-standing communist administration in Kerala has invested heavily in education, with the result that Kerala has a very high literacy rate, and also a very high proportion of English speakers. However, this combination of high-quality education and widespread fluency in English has had unanticipated consequences. It has been difficult for well-educated people to find jobs in the major cities such as Cochin, and hence they have been forced to become migrant workers, often in the Middle East. Such workers return very large amounts of money to the Kerala economy. The other main source of income for Kerala is from tourism. As the economy has come to rely upon these two income streams, there has been relatively little industrial investment, leading to urban unemployment levels of 19.9% (George, 2011).

The well-educated elite can thus normally find work overseas, while others have to move to other parts of India. Those who remain in Kerala are struggling to find work in an economy that rests for the most part upon tourism – an industry in which many of the jobs are lowly paid. The families who have members working overseas, many in highly skilled jobs, are normally able to live in the wealthier areas and send younger children to private schools. Meanwhile, the state government with reduced sources of income from taxation has difficulty sustaining adequate levels of health care and of education.

It is important also not to ignore the potential social consequences of large-scale migration. Many families have one or more absentee wage-earners and this can have consequences for the cohesion of the family unit. Nevertheless, Kerala is attracting external investment, notably in Cochin, for new information technology parks that are being constructed. In the meantime, however, there tends to remain a division in society between the highly paid technocrats and their families, and those who work in the lower-paid service jobs, such as catering and housekeeping, attached to the tourism industry.

Sociologists such as Amitai Etzioni (1929–) have argued strongly that we should be aiming for a type of society in which the talented, well-educated minority are encouraged to innovate and generate wealth, while at the same time doing as much as they are able to help those less fortunate. Etzioni has used the term communitarianism to describe this balance between individual autonomy, and a sense of responsibility towards society. This approach is difficult to negate on philosophical grounds, and yet there remains the practical problem of the methodology by which wealth would be redistributed.

It is evident that wealthy entrepreneurs cannot live their lives as totally separate from a poorer sector of society who normally purchase the products that they make. Wealthy manufacturers and industrialists are very much dependent on the numerous poorer people in their society to create a market for their goods. Hence it can be argued that a sense of communitarianism and a concern for all communities is important for a healthy and moral society. As Selznick argues:

> *'We are or should be "communitarian liberals" or, if you prefer, liberal communitarians. Like John Dewey, we should combine a spirit of liberation and a quest for social justice, with responsible participation in effective communities. This is not a wholesale rejection of liberalism. Rather, it is a call for a deep reconstruction of liberal theories and policies.'*
>
> Selznick, Philip (1998), 'Foundations of Communitarian Liberalism' (p. 3).

Poverty, deprivation and exclusion

Poverty is a difficult and complex concept to define, and yet it is important that we attempt the task, otherwise we cannot begin to analyse some of the economic and social differences in society. We can think of poverty in absolute terms, such as the living conditions of many people in developing countries. If someone does not have sufficient food to sustain life, nor the means to maintain hygiene, nor medical care or shelter, and consequently is at risk of dying, then we would have little doubt in describing them as living in poverty. On the other hand, we can imagine an unemployed person living in a developed country, in a dilapidated inner-city flat, yet having access to food, water, heating and a free health service. We might still describe such a person as poor, yet there would be no comparison with the person who was just surviving in a developing country. In other words, poverty is often thought of as a relative concept, the use of which depends very much upon the context.

Did you know?

The National Health Service in the United Kingdom was established in 1948, following the earlier Beveridge Report, in order to try to ensure that all citizens had access to free health care when necessary. This was seen as an important element of social equality, and was particularly necessary following the consequences of six years of war, ending in 1945. The National Health Service has continued to expand since the 1940s, yet it remains a question of much debate as to whether it can be sustained financially according to its original framework and principles.

We also use the term poverty depending upon the perceived life chances of a person. We may imagine an undergraduate at a prestigious university, who owes money in overdrafts and tuition fees, and lives a fairly impoverished life. In such a context, we may be reluctant to describe the student as poor, as we know that when he or she leaves university there will be a very high earning potential. On the other hand, a young person with low educational levels, few job prospects, yet in exactly the same financial circumstances as the student may be considered as living in poverty, since there are limited prospects to improve the situation.

Key idea: Poverty

The concept of poverty may be thought of as a relative concept which depends to a large extent upon the context of the example being considered.

Thus the use of the term poverty may not depend upon the actual income of a person, but rather upon their overall life chances. Nevertheless, the use of income levels is a useful and practical means of judging levels of poverty. The analysis of poverty is sometimes complicated by the lifestyle choices made by individuals. One can imagine an artist or musician who chooses to take on only a small amount of part-time work in order to leave time for their creative work. In this case their frugal lifestyle is of their own choice, in order to achieve specific ends. We would probably be reluctant to describe them as poor, partly since they are managing to achieve their goals in society. On the other hand, a person with the same frugal life, although not through their own choice, may be described as living in poverty.

Dig deeper

Dorling, D. (2011), *Injustice: Why social inequality persists.* Bristol: Policy Press.

Fraser, D. (2009), *The Evolution of the British Welfare State: A History of Social Policy since the Industrial Revolution* (4th ed.). London: Palgrave Macmillan.

Klein, R. (2013), *The New Politics of the NHS: from Creation to Reinvention.* (7th ed.). London: Radcliffe.

Lister, R. (2004), *Poverty.* Cambridge: Polity.

Lowe, R. (2004), *The Welfare State in Britain since 1945* (3rd ed.). London: Palgrave Macmillan.

Test your knowledge

1 The assumed economic difference between the south-east of England and the rest of the country is known as?
  a the London separation
  b the North–South divide
  c the fiscal divide
  d the financial differentiation

2 A society in which the state tries to ensure a minimum provision for all citizens is known as...?
  a an additional condition
  b a supplementary state
  c a welfare state
  d a charitable approach

3 Bangalore is known as India's...?
  a artistic heritage capital
  b agricultural centre
  c space-age city
  d silicon valley

4 Kerala has...?
  a the largest steel industry in India
  b a very high literacy rate
  c a large number of coal mines
  d a large offshore oil industry

5 Who used the term communitarianism?
  a Etzioni
  b Einstein
  c Blumer
  d Durkheim

6 In what year was the UK National Health Service founded?
  a 1930
  b 1951
  c 1953
  d 1948

7 If we argue that poverty as a concept depends upon the circumstances, we are saying that it is a...?

  a relative concept
  b absolute concept
  c real concept
  d parallel concept

8 Kerala provides a lot of migrant labour to...?

  a Sri Lanka
  b Australia
  c Greenland
  d the Middle East

9 Kerala's main industry is...?

  a tourism
  b fishing
  c manufacture
  d finance

10 William Beveridge was the architect of the...?

  a education system
  b the British nuclear strategy
  c the welfare state in Britain
  d the European Community

12

The changing nature of work

Chapter 12 will analyse the transformation taking place in the world of work within the postmodern age. One of the trends is in the subdivision of work roles into separate activities. These activities are then grouped into those that are highly skilled and require specialized education and training, and those that are to some extent routine, and can be carried out without specialized training. The less-skilled work can then be carried out by employees on casual contracts or zero hour contracts. The result is the deprofessionalization of work, with employers needing fewer highly trained professionals. There is also a reduction in the number of people with an overview of the total work role. When this kind of deskilling is repeated across the labour force, then there is a saving of money as fewer professionals are required. There are also savings to be made by having more people working on a casual basis. These are only some of the changes taking place in the world of work. The sociology of work seeks to examine such changes critically with a view to understanding how they may affect individual social groups.

Different approaches to work

In the pre-industrial age the majority of people worked on the land, either on family-owned smallholdings or as labourers for large landowners. In an agrarian society, the precise manner in which people worked was often conditioned by such factors as the weather and the seasons. They might harvest wheat, care for livestock, repair barns and, in general, respond to needs as they arose. People were not restricted to working in one place. A shepherd, for example, might range over a large geographical area. In addition, landowners left their workers to complete their duties without watching them at all times. With the advent of the Industrial Revolution, however, work became much more localized.

When people worked in a coal mine, a textile mill, or a factory, they reported to the same site each day and, as industrialization developed, workers were increasingly subject to strict hierarchical management styles. In a system dependent upon carefully monitored output, the performance of workers was closely managed.

Key idea: A day's work

With the Industrial Revolution came the concept of 'going to work' i.e. of going to an office, a factory or other workplace, for a fixed number of hours each day.

Did you know?

F. W. Taylor (1856–1915) studied the process of work, and concluded that it was possible to analyse a work-based task in order to determine the most efficient way in which it should be conducted. The role of management was then to train workers appropriately and to ensure that they carried out their work in the most effective way. This scientific approach to the management of work was influential when first introduced, but also alienated some groups of workers.

This style of working was particularly characterized by the industrial production line, where workers carried out routine, repetitive tasks all day, with little rest or respite. In a post-industrial age, however, much of this either has changed or is changing. Although many people such as shop workers or those in the catering industry work in the same place each day, there is nowadays a much greater trend for people to manage their own working situation. Workers are much more involved in planning and decision-making relating to their work role, and may not be as closely managed as in previous times. They may be given a statement of their duties and responsibilities, but then to a certain extent left to decide exactly how they will meet those responsibilities. Workers may be invited to develop new work strategies, and to make recommendations to management, rather than simply carrying out instructions in a prescriptive way. Some of these types of change did much to reduce the alienation felt by workers in the industrial age. So routinized and controlled were the lives of industrial production workers that they felt dehumanized and unable to contribute in a meaningful way to their work role. Their work life involved merely the following of instructions with no opportunity to provide their own insights into the employment situation.

Work in the electronic age

The advent of computers has revolutionized the world of work. It has removed the need for a paper-based workplace, opening the possibility of the majority of documents in a workplace being held electronically. Large amounts of office storage and filing space is no longer necessary, with workers relying on laptops and cloud technology to store and access essential documents. One of the results is that large offices are not necessarily required, with workers only calling in to the office when necessary, and then simply docking into a workstation for the duration of their visit ('hot desking'). This concept is related to that of remote working, where employees are free to work from home, or indeed anywhere of their choosing, as long as they meet the needs of their work role.

Key idea: Changing work patterns

In the electronic age, there has been a move from working for a fixed period of time, to the requirement to complete a predetermined task to a certain standard.

This pattern of working places employees in charge of the planning of their work, and also enables them to save time and energy in commuting to the workplace. Such factors may in the future determine the kinds of jobs employees seek. As Burke and Ng point out:

'As the global competition intensifies and the demand for talent heats up, it will be the workers who will be selecting which organizations they want to work for, based on the kinds of working conditions and flexibility employers offer in terms of location, technology, workspace, and human resource policies.'

Burke, Ronald & Ng, Eddy (2006), 'The Changing Nature of Work and Organizations: Implications for Human Resource Management' (p. 87).

However, managers are sometimes uncertain about the process, as they fear loss of control over their workforce.

Key idea: Changing employment considerations

When seeking a new job, workers are often considering the expected approach to work, as much as the salary being offered.

The use of communication technology has created the possibility of employees working together, despite the fact that they might be in different time zones, different countries and carrying out widely different activities. Such teams are often known as 'virtual teams' and are brought together in order to work on the solution of a specific task.

In the past, teams of workers had to be constructed from those personnel available in a specific place or part of an organization. Nowadays, however, when there is a problem to be solved the best team of experts can be put together, irrespective of where they are working, knowing that they can be in contact electronically. Such web conferencing and web seminars ('webinars') have become an almost essential element in work communications.

One strength of remote working is that employees are no longer restricted to interactions with those who work in their own organization. They are freer to make professional connections with people across a range of organizations, and to work with them as appropriately ('co-working'). Within this newer approach to working, the ability to function effectively in a team becomes more important than the capacity to work well as an individual. In addition, the medium of self-managed work time enables employees to distribute their work and leisure time in the most effective way possible. If they wish to work in the very early morning when their minds are fresh, then they can do so and take time off later in the day when they are more tired. Equally, and very importantly, these new ways of working can favour female employees who are trying to balance work and family commitments.

Key idea: Work-life balance

In considering equal opportunities in the workplace, it is very important that managers provide both women and men with appropriate opportunities to achieve a work-life balance.

There should be more opportunities in the post-modern world for women to resume work when family commitments diminish, and to work in a manner that suits their other responsibilities. It is essential that as these new ways of working evolve and become the norm, the needs of women are considered in detail. As Sullivan argues:

The nature of work tasks

The actual nature of work itself has also changed in the computerized, post-modern world. Work is often project-based, incorporating tasks that have precise deadlines. This is a further argument for reducing standardized working practices, and encouraging self-managed work where the employee can work longer hours when necessary to complete a project, and then compensate by taking time off at other occasions.

Work tasks are continually being adapted as they use more and more advanced technology. This places greater importance upon education and training to ensure that employees remain up to date in terms of technological skills. The tendency to divide work activities into discrete tasks and projects makes it easier for managers to employ workers for short-term contracts. This may not be desirable for the employees, but it is a feature of many aspects of the nature of contemporary work.

Did you know?

Henry Ford (1863–1947), who established the Ford Motor Company, was responsible for the widespread use of the assembly line process to manufacture motor vehicles. Interestingly, he took a great interest in the welfare of his workers, and encouraged them to lead a sober lifestyle. Moreover, he was noted for paying his workers very generously, while at the same time asking them to work hard for the company.

There is also the possibility of companies putting out work to tender. Once work tasks can be compartmentalized, they can be offered outside the organization where they might be carried out more cheaply than internally ('outsourcing').

Nevertheless, it is not only employees who need to adapt to new working conditions. Managers and employers are having to accept that a dispersed workforce requires different strategies in terms of management. Narrow hierarchical management systems are difficult to implement when, for instance, employees are working across different time zones. An employee may simply not be able to make contact with his or her line manager. The power of decision-making has to be dispersed to either individuals or democratically operating teams. Such management styles are difficult, however, for some managers, who find it rather daunting to hand over many of their responsibilities in this way. Managers realize that they have to learn to trust their employees to act in a responsible fashion, and that they cannot exercise authority over their staff at all times.

Key idea: Decentralization

The modern workplace and work tasks are so complex that managers are having to adjust to decentralized management styles.

These changes in working patterns are the subject of a great deal of research, very often qualitative studies of the lives of individual workers, as indicated by Perlow:

'In many ways, the research that the emerging sociology of work time calls for is a structuration approach to writing work ethnographies. Individuals' interdependent work patterns would be the basic unit of analysis, and researchers would consider simultaneously the role that these interdependent patterns play in the work process and both the social and temporal contexts that perpetuate and are perpetuated by these patterns.'

Perlow, Leslie A. (1999), 'The Time Famine: Toward a Sociology of Work Time', *Administrative Science Quarterly*, Vol. 44 (pp 77–8).

Linked to the development of information technology, and electronic communications, is the general phenomenon of the increasing sophistication of the world of work. Tasks that several decades ago were completed manually and with notes taken with pencil and paper have now become technologically advanced. Not only that, but the technology is changing and adapting very rapidly. It is not possible for workers to attain knowledge and skills, and then to hope that they will be relevant for the next 10 or 20 years. Employees will need to continually upgrade their knowledge, if they are to remain employable. Those people who succeed in the world of work will need to recognize that we live in a knowledge-based society, in which those with the most extensive knowledge base will be those who are most employable and successful.

During the industrial, modern period there had been a gradual deprofessionalization within the world of work.

The deprofessionalization of teaching

School teaching has many of the characteristics of a profession, including stipulated entry qualifications and a clearly delineated programme of professional training. However, there are also trends within the profession that can be viewed as undermining that professionalism. For example, there is a broad tendency to be very prescriptive in terms of the subjects taught in schools, and also in terms of the curricula within those subjects. The key issue is the extent to which these curricula should be specified. Teachers are normally considered to be subject experts, and to adapt what they teach to the needs and requirements of their pupils. If the curriculum is so precisely specified that there is little room for the judgement of the teacher, then one might see this as counteracting the professionalism of the teacher.

In addition, there is an increasing tendency to judge the performance of teachers on the basis of the achievement of their pupils. When pupils are assessed on their knowledge and understanding of relatively narrow curricula, then there will be a tendency for teachers to concentrate on teaching the kind of narrowly based information and skills that should result in high scores by their students. They may not deviate into interesting areas for fear of jeopardizing their student marks and hence their own performance rating.

Equally, as the school curriculum becomes narrower and narrower, and much of it can be produced as self-learning computer packages, there is the possibility that teaching assistants can be employed instead of professional teachers to help the pupils learn. Teachers may become, in effect, curriculum designers and authors, while less well qualified people interact with the pupils. Overall, this can be perceived as a form of deprofessionalization.

As more and more technically advanced processes were developed, workers were reduced to simply managing the machinery rather than developing and using their own skills. For many workers this resulted in a sense of alienation from the work enterprise, and a feeling that they were just being used by the industrial process.

Did you know?

Typical of this approach was the so-called 'time and motion' study, based partly upon the work of F. W. Taylor. The idea of this approach was to consider an individual work task, and then to break it down carefully into its component elements. Each separate subtask within the overall job was analysed in terms of the most effective and efficient way of carrying it out, and also in terms of the time taken for each subtask by the average worker. It was then possible to determine whether a person was achieving the average performance for the task. 'Time and motion' studies provided a benchmark by which work-based performance could be measured but alienated many workers who felt that the approach was intrusive, and did not take into account all of the variables inherent in performing work-based roles.

This was in many ways a Marxist analysis of the status of work, but was taken up and extended in the mid-20th century by the American sociologist Harry Braverman (1920–76). He wrote particularly about the loss of pride in their jobs felt by many workers (Braverman, 1998). Although some aspects of contemporary work using computers encourage high-level cognitive skills, there are others that arguably result in a deskilling.

For example, when school students are provided with detailed teaching materials that they access via their laptops, there is less need for the well-qualified teacher. Perhaps a less well qualified person can be present in the classroom to act merely as an assistant or mentor when needed. The high-level cognitive material is included in the computer-based materials, rather than in the traditional teaching process.

Dig deeper

Ackerman, F., Goodwin, N. R., Dougherty, L. & Gallagher, K. (Eds.) (1998), *The Changing Nature of Work*. Washington D.C.: Island Press.

Gershuny, J. (2003), *Changing Times: Work and Leisure in Postindustrial Society*. Oxford: Oxford University Press.

Grint, K. & Nixon, D. (2015), *The Sociology of Work*. Cambridge: Polity.

Mullins, L. J. (2013), *Management and Organisational Behaviour* (10th ed.). Harlow: Pearson.

Tholen, G. (2014), *The Changing Nature of the Graduate Labour Market: Media, Policy, and Political Discourses in the UK*. Basingstoke, Hants: Palgrave Macmillan.

Test your knowledge

1 A strict, hierarchical management style was typical of...?
  a medieval Europe
  b the period of the Industrial Revolution
  c artistic, creative communities
  d the Iron Age

2 F. W. Taylor was known for the development of...?
  a scientific management
  b creative intelligence
  c the sociology of computer science
  d the silicon chip

3 In the industrial age workers were often...?
  a very happy
  b well remunerated
  c secure in their jobs
  d alienated from the world of work

4 When workers do not have a fixed office, but call in at their employers and plug in their laptops in an available space, this is known as...?
  a informal working
  b distance learning
  c ad hoc working
  d hot-desking

5 When members of a team who live in different places – and are linked by information technology – work together, they are known as...?
  a an international team
  b a virtual team
  c a project group
  d an integrated team

6 When workers have a meeting, conference or seminar using communication technology, this is often known as...?
  a a webinar
  b an electronic meeting
  c a distance meeting
  d an electronic conference

7 Henry Ford was responsible for the widespread installation of...?

a airplanes

b motorways

c assembly line production

d pedal cycles

8 The analysis of industrial jobs to determine the most efficient way of carrying them out is known as...?

a time and motion study

b subtask analysis

c forward projection

d management study

9 Harry Braverman wrote about...?

a the degradation of work in society

b the levels of unemployment

c the impact of laptops

d rural work

10 When employers need fewer highly skilled and educated workers, this is known as...?

a deprofessionalization

b synergy

c coordination

d task analysis

13

Transition in the natural world

Chapter 13 examines the interaction between society and the natural world. On the one hand human intervention undoubtedly affects the environment. Examples include deforestation in both tropical rainforest regions and in mountainous areas such as in Nepal; open cast mining; overfishing; and the deposition of refuse and toxic substances. The consequences include climate change, soil erosion and the poisoning of the soil making it unfit for agriculture. As a discipline, the sociology of the environment analyses some of the reasons for the adverse interventions of human beings. The key reasons are often variants of economic factors. It is often cheaper to ignore the long-term effects of human action on the natural world than it is to adopt prudent measures designed to conserve it.

Social influences on the environment

The social, commercial, political and economic lives of human beings are inextricably linked with the nature of the environment. In some ways, human beings directly employ the resources of the environment in order to profit from them. There are many examples of this. The destruction of the rainforests in the Amazon in order to export hard woods to parts of the world that will pay well for this timber has adverse results both locally and on a global scale. The rainforest is a habitat for both wildlife and for some indigenous peoples, who live in intimate contact with the tropical ecosystem.

The deforestation has a destructive effect upon this ecosystem. Such exploitation is short-sighted, however, since the timber of the rainforest has a finite life, and once the trees are felled it will take many years for them to be replaced.

Other forms of exploitative activity, such as mining, fishing and whaling, fall into the same category. Human beings, of course, need to use some of the resources of the planet in order to survive, but all too often this is done in a manner that does not take into account the survival and the continuation of these resources.

Did you know?

In the recent history of agriculture there has been a regular practice of systematically killing wild animals, notably predators, which were deemed to have a negative effect upon the stocks of domestic animals. However, there has also been a parallel movement to reintroduce wild predators where these have been excessively culled in the past, and where they are seen as a legitimate element of the local ecosystem. Such a reintroduction often benefits the local tourism industry, and people generally like to see indigenous animals in their natural habitat. An example includes the reintroduction of wolves in the Pyrenees. Nevertheless, such reintroduction does not always find favour with local farmers, who are afraid of deaths among their livestock.

Ecotourism

Much modern tourism is organized through the medium of large multinational companies, which are primarily concerned with generating a surplus for their shareholders. Almost inevitably this method of funding holidays involves investment in modern hotels and clubs that are sometimes built in areas where the priority is providing facilities for tourists rather than ensuring that there is no undermining of the local environment. Ecotourism, however, takes a different view. It places emphasis upon sustaining the environment, wherever possible, upon investing in local indigenous communities and in trying to maintain the local fauna and flora. Clearly such holiday or tourist activity will need to generate a profit, although within ecotourism the emphasis will be upon using some of that profit to sustain the local environment. There will be an attempt to minimize any impact upon the natural environment and to ensure that wherever possible the ecosystem remains undisturbed.

Key idea: Precious resources

Human beings always need to use some of the Earth's resources in order to survive, but it is how they go about this that is significant. The use of resources needs to be done in a way that enables those resources to replenish themselves.

Traditionally, capitalism has tended to use resources in order to generate a short-term profit, and without concern for renewing the resources being used. In other examples, capitalist development may not directly utilize environmental resources, and yet there are still adverse consequences for our surroundings.

Did you know?

Alfred Sloan (1875–1966), the chairman of the General Motors automobile company for many years, developed a number of concepts in corporate manufacturing capitalism. These concepts included regular changes in the styling of products, and also built-in obsolescence. He restyled car models so that consumers would want to buy the latest model. He also ensured that cars would not have an unlimited life, so that consumers would have to make regular purchases. As a general principle, such consumer demand tends to have a negative effect upon the environment as it causes additional resources to be used.

The construction of a new airport, the building of new motorways or railways, or new large-scale housing developments, can all have substantial consequences for the environment, even though they may not be as directly exploitative in the same manner as say tree felling. Much the same can be said of such activities as waste disposal. If carried out responsibly, then this may have a minimum effect upon the environment, although the indiscriminate disposal of industrial waste may have serious consequences.

Did you know?

The majority of waste materials discarded in the world's oceans are made of plastic. These have an adverse effect on sea mammals and other wildlife through ingestion or by trapping animals. Much of this packaging is used to enhance the marketability of products, and provides an example of the clash between capitalist endeavours on the one hand, and the need to care for the environment on the other.

There are an increasing number of strategies designed to generate energy without the use of fossil fuels. These include solar power generators, wind farms and tidal energy generators. While avoiding the generation of carbon dioxide in the atmosphere, some people may argue that these forms of energy generation have adverse consequences for what we might term the aesthetics of the environment.

Issues concerning the sociology of the environment are becoming increasingly political, as voters make their feelings felt about, on the one hand, the generation of electricity from fossil fuels and, on the other, the visual impact of some ways of generating 'clean' energy. The exploitation of the environment is perceived more and more as a result of political policies. As Matten argues:

> 'Consequently, governments – formerly quite successful in managing environmental problems – have so far been very reluctant to threaten their electorate's standard of living by, for instance, decreasing of mobility and freedom of choice.'
> Matten, Dirk (2004), 'The Impact of the Risk Society Thesis on Environmental Politics and Management in a globalizing economy – principles, proficiency, perspectives.' (p. 378).

In the area of the development of new housing, for example, there are choices to be made between the renovation of unoccupied housing stock in the cities, and the building of large numbers of new houses on 'green belt' land.

Key idea: Environmental policies

Political policies and the sociology of the environment are increasingly linked as politicians try to determine the approaches that will be acceptable to the electorate.

The issues here are complex, but ultimately reflect political priorities about the manner in which we use our environmental resources.

As we consider the environmental disasters, famines and droughts that occur across the planet, there is an argument that these are not simply the result of ecological events over which we have very little control. In fact, many would argue that they are often the result of political decisions by regimes that are undemocratic and unaccountable. In some cases, countries receive considerable amounts of overseas aid that could be used in improving agriculture, the environment or animal husbandry, but in fact is often wasted through political corruption or inappropriate spending.

Capitalism, as the dominant ideology of the majority of Western countries, is characterized by a continuous need to generate profit. In order to produce a surplus for the shareholders, companies need to consume raw materials. These may be as a source of energy generation, or as materials from which to make saleable products. The problem with the need to continually consume materials is that it leads to an endless depletion of parts of the environment. As companies in a capitalist society are usually in competition, this merely increases the need to generate profits and thus the use of environmental materials. It can be argued that there needs to be a broad consensus about the need for environmental change before this can be brought about. As Beck argues:

'Or, to put it in sociological terms: How can a kind of cosmopolitan solidarity across boundaries become real, a greening of societies, which is a prerequisite for the necessarily transnational politics of climate change?'
Beck, Ulrich (2010), 'Climate for Change, or How to Create a Green Modernity?' (p. 255).

Risk and the environment

Human existence has always involved risk, particularly in historical times before the advent of science and technology, which could to some extent insulate humans against the vagaries of the natural world. When humans were forced to live in close contact with the environment there were potential risks from wild animals, extreme cold or heat, lack of food, and events such as floods or forest fires. The continual potential for inter-human conflict was also an ever-present source of risk. Under such circumstances human societies did their best to minimize risks by taking whatever measures they could. They constructed villages on high land, in defendable positions. They surrounded habitations with thorn fences to protect themselves from predators, and took whatever measures they could to store food against the possibility of poor harvests or famine.

However, in the modern and indeed postmodern ages, risks have come increasingly not from natural occurrences but from the results of the activities of human beings. It is thus becoming increasingly necessary for human beings to try to predict the consequences of their actions in order to militate against the possibility of dangerous risk. As a general principle, when we interfere with the environment, change the natural cycle of events, add unnatural materials to the environment or cause a lack of balance in the ecosystem, then there is a risk that the environment will be damaged.

Key idea: Caring for the environment

Actions that create an imbalance in the environment are sometimes the cause of risks that can have a widespread effect upon the lives of human beings.

Before any action is undertaken, it is important for human society to try to predict the possible results, so that the natural world can be safeguarded.

An important sociological dimension to this issue is that in the past the rich, powerful and influential were often able to reduce the impact of risks upon themselves. They might be able to do this by the judicious purchase of land, or opportunities, or by ensuring that there were people who could protect them in times of danger. However, in the modern and postmodern worlds, this is not necessarily any longer possible. If human beings, for example, do not take adequate steps to maintain nuclear power stations, chemical engineering complexes or other industrial facilities, then there may be consequences for large groups of people. Interestingly, the people affected by such events may belong to a wide range of social classes, and not be restricted to the working class. If airplanes or other means of transport are not maintained adequately, and there is an avoidable accident, those killed or injured may again come from a range of social classes. In the modern world, where there is an increasing potential for technological events that affect the environment in different ways, there are likely to be consequences for many subgroups in society. While it is true that workers are often disproportionately affected in industrial accidents, where the event affects different aspects of the environment there are likely to be widespread consequences for many groups.

In 1984 at Bhopal, in the Indian state of Madhya Pradesh, there was a major malfunction at a large pesticide works that resulted in the release of a large cloud of poisonous gas. Many workers who lived in close proximity to the chemical plant were killed, and there were also long-lasting environmental consequences. The water table was seriously polluted, affecting many people in the area, and great numbers of livestock were also killed, resulting in adverse consequences for farmers.

One of the significant elements of large-scale industrial and chemical accidents is that the environment is often affected across national boundaries or more widely than normal because of the movement of tides, ocean currents and winds. Nuclear accidents such as at Three Mile Island (1979) and more particularly at Chernobyl (1986) have had international consequences through the release of radioactive materials. In addition, oil spillages from tankers such as the *Torrey Canyon* (1967), the *Amoco Cadiz* (1978) and the *Exxon Valdez* (1989) have had enormous consequences for marine wildlife, and for coastal flora and fauna. As is often the case in large-scale industrial and environmental disasters, cause and responsibility are often contested.

Key idea: Industrial accidents

The effects of some industrial accidents today are often so widespread that consequences may traverse national boundaries.

The environment and equilibrium

The essence of treating the environment in a responsible manner is arguably one of trying to maintain the equilibrium and balance that are a feature of an ecological system. The addition of chemicals, the destruction of aspects of that environment, or the failure to maintain a sensitivity to ecological interaction, all have adverse consequences for this sense of balance.

The demands of business, manufacturing industry and the extraction of raw materials are sometimes at odds with the maintenance of an ecological equilibrium. In sociological terms one can argue that there is an intrinsic conflict between the principles of capitalism in generating profits for investors, and the principles of environmentalism in sustaining a sense of equilibrium in the living world.

One of the early advocates of a sensitivity towards the environment was a biologist called Rachel Carson, who, in 1962 published a book called *Silent Spring*. In it she argued that artificial pesticides such as DDT accumulated in many animal species, resulting in large-scale death, particularly among the bird population. Although Carson met much opposition from the manufacturers of such pesticides, there was a gradual reduction in the amount of such pesticides being used.

Key idea: *Silent Spring*

There are sometimes conflicts between those who defend the environment, and those who are exploiting it for commercial advantage. Rachel Carson (1907–64) was a famous example of a person who tried to protect the environment from the spread of poisonous chemicals, and thus entered into conflict with chemical manufacturers.

Mohandas Gandhi is not specifically thought of as an environmentalist, and yet many of his approaches to existence were consistent with caring for all living things. He was much influenced by the Jain religion, whose members are well-known for their adherence to a philosophy of non-violence or *ahimsa*. Gandhi's approach to non-violence has been influential in many areas of Indian life, notably in the Chipko Movement, which tries to discourage the systematic felling of trees, particularly on the lower slopes of the Himalaya. There are really two elements to this movement. The first is the caring for trees as living organisms in the tradition of Gandhian *ahimsa*. The second is a form of socialism that encourages Indian villagers to sustain their forests, since the availability of timber is essential for their daily lives in terms of cooking and heating homes.

There continues to be some debate as to whether trees should be cut down at all, as Ishizaka points out:

'In other words, in the past, movement participants insisted that their local communities, not corporations outside the locality, had the right to cut down trees and aimed at revitalizing local economy through promoting forest-related industry (lumbers and resins) but the Advani village residents called for abandoning local community's right to cut trees as well and insisted that forests should be preserved for environment conservation purposes.'

Ishizaka, Shinya (2009), 'What has the Chipko Movement brought about?' (p.6).

Ultimately, human beings will have to make a choice between shorter-term benefits whether in terms of wealth or energy production, and the longer-term advantages of maintaining the quality of the environment.

Dig deeper

Beck, U. (2009) (trans. C.Cronin), *World at Risk*. Cambridge: Polity.

Button, G. (2010), *Disaster Culture: Knowledge and Uncertainty in the Wake of Human and Environmental Catastrophe*. Walnut Creek, CA: Left Coast Press.

Carson, R. (2000), *Silent Spring*. London: Penguin.

Schnaiberg, A. (1980), *The Environment: From Surplus to Scarcity*. Oxford: Oxford University Press.

Smith, K. & Petley, D. N. (2008), *Environmental Hazards: Assessing risk and reducing disaster* (5th ed.). Abingdon, Oxon: Routledge.

Test your knowledge

1 A form of travel and tourism that tries to sustain the environment is often known as...?
   a a package tour
   b a short-haul tour
   c a sustainable holiday
   d ecotourism

2 The manufacture of a product that has a pre-planned and finite life is known as...?
   a pre-aging
   b built-in obsolescence
   c limited life manufacture
   d time-scale manufacture

3 The majority of refuse in the oceans of the world consists of...?
   a food
   b plastic
   c wood
   d cardboard

4 In 1979 a nuclear accident took place at...?
   a Delhi
   b Three Mile Island
   c Cape Town
   d Berlin

5 The *Exxon Valdez* was an oil tanker involved in an oil spillage in...?
   a 1989
   b 1979
   c 1968
   d 1960

6 Rachel Carson's celebrated book on the environment was called what?
   a *Silent Summer*
   b *The Death of Plants*
   c *Silent Spring*
   d *The End of Life*

7 The environmental movement based on Gandhian principles was called...?

   a Chipko

   b *ahimsa*

   c sustainability

   d ecosocialism

8 Gandhi was influenced by the Jain religion, which placed great emphasis upon...?

   a meditation

   b non-violence

   c yoga

   d ecology

9 A large and fatal leak of poisonous gas took place in 1984 – where?

   a Bhopal

   b Chernobyl

   c Newfoundland

   d Enschede

10 Excessive felling of timber does not result in one of the following – which?

   a an increase in factory construction

   b deforestation

   c soil erosion

   d damage to the forest ecosystem

14

Globalization and the world state

During the period of modernity, relationships between countries were often based upon a colonial system, which gradually diminished in importance in the early 1960s as countries in Africa and Asia gained their independence. Groupings of countries based either on ideology or economic relationships, such as the Soviet bloc or the EEC, grew in significance. In the postmodern world, the facility for electronic communication reduced any remaining restrictions on commerce, fiscal exchange and technology sharing. Goods could be bought and sold, with few limits imposed by national barriers. Money could be transferred between banks in different countries. Despite this delocalization, and the disappearance of traditional colonialism, there remained a considerable degree of economic hegemony, where a few large industrial powers exercised disproportionate control over large numbers of other countries. This chapter will explore the causes and consequences of these global systems.

The concept of globalization

For millennia there has been trade, communication, cultural exchange, migration and the movement of labour around the world, but only since the Industrial Revolution and, more importantly, the computer revolution has there been true globalization. With the advent of computerized information technology, people in widely separate parts of the world have been able to communicate in real time, making it possible to engage in commerce, and facilitating the exchange of knowledge, culture and ideas.

The critical feature of the modern world has become the rapidity of communication, making it possible for different countries to be genuinely connected. Globalization has created the potential for multinational companies to effectively operate across national boundaries, and they can manage different aspects of their functions in different parts of the world. This has led to a great expansion of the possibilities for capitalism, enabling, for example, the movement of labour to a much greater extent than previously. It has also, however, resulted in a large amount of aspirational migration. People in very poor parts of the world have been able to see and understand through information technology the facilities available in rich parts of the world, and have been determined to try to gain access to a new lifestyle.

People have become aware of the ways in which the cultures of the world are interconnected, and indeed dependent upon each other. To some extent this was also true in the days of colonialism in the 19th and 20th centuries. Raw materials were exported from colonial countries to the industrial powers of Europe, to be converted into products that were often then resold to the colonial countries, creating a cycle of dependency. The difference with a globalized economy rests in the speed of communication and transfer of goods, the complexity of the economic networks involved, and the extensive involvement of corporate capitalism.

Globalization and communication networks

The mobile phone has transformed the way in which people can communicate, particularly on an international basis. People can simultaneously be involved in economic activities, without being in face-to-face contact, through the use of social networks and email. This is transforming the way in which people work. Instead of working for fixed periods of time, they can be engaged in economic activities at any time of the day or night using their smartphones. We can order goods and services, book hotels and conduct banking transactions at any time.

On the other hand, we have yet to experience or understand the social consequences of these new ways of working. We have become conditioned over the years to the nature of work. We often rely upon a workplace to provide us with social contacts, to give us a sense of self-worth, and broadly to provide us with a feeling of meaning in life. Working within the new electronic media can reduce the scale of our face-to-face social contacts, and mean that we have far fewer breaks from the world of work.

The introduction of call centres has arguably resulted in a much less personal customer service for many people. This can be exacerbated where such centres are located overseas, and despite the linguistic competence of many of the call centre workers, it can be disorientating to be discussing events and circumstances from one's home country with someone in a distant country. The prime motivation among multinational companies for locating some call centres overseas is the cost reduction in terms of staff salaries. However, there is also the issue of job reduction in the home country.

Globalization and risk

It is one thing of course to talk about the speed and complexity of networks, but there are also major risks involved. As we become more and more dependent upon computer systems, it is increasingly difficult to plan for computer malfunctions. Computer systems are very complex to develop and costly to install. If they prove unsuited to the work for which they were planned, then it can be a costly mistake.

The ready availability of mobile phones along with their cameras is transforming the nature of photojournalism. In the past we relied upon journalists to be sufficiently astute to capture images that represented the essence of a particular news event or story. Now, however, the people who are actually making the news, through being involved in an event, are able to record it photographically. It is difficult to understand the potential effect of this upon journalism since news reporters are educated to appreciate the context of news events. In effect, the smartphone enables those who formerly were consumers of news reporting to start to contribute to the news collecting process. As Movius suggests:

'The expansion of communication flows and global online networks raise the possibility of a new dimension of globalization, and new forms of global/local media flows. Broadly speaking, new media technologies allow for media content to flow easily across borders and enable users to become producers, which in turn lead to hybrid media forms.'
Movius, Lauren (2010), 'Cultural Globalisation and Challenges to Traditional Communication Theories' (p. 9).

The new possibilities for international trade created by globalized networks have greatly increased both the volume and complexity of trade. Formerly, it was usually the case that the food we purchased was produced locally, close to point of consumption. Milk came from the local dairy herd; meat from local livestock; and vegetables and fruit from the local market garden. In many cases, of course, families grew or raised their own food. Much of the food would be naturally organic, since it was produced in a family garden or allotment. It is also interesting to recall that, traditionally, people only ate the types of food that were indigenous to their own locality. There was thus a very good chance that such food would be fresh, because it was grown in the vicinity.

With the globalization of food, however, it is much more difficult to be assured of the quality of food, and indeed whether it is fit for consumption. In the case of meat, for example, despite systems in place to authenticate the origins of meat, there still appear to be cases where this is less than certain. In a globalized world food is transported across large distances, sometimes raising questions about its freshness and quality. As Labonté et al argue:

> 'The pathways linking trade and foreign direct investment from food to chronic disease are described below. We identify three general pathways which relate to the changes in the food system: growth of transnational food corporations; liberalization of international food trade and investment and global food advertising and promotion.'
>
> Labonté, Ronald, Mohindra, Katia S. & Lencucha, Raphael (2011), 'Framing international trade and chronic disease' (p. 3).

The increase in the use of computer-based communication systems has led to an increase in the number of call centres. Although many are located in the home country of a particular company, there is also the tendency for them to be located overseas. The usual strategy is to identify a country in which there is a reasonably large number of appropriately educated people who speak the language of the mother company and potential clients. There is a risk however of security lapses in general in call centres, and arguably to a rather greater extent when the centre work is outsourced to a distant country. In the latter case, it is more difficult to establish regular quality control measures based on face-to-face contact. However, most call centres are subject to monitoring, in both the home and outsourced country.

Supply chains and outsourcing

In conventional terms a supply chain is the process whereby a company moves from the purchase of raw materials through a series of manufacturing and production procedures to the final saleable product. A traditional manufacturing company may house all of these processes on a single site, albeit with different stages of the process taking place in separate buildings. When this is the case it is relatively easy for a company to monitor the different stages of the supply chain, in order to ensure that, for example, staff are adhering to health and safety standards; the conditions under which staff are working are appropriate; and the final products are suitable for sale in the country in which they are marketed.

One of the key difficulties with multinational companies, and with companies operating within a global market, is that the supply chain can become very extended. Raw materials may be sourced in one country, and then transported to a different country for processing and manufacturing.

Key idea: Extended supply chain

In global organizations the supply chain can become very extended. The sourcing of raw materials may take place in one country; manufacture in another; and then storage and distribution of final products in another. In such a situation it can be difficult to sustain adequate standards of health and safety.

The product may then be moved elsewhere for finishing and packaging. The completed product may subsequently be marketed electronically and distributed globally. Under these circumstances it can be difficult to monitor and to manage the supply chain. In practical terms it may not be possible to achieve this effectively through electronic communication, and may require expert staff to be present to oversee different elements of the manufacturing process. There can be particular problems in this regard when important parts of the manufacturing process are conducted in developing countries, which may not have as rigorous standards of health and safety as exist in the West.

The Rana Plaza building collapse

In 2013 the so-called Rana Plaza building in Dhaka, Bangladesh, collapsed with the loss of more than 1,000 lives. This was a multi-use building, but the principal activity was as a clothing factory. Much of the work in the factory involved the manufacture of fashion clothing for well-known clothing brands in the West. Questions had been raised concerning the structural safety of the Rana Plaza building. Some tenants had moved out, but the work in the clothing factory continued. The deaths in the building collapse raised a number of questions about the monitoring of the state of the building. There were questions about whether the design and construction of the building complied with Bangladeshi regulations. In addition, questions were raised about the degree of monitoring of the working conditions of the people making the fashion clothing by the global companies involved (including the state of the building). Overall, this case appears to illustrate the kinds of problems that can occur when globalized companies contract work in developing countries.

Outsourcing occurs when a company identifies a particular function that at the time is carried out within the company, and decides to have that function carried out externally, by a separate company. The usual reason for outsourcing is an economy of scale, or because the company now carrying out the work can do it more cheaply than the in-house provision.

Suppose, for example, that a manufacturing company has need of a particular specialized component for its production. It has previously made this component itself, but then finds a different specialized organization that can make the component more cheaply simply because it has all the specialized equipment, and can make such components on a large scale. The original company outsources the work. On the negative side, this may result in some job losses, but on the other hand there will be cost savings, and that money could be used to employ new staff in different areas of the firm. Alternatively, it could also be used to retrain staff.

Key idea: Outsourcing

It may not be functional for a single company to carry out a very wide range of activities and processes. It may be more advantageous to 'outsource' aspects of the work to a specialized company.

As with many such strategies, it can be argued that there is nothing intrinsically right or wrong about them; rather that much depends upon the reasoning and motives behind them, the consequences for the workforce, and the manner in which they are carried out.

Anti-globalization

There is an increasing movement of people and organizations who are opposed, both ideologically and in practical terms, to the philosophy of globalization. Many were difficult to persuade that globalization would benefit individuals rather than large multinational companies. As Stiglitz pointed out:

> *'Environmentalists felt that globalization undermined their decades-long struggle to establish regulations to preserve our natural heritage. Those who wanted to protect and develop their own cultural heritage saw too the intrusions of globalization. These protestors did not accept the argument that, economically at least, globalization would ultimately make everybody better off.'*
>
> Stiglitz, Joseph (2007), *Making Globalization Work* (p. 7).

Different groups have their own particular perspective on globalization, but the general arguments are as follows. Multinational companies are perceived as having grown too large and powerful, and in some cases to appear to eclipse the power and influence of nation states. Whereas many states are governed through democratic processes and view themselves as having responsibilities both at home and towards less developed parts of the world, multinational companies see themselves as having a prime responsibility to their investors and shareholders. Their objective is to enhance profits and hence to expand and to attract even more investment.

In order to do this, it is argued by some that multinationals do not place ethical trading and business practices at the top of their priorities. It is suggested by their opponents that multinationals are able to operate in a liberal economic and fiscal environment, within which there are insufficient controls. It is suggested that they do not need to concern themselves overly with the way raw materials are sourced, with the working conditions of their employees, and with the strategies by which their products are marketed. As they operate across many different national boundaries, each often with its own legislative, trading and business conventions, they may be able, it can be argued, to operate in a variety of ways that are principally of benefit to themselves. Not everyone who is opposed to a liberal capitalism is necessarily against globalization. For some, the opposite of being anti-globalization is to support a form of economic nationalism, and this equally may not appear to be the most relevant strategy in the modern world.

A knowledge society and globalization

Knowledge has always been important, and we have seen the significance of scientific and technological knowledge during the Industrial Revolution. Since then, however, the pace of knowledge advancement has increased and increased. As an example, we could take the construction of large commercial buildings during the Victorian era compared with during contemporary times. During Victorian times large buildings such as banks, railways stations or town halls usually employed large numbers of skilled workers, as the buildings included complex, decorative architectural features. Construction was slow, although the final product was often of great artistic interest. As time passed the trend was towards simpler and less decorative architectural designs and more mass production. A social consequence of this was a decline in the number of skilled craftsmen, such as stonemasons, required in the construction process. Tradesmen found that they needed to diversify into other trades or occupations.

Nowadays, many such buildings are prefabricated with very large sections being lifted into position with cranes. The original designs are created on computers, and the data transferred to large-scale engineering machinery in order to create the steel support structure, and prefabricated wall sections. The final building can then be erected very rapidly. The key aspect of this transition from worker-centred to technology-centred construction is the role played by a sophisticated level of technological understanding. In other words, it is a knowledge-based industry rather than one founded on human strength.

Key idea: Information technology

New forms of manufacture, where the processes are based upon information technology, often enable the job to be completed more rapidly. A major disadvantage of this is that there can often be a concomitant loss of employment.

Did you know?

One of the leading writers on the phenomenon of a society founded upon its knowledge base was the Harvard sociologist Daniel Bell (1919–2011). He outlined what he saw as the characteristics of a 'post-industrial society'. One of the key characteristics was that such a society is concerned with the generation of high-technology ideas, the implementation of which can help in the more efficient use of society's resources. As the majority of such ideas depend upon information technology, the parallel development in a post-industrial society is an increase in the number of information technology literate researchers, and a corresponding decrease in the number of traditional, non-IT-oriented workers. The computer-oriented nature of such a society also means that it is likely to be linked with other parts of the world in a variety of computer-mediated networks.

Manuel Castells (1942–) has argued that it is not simply the increasing importance of the knowledge base of society that is transforming its nature, but also significantly the networks that have developed as a result of the rise of digital communication. There is a variety of important networks, ranging from academic ones to social networks and to a variety of professional, technical and business networks. Their key significance is that they not only enable people to be in contact with others of similar professional interests, but that, by means of this social process, they enable knowledge to be exchanged, processed, evaluated and developed.

When discussing the knowledge society however, it is worth distinguishing between 'information' and 'knowledge'. The new global networks and computerized communication have enabled a dramatic increase in the dissemination of information. However, unless people possess the background education, and ability to interpret and analyse information, they will not be able to transform that information into understanding. This may be the situation in a good deal of the developing world, where the resources have not been available to establish an education system that provides children with a sufficient level of analytical skills.

Did you know?

Peter Drucker (1909–2005), the thinker and writer on management issues, was one of the first people to argue that society was evolving from one in which manual skills were of primary importance, to one in which the most successful people were those who placed significance upon cognitive skills. Although he wrote extensively on management issues, he tended to take a very balanced viewpoint in his writing, in terms of what should be the priorities within a company. He conceded that it was essential for a company to generate a surplus but that companies also needed to think carefully about their priorities and to take a moral stance in the world.

Key idea: Cognition in the workplace

Employment patterns of the modern world are placing much less emphasis upon physical labour, and much more importance upon intellectual, cognitive activity.

Globalization and commodification

Commodification is the treatment of an object, process or other entity as a product that can be allocated a price and sold on the market. Arguably one of the characteristic features of a globalized world is the increase in the range of commodification, and the diversity of objects that are treated as commodities.

Did you know?

For many people one of the most unethical aspects of commodification is the selling of human organs, or indeed human beings, on the open market. It is not unusual for blood, for example, to be sold in some parts of the world, but it can be argued that although this practice may help some people, the principle of treating a human product in this way is unethical. Undoubtedly, the most immoral aspects of this practice involve human slavery, for purposes of forced labour or sexual exploitation. Other aspects of this type of commodification include the sale of human organs such as kidneys for transplant. In this case, of course, such transplants may be carried out as a normal means of medical treatment.

Multinational companies are able to take advantage of globalization in order to market products, and this process illustrates some of the changes that can and have taken place in the commercial world. For example, the sale of drinking water as a commodity is a relatively recent phenomenon, and yet is now a worldwide practice. Water has also been successfully 'branded' in the sense that clearly identifiable labelling is used to market different types of water. The branding of commodities has become an essential element in globalization, with the result that successful brands can become very valuable.

Key idea: Branding

The branding of goods, and the developing reputation of a brand, result in customers often attaching more importance to the brand name than to the product. This can happen particularly in the case of globalized companies and brands.

Dig deeper

Baylis, J., Smith, S. & Owens, P. (2014), *The Globalization of World Politics: An Introduction to international relations* (6th ed.). Oxford: Oxford University Press.

Held, D. & McGrew, A. (2007), *Globalization/Anti-globalization: Beyond the Great Divide* (2nd ed.). Cambridge: Polity.

McNally, D. (2002), *Another World is Possible: Globalization and Anti-capitalism.* Winnipeg, Canada: Arbeiter Ring Publishing.

Steger, M. B. (2013), *Globalization: A very short introduction* (3rd ed.). Oxford: Oxford University Press.

Stiglitz, J. E. (2003), *Globalization and its Discontents.* London: Penguin.

Test your knowledge

1 The sequence of events by which raw materials are transformed into a finished product for the customer is known as...?

   a a supply chain

   b automated processing

   c computerized programming

   d IT manufacture

2 If a company engaged another business to carry out an element of its work in the same, or a different country, this is known as...?

   a differentiation

   b shared manufacture

   c outsourcing

   d supplementary manufacture

3 When a supply chain becomes too extended, there is a danger of risks in terms of...?

   a failure to obtain raw materials

   b poor production continuity

   c health and safety

   d manufacturing quality

4 The 2013 collapse of the Rana Plaza building took place in?

   a Bangladesh

   b Turkey

   c China

   d Australia

5 In the world of globalization there has been a transition from a physical labour economy to an economy based on...?

   a transport

   b flexibility

   c wealth

   d knowledge

6 The sociologist Daniel Bell discussed the characteristics of a...?
   a manufacturing process
   b sociology course
   c computer
   d post-industrial society

7 Manuel Castells wrote about the nature of...?
   a a networked society
   b a paperless office
   c an open access qualification
   d analogue communication

8 Peter Drucker argued that companies should strike a balance between ethical responsibility and...?
   a profitability
   b redundancy
   c losing money
   d employment

9 The treatment of an object solely as a product to be sold is known as...?
   a quality support
   b management
   c profit
   d commodification

10 The identification of a product with a logo or name is known as...?
   a residue
   b branding
   c support
   d identification

15

Caste, class and strata in society

Most societies are to varying degrees stratified, and sociologists have been interested to relate individuals in such strata to various other factors such as social opportunity, education, economic success and political power. In India, castes are essentially occupational groups, although they are also related to socio-economic power. They probably originated at the time of the invasion of India by Aryan tribes from the Asian steppes, and the divisions have been consolidated over time. They are probably more rigid than social classes, within which there may be opportunities for social mobility depending upon access to education and economic opportunity. This chapter will explore such social stratification and relate it to differential opportunity in such areas as education and health care.

Different types of social stratification

It is almost inevitable that in any society some individuals will occupy prestigious positions of power and authority, while others will have an inferior status with little influence. Social status may be acquired in a variety of different ways. It may be inherited or in more primitive societies it may be acquired through expertise in warfare or in defending the tribal territory. Social status may also be strengthened through the acquisition of wealth, perhaps by participation in trade, or as plunder during warfare. In more complex, advanced societies, status may be enhanced through gaining political power, or by understanding the way in which legal authority functions.

Nevertheless the hierarchical nature of society, and the way in which social stratification functions, are important elements in society, as they are often related to access to health care, the education system and to social opportunities in general. For these reasons, sociologists are very interested in social stratification.

Key idea: Social stratification

Social stratification is the separation of society into various layers or strata, arranged in a hierarchical order. Membership of a particular stratum may be brought about by birth or through personal achievement. Access to privileges in society is often related to social stratification.

One of the main characteristics that distinguishes people of different social classes is employment. The latter determines many different factors in the lives of people. By affecting their disposable wealth, it usually determines the type of education they receive, the health care to which they have access, their housing and the nature of their material possessions.

Social class is a very important issue politically, since it inevitably concerns the unequal distribution of wealth, services, goods and status in society. Politicians are generally keen to support individual effort, since it can lead to the wealth creation needed to provide growth in society. On the other hand, they do not want to be seen as supporting the unequal distribution of assets, as this may seem that they are advocating policies that do little for the mass of poorer people.

Superficially at least then, politicians are not in favour of extremes of social class differentiation, since this emphasizes and exacerbates the kind of differences in opportunity and attainment that the policies of politicians tend to claim to reduce or eliminate. On the other hand, both politicians and members of the public are only too well aware of genetic differences between human beings that render some likely to be more successful in life than others. In addition, some people, by accident of birth, inherit wealth and social status to an extent that they start in life with a considerable advantage.

Historically, it was difficult for a person to transcend the social class into which they were born. It was in theory possible for someone to be born into an impoverished family and yet by virtue of their own efforts, abilities and determination to become wealthier and to improve their social status. This was however relatively rare – although not impossible. In the case of social class, most people assumed the occupation of their parents. Through the difficulty of enhancing their status through education, it was difficult to radically change their occupational standing.

Key idea: Social mobility

Social mobility is the capacity of individuals to be able to change their social status through their own efforts. Some of the factors that help people to improve their status are education, employment, wealth and material possessions. A meritocracy is a society in which social mobility is possible, based upon the abilities and efforts of individuals.

Employment and social stratification were thus very closely linked, although in some societies the link was even stronger through a concept known as caste. Hindu society in India was, and to a large extent still is, the paradigm example of caste.

A caste, or more strictly speaking, a *jati* in India, is a social group that is normally linked to both a religion and to a particular occupation. The caste is very strictly defined and organized. Whereas it is possible to marry outside one's social class, it is difficult, if not impossible to marry outside one's caste.

The concept of social class

We have already explored one concept of class, that of Karl Marx. For Marx, social class was inextricably linked with the economic relationships in society. In a capitalist society, the minority of people who owned the means of production, the bourgeoisie, were dependent on the majority, the working class or proletariat, who worked in order to generate a surplus for those who owned capital. The concept of class for Marx was hence a socio-economic concept. According to Marx the bourgeoisie exploited the working classes, whose labour generated a surplus that made the bourgeoisie even richer.

For Marx it was very difficult for the proletariat to escape this cycle of exploitation and alienation. The real problem was, according to Marx, the nature of the capitalist system, within which there was an inevitable division of society into two social classes.

Max Weber (1864–1920), the German sociologist, adapted much of Marx's theory of social class, and called it the 'Three component theory of stratification'. According to Weber, the differentiation of society could be explained by three key concepts: class, status and power. For Weber 'class' was a reflection of the economic position that one held in society. This could be determined in a variety of different ways.

The most straightforward determinant of economic position was based upon the family into which one was born, and its level of wealth. It was possible however to be born into a wealthy family, but for older siblings to inherit much of the wealth. Class was also a reflection of individual achievement in society. Hence, it was possible for a person to be economically successful, even though they had not received the benefit of being born into a wealthy family.

The second main factor in Weber's typology was that of 'social status'. This could be thought of as the social standing possessed by an individual and which derived from a variety of sources. Status could, of course, be derived from class in the sense that wealth or economic success can easily have a profound influence upon social status. However, there are many other factors that can affect status.

Many people acquire moral status derived from the manner in which they conduct themselves and behave towards other people. A historical example would be Mohandas Gandhi, who although acting politically in opposition to the British rulers in India, nevertheless won their respect by the dignified and ethical manner in which he behaved towards his political opponents.

People can gain social status in a variety of ways, which often involve acting in a selfless manner, and one which is devoted to the welfare of others. Doctors may risk their own health through the devoted manner in which they care for their patients; religious people may call for changes in society in a context that may endanger their own lives; and in any walk of life a person may act in order to save another person, but in a manner that risks their own life.

A third way in which society may be stratified is according to the people who possess power, and the ability to transform society in the way that they consider appropriate. Power can be of various types, including economic, political, spiritual and military power. To a certain extent, the exercise of a certain type of power requires those upon whom the power is used to submit to its influence. For example, spiritual power cannot be exercised upon those who do not recognize its essential spiritual precepts. Economic power can only be exercised upon those who are influenced by the possession of wealth. Nevertheless, the exercise of power does in general enable people to influence society in the way in which they desire.

Caste in Hindu society

In India, Hindu society has historically been divided into four main groupings known as 'castes'. These developed several thousand years ago during the so-called Vedic period, which started approximately 2,000 BCE. The name of this period derived from the name of the *Vedas*, or Hindu scriptures, which were written in Sanskrit.

The caste system was divided into four main groupings. The Brahmins were traditionally the caste of Hindu priests; the Kshatriyas were the warriors; the Vaishyas were involved in business and commerce; while the Shudras were typically agricultural labourers. The Brahmins had the highest social status; then the Kshatriyas, then Vaishyas and finally Shudras. There was also a large group of people who did not formally belong to a caste. These were the 'outcastes' or 'untouchables'.

Key idea: Caste

Caste is a relatively rigid form of social stratification particularly associated with Hinduism and the Indian subcontinent. A person's caste is often related to their job. Social mobility between castes is usually very hard to achieve.

In traditional Vedic society the Brahmins were very important because they knew the religious rituals that enabled them to enlist the help of the Gods in looking after the population. The ability to administer these rituals gave them considerable power and status in society, and with that they often accumulated a good deal of wealth. Apart from the Brahmins and the other three main divisions of society, Hindu society was divided into many hundreds of other groupings that were often related to a specific type of employment. Thus people belonged to both one of the traditional Vedic divisions and also a smaller employment-based caste. Many of these castes were 'endogamous', signifying that people could only marry someone from the same caste.

Caste is very much linked to social status, and this has continued to this day. It is possible, for example, for someone to belong to a Brahmin family and even though not very wealthy to have more social status than someone from another caste.

The position of the 'untouchables' has slowly changed somewhat, and this is partly due to the types of nomenclature that have been used. Gandhi, for example, called them *harijans*, which means 'children of God'.

Did you know?

In the early 1920s it was quite common for temple authorities in India to ban 'untouchables' from visiting temples, and even from walking on the roads around temples. Gandhi recognized that this was happening particularly in the region of what is now the state of Kerala, and mounted a campaign against the practice. By 1926 the temple authorities changed their attitude and admitted 'untouchables'. Later, in 1932, Gandhi founded the All India Anti-Untouchability League in Mumbai in order to extend opportunities for 'untouchables'.

Gandhi was pointing out that we can define people in any way that we wish to, and do not have to accord with traditional perceptions. In a way he was making here a sociological point, that society and individuals can be defined according to the criteria that we wish to use. 'Untouchables' are also termed 'Dalits' or by using the official term of the government of India – 'scheduled castes'. Since India gained independence many steps have been taken to improve their position through various positive discrimination measures. The position of Dalits is slowly improving, with a greater proportion gaining a good education and professional jobs.

Dalits were traditionally excluded from activities that meant contact with the higher castes. This included such normal activities as cooking or eating together, or as drawing water from the same well. There have also been many examples of almost routine violence and assaults against Dalits. Much has been done to reduce the incidence of such events, but they still occur. Without doubt, however, when we measure the transformation in Dalit society, we can see many improvements. Undoubtedly significant in this regard was the election in 1997 of K. R. Narayanan, a Dalit, to the role of president of India.

Did you know?

K. R. Narayanan (1920–2005) was born in a small, poor village in the state of Kerala in southern India. His family belonged to a caste that was responsible for collecting coconuts, and was considered to be part of the Dalit community. His father was a specialist in Ayurvedic medicine. With the help of several scholarships he pursued university studies in India and in London. Jawaharlal Nehru recognized Narayanan's ability and employed him in India's foreign and diplomatic service. He later became the Indian ambassador to the United States, and also the tenth president of India. As a noted academic he was also appointed as vice-chancellor of the Jawaharlal Nehru University.

It is relatively difficult to summarize the main features of the caste system, such that the criteria match all of the different castes. However, there are arguably certain generalizations that relate to all castes to some extent or another. Different castes tend to live separate lives, whether physically in terms of the area that they occupy in a village, or socially in terms of the groups with which they mix. Wherever possible, one caste will avoid mixing with other castes.

The caste to which a person belongs is largely determined by birth, and in reality there are very few ways in which caste can be changed. Castes are arranged in a social hierarchy with the result that there is a clear sense in which members of higher castes can often give instructions to members of a lower caste. The kinds of establishments that people attend, be they educational institutions or places of entertainment, are determined by their caste allegiances. This still applies very much to food, just as it did hundreds of years ago in an Indian village. Since occupations and employment are very much linked to caste, or to the sub-caste to which a person belongs, people are restricted in terms of the training and jobs that they can undertake.

Finally, in terms of marriage, it is unusual for a person of one caste to marry a person from a different caste. Technically this is possible, but is not the norm. The caste system of India is changing, although this is more a question of gradual adaptation and evolution, rather than a sudden transformation.

Dr B. R. Ambedkar (1891–1956)

One of the leading campaigners for the rights of Dalits, and against the unfairnesses and exploitation of the caste system, was Dr Ambedkar. He was born into a family whose caste was considered 'untouchable'. As a schoolboy he suffered a great deal of discrimination as he was a Dalit, but he was nevertheless extremely able academically. He ultimately graduated in economics from the University of Bombay, and was subsequently employed as a lecturer at Sydenham College in the same city. He continued studying for higher degrees and later in his life was awarded doctorates from London University and from Columbia University in the United States. In 1936 he established the Independent Labour Party in India, and at the time of Indian Independence he was appointed the chair of the committee given the responsibility of drafting the new Indian Constitution. After Independence he was also made the law minister in the new administration of Prime Minister Jawaharlal Nehru. In 1950, still frustrated by the continuing examples of discrimination against 'untouchables', Dr Ambedkar decided to adopt the Buddhist religion.

Social class and education

Generally speaking, working-class children tend to have lower levels of educational attainment than middle-class children. Reay commented on this issue as follows:

'It is clear that historically the working classes have been constructed as the inferior 'other' within education but what about the present? Surely such attitudes have been transformed in the twenty-first century? Unfortunately all the evidence seems to indicate that the contemporary education system retains powerful remnants of past elite prejudices. We still have

Some people, including some teachers, would explain this by arguing that the reasons lie with the working-class children themselves. Such reasons may include that the children have no interest in schoolwork; they do not try hard enough; they rebel against the school system; they prefer out of school activities to academic work; they have no ambition to get a professional job; and they do not understand the principle of deferred gratification – that if they work hard now, they will eventually have a good career.

Key idea: Class and education

In general, working-class children appear to fare less well in the educational system than middle-class children. The reasons for this are complex, but probably relate to aspects of working-class culture such as the degree of parental support and understanding of the educational system.

This kind of explanation is straightforward and simple to understand, but does not take into account the subtleties and complexities of the differences between working-class life and middle-class life. It can be argued that there is a much closer fit between school culture and the culture of middle-class family life. School culture values order; politeness; discipline; academic success; professionalism; hard work; smart, conventional dress; fair play; and respect for those in authority. These are many of the qualities that are respected in a middle-class household. It follows that in a comprehensive school pupils who exhibit these kinds of qualities will be liked by the teachers, who will make it clear that they have high expectations of them. The teachers may support those pupils and encourage them in their academic studies so that they achieve to the best of their ability.

There are also many ways in which middle-class parents are able to use their own cultural capital in order to assist their children. The probability is that they will be better educated than their working-class peers and hence will be able to help their children with their studies and homework. They are likely to have collections of books in the house, which may encourage their children to read and to widen their knowledge. They may have a greater variety of IT equipment in the home, and encourage their children to use it for educational purposes. Middle-class parents may be bilingual or multilingual and thus able to help their children learn foreign languages. Through their own educational experiences they will also normally have a sound understanding of the educational system, which will enable them to offer informed advice to their children on such questions as option choices or university applications.

Unlike working-class parents, middle-class parents will generally possess a higher level of social skills that enable them to engage in meaningful discussion with educational professionals. The social capital possessed by middle-class parents enables them, for example, to discuss their child's progress with a headteacher or college principal, in such an informed way that they are regarded as equals. Their general knowledge, demeanour and understanding of the educational system will enable them to ensure that their child receives the best attention from the educational institution.

Key idea: Social capital

Middle-class parents often possess a range of social and interpersonal skills that enable them to have well-informed discussions with teachers, lecturers and potential employers for their children. These skills are often known collectively as social capital, and enable them to support their children in the development of their career.

Many of the systems in a school may disadvantage working-class children and favour middle-class children. Middle-class children may be familiar with ideas of order and discipline in the family, and hence will respect these at school. They will probably support the idea of a prefectorial system, and of an ordered system of punishment for contraventions of school rules. They will feel quite happy in an environment that requires lining up in the playground; moving in order along corridors; showing respect to teachers and doing what is asked of them; keeping the classroom and their belongings tidy; and cleaning up after themselves when practical activities are finished. They will also generally take a pride in wearing their school uniform; will wear it in the accepted manner; and will act in an appropriate manner on their way to and from school. Although these middle-class behaviour patterns may not be directly related to academic success, nevertheless teachers will tend to look favourably upon pupils and students who behave according to the accepted norms of the school.

Those pupils who do not tend to follow the school 'rules' or the established behavioural norms are sometimes defined as 'deviant'. When pupils are required to 'line up' in the playground before entering school, there may be one or two pupils who regularly do not comply with this. They may enter the school by a different door; they may be slow to line up; or they may misbehave. These pupils may be considered deviant, or alternatively they may be thought of as creative, lateral-thinking children who do not simply accept what they are told to do, but develop their own strategies of behaviour. Deviance, within this viewpoint, becomes less a question of the facts of someone's behaviour, and more of a question of the degree of compliance with artificially created norms. As Grattet puts it:

'The societal reaction perspective views deviance as a product of the social interaction between individuals and various types of audiences, such as peer groups, anonymous onlookers, and representatives of formal social control organizations. Deviance is a designation – a label – that is attached to some individuals and not to others.'

Grattet, Ryken (2011), 'Societal reactions to deviance' (p. 186).

Children who are thought of as non-compliant in terms of behaviour may also be defined as non-compliant or dysfunctional in academic terms. They may not follow instructions when it comes to academic matters. When they fail at an academic exercise, this may be seen by teachers as a symptom of a general desire not to cooperate in academic matters. Poor behaviour may hence be linked to poor achievement in academic matters. In general, such children may be 'labelled' as underperforming or as dysfunctional. Labelling can therefore be an assumption, made by a teacher, that because a pupil has not achieved very well in terms of one criterion (such as behaviour, for example) they are unlikely to do well in terms of a second criterion (such as academic achievement) for example. Such an assumption is sometimes termed a 'self-fulfilling prophecy'. Teachers can assume that pupils who do not comply with behavioural norms will do badly at scholastic work. The teachers may actually send this message to the students, giving them the feeling that very little is expected of them. This may engender a lack of self-belief in the students and hence a poor academic performance.

Did you know?

Howard S. Becker (1928–) is one of the leading writers on labelling and deviance. He has also been a lifelong musician playing in clubs in Chicago as a teenager and through his years of academic study at the University of Chicago. He was eventually able to take advantage of his experiences in those clubs by writing about the subcultures that he observed. He obtained his PhD when he was 23 years of age, and embarked on a career as a university professor and researcher. His interests were eclectic, discussing the art of academic writing and taking an active interest in French culture and society.

A similar effect operates in relation to students being streamed in school. If students are classified in a lower stream then they will probably assume that they are held in low esteem in the school, certainly in the streaming subject. Even if they have generally performed better in subjects other than the one in which they are streamed, their performance may generally decline because they believe that they are less bright than students in higher streams.

The problem with streaming is that once pupils are classified into the lower streams, there is a tendency that they will not improve, but will reflect the expectations that the teachers appear to have of them. This can have an adverse effect upon working-class children, because teachers can very well make assumptions about their academic potential. Even though the classification of working-class children may be based upon 'objective' tests and criteria, this may not prevent the pupils developing a very negative self-image. This will not be the case with middle-class children who are classified in upper streams, and who may develop a positive self-image.

There are other differences between working-class and middle-class children. One of the distinctions is economic. Middle-class children have access to the financial resources that enable them to take full advantage of the opportunities of the educational system. Their parents are able to afford resources such as a sports equipment to enable them to participate in school teams; they can purchase books and computers; and fund their children to go on study trips. It is difficult for children from poorer, working-class homes to play tennis or hockey without a good tennis racquet or hockey stick.

Even though children from different social classes attend the same school, and at least notionally have the same opportunities, the reality can be somewhat different. Material deprivation has a number of consequences at school in creating differential opportunities, but there are also rather more hidden effects at home. Working-class children may have limited resources at home, such as the lack of a quiet space to do homework, and a lack of time to study because they are expected to help with activities around the house.

One might sum up a lot of the differences between working-class and middle-class children under the general heading of socialization. From their earliest years middle-class children are introduced to ways of speaking and communicating, different ways of dressing, manners and ways of interacting, up to and including higher education and work. As Cohen-Scali comments:

> 'Socialization for work appears to be a long process which has its origins in childhood, becomes more and more complex, and is enriched throughout adolescence and adulthood, notably through professional training courses which are vectors of diffusion of culture and new values. For teenagers, socialization for work takes place, in family, social, and educational circles.'
>
> Cohen–Scali, Valérie (2003), 'The Influence of Family, Social, and Work Socialization on the Construction of the Professional Identity of Young Adults' (p. 242).

All of this will help to distinguish them as potentially fitting in to certain strata of society. In short, they will be socialized into the customs and behaviour patterns of their peer group. Working-class children will also be socialized, but into different customs and behaviour patterns, and in future life it will be more difficult for them to integrate themselves into a middle-class social stratum.

Dig deeper

Becker, H. S. (1963), *Outsiders: Studies in the Sociology of Deviance*. New York: The Free Press.

Kramer, M. (2010), *Organizational Socialization – Joining and Leaving Organizations*. Cambridge: Polity.

Moncrieffe, J. & Eyben, R. (Eds.) (2007), *The Power of Labelling – how people are categorized and why it matters*. London: Earthscan.

Saunders, P. (1990), *Social class and stratification*. Abingdon, Oxon: Routledge.

Woodward, K. (ed.) (2004), *Questioning Identity: Gender, Class, Ethnicity* (2nd ed.). London: Routledge.

Test your knowledge

1 The separation of society into various layers, arranged in a hierarchical order is known as...?
   a a managed hierarchy
   b socialization by layers
   c social stratification
   d hierarchical stratum

2 A society in which people rise to a level that reflects their ability is known as...?
   a an oligarchy
   b an autocracy
   c a democracy
   d a meritocracy

3 A caste system is typically related to which religion?
   a Islam
   b Buddhism
   c Hinduism
   d Christianity

4 A social group in which people may only intermarry within the group is described as...?
   a endogamous
   b secular
   c monogamous
   d profligate

5 In India, 'untouchables' are now normally known as...?
   a casteless
   b Dalits
   c upper caste
   d lower caste

6 The first Dalit to become president of India was...?
   a Shankara
   b Nehru
   c Narayanan
   d Gandhi

7 One of the leading campaigners for the rights of Dalits was...?
   a Sri Aurobindo
   b Ramakrishna
   c R. K. Narayan
   d Dr Ambedkar

8 One of the leading writers on deviance was..?
   a Hughes
   b Weber
   c Becker
   d Durkheim

9 If a child is described in a certain way, and he/she comes to believe that claim, even when it may not be true, this is an example of a...?
   a corollary
   b assumption
   c social fact
   d self-fulfilling prophecy

10 The accepted standards by which society functions are termed...?
   a assumptions
   b norms
   c statements
   d syllogisms

16

Evolving concepts of gender

During the Second World War, the male domination of society was shaken somewhat when, through economic necessity, women assumed roles in, for example, heavy engineering, which previously had been a male preserve. After the war, however, there was a tendency for women to revert to traditional roles of home making and child-rearing. However, society was gradually beginning to view gender as a social construction, and Simone de Beauvoir famously argued that women do not have to accept society's social definition of their gender role, but can be what they wish to be. The feminist perspective further argued that there were distinctive ways of viewing the social world that one could attribute to women, and which should be viewed as a strength, for example, in the workplace, in organizations and the professions. Legislation was introduced in the 1970s to combat gender discrimination, and the struggle has continued for genuinely equal rights for women. This chapter will review these issues and the sociological arguments which are inherent in them.

The nature of patriarchy

Feminists do not necessarily share exactly the same concept of society and of the role of women in it. However, most feminists are of the view that society is patriarchal in nature, with men having decision-making authority over women in most situations. Whichever hierarchical organization one examines, from say the Church to the armed forces, to business and commercial organizations, feminists argue that it is almost certain that crucial decisions will be taken by men, with women finding it extremely difficult to position themselves in a locus of power. Patriarchy has enabled men to give voice to their opinions and feelings about the world in such a way that they are able to influence the flow of events in both the family, in organizations and on a global level.

Did you know?

Harriet Martineau (1802–76) is commonly considered to have been the first sociologist. She was an authority in many different fields, especially economic theory. She wrote a great number of books, many of which were written from a feminist perspective. She commented on many aspects of the relationship between the genders. Eclectic in her interests, she produced a translation of the writings of Auguste Comte on positivism. This translation proved very popular. When she wrote about society, and particularly from a feminist perspective, she tried to base her writings on as many different facets of society as possible. Harriet Martineau knew many different intellectuals, politicians and writers on both sides of the Atlantic, including James Madison, John Stuart Mill and Thomas Carlyle.

In order to understand sociologically the nature of feminism or of patriarchy, it is necessary to ask the kind of questions that truly analyse the nature of society. As Hemmings points out:

> 'Such critical historiographic accounts of power, history and authorship allow a different set of questions to be asked about the feminist past. Rather than asking for example, "What really happened in the 1970s?" I want to ask "How does this story about the 1970s come to be told and accepted?"'
> Hemmings, Clare (2005), 'Telling Feminist Stories' (p. 119).

The power exercised by men has made it very difficult for women to have the same kind of influence. Men have been able to exercise authority and power particularly through the context of the workplace. This has historically enabled them to obtain a monopoly of influence over the professions, such as law and medicine, and although this monopoly is gradually being eroded, it still exists in many ways.

During the Second World War women were actually encouraged to work in factories and on farms to assist the war effort. This experience did a great deal to indicate the potential of women to contribute to the economy. Moreover, it suggested that if a country failed to employ women in key roles, then the economy of that country was failing to take advantage of an important resource. However, despite these arguments, once the Second World War was over, women tended to assume the kinds of roles they had held before the war. They took control of household duties and of care of the children. They perhaps worked part-time while their children were still at home. However, they had no real influence in the world of work, other than that mediated via their husbands and children.

Despite the fact that they may have achieved a high academic standard at school, it was relatively rare that they were encouraged to proceed to higher education and the professions. The ambitions of young women in the 1950s and early years of the 1960s were generally limited to a romantic ideal of getting married and starting a family, with no real ambition of embarking on a career.

Did you know?

The writer Mary Wollstonecraft (1759–97) wrote and argued extensively on female rights, and was a significant influence upon the burgeoning feminist movement of the mid 20th century. She travelled to Paris in 1792 at the height of the French Revolution. Among her writings, one of her best-known volumes was *A Vindication of the Rights of Woman*. One of her children, Mary Shelley, became famous in her own right, as both a feminist and as the author of the novel, *Frankenstein*.

The fact that men were able to integrate themselves in the world of work enabled them to articulate their views on different issues and to exert a range of power and influence. As men were familiar with stating their views and with influencing events, they were often able to transfer these skills from the workplace to a whole range of contexts in society. MacKinnon comments further:

'Where liberal feminism sees sexism primarily as an illusion or myth to be dispelled, an inaccuracy to be corrected, true feminism sees the male point of view as fundamental to the male power to create the world in its own image, the image of its desires, not just as its delusory end-product.'

MacKinnon, Catharine (1983), 'Feminism, Marxism, Method and the State: Toward Feminist Jurisprudence' (p. 640).

Men thus had the skills and expertise to lead social and leisure organizations and to serve on committees. Women, however, would typically lead their lives in the home, and most men during the period of, say, the 1950s and early 1960s would normally have assumed that women had no wish to assume responsibility. Worse still, many men would assume that women were not suited nor had the ability to hold responsible positions. In some cases at the time, women were excluded from membership of some organizations, such as golf clubs.

Family life and the relations between men and women were thus very much 'gendered'. That is, the dynamics of the interactions between men and women were very much influenced by the nature of the two genders. Family life was thus not merely the meeting of two equal genders, but of two people who each held very different degrees of power.

Simone Weil

Not all women decided to adopt stereotypical female role models in their lives. Simone Weil (1909–43) was a French philosopher, Christian mystic, left-wing political activist and sociologist. She was born into the Jewish faith, but later adopted a Christian perspective. Throughout her adult life Weil was also very interested in Eastern religions such as Hinduism and Buddhism. She was widely read and extremely intelligent. She studied at leading institutions in Paris such as the Lycée Henri IV and the École Normale Supérieure, in one examination coming ahead of Simone de Beauvoir.

Weil was born into a Jewish family from eastern France. She was always committed to helping people. In fact she obtained a post in a car factory in eastern France in order to learn more about working-class customs. In 1936 she fought with an anarchist group in the Spanish Civil War. After the Second World War had broken out, in 1942 she travelled first to the US with her parents and then to London to join de Gaulle's Free French movement. She hoped to be able to move back to France and to join the Resistance. However, as a consequence of contracting tuberculosis, she died in a hospital in Kent in 1943.

Throughout her life, Weil refused to adopt a conventional lifestyle. Although she could have had a fairly affluent life, she avoided luxuries of all kinds in order to exhibit an empathy with the poorer people of society. She wore unkempt and dishevelled clothes, which did not in any way enhance her femininity. During the Second World War she ate very little food to reflect the enforced lives of people in Occupied Europe. This very basic diet probably exacerbated the illness that finally led to her death.

The gendered divisions in family life left women responsible for tasks of lower status, while men generally assumed responsibility for issues such as the distribution of financial resources.

At this stage it is worth pointing out the conceptual difference between 'sex' and 'gender'. The functional differences in terms of reproduction define what we mean by 'sex'. It is determined by our genetic inheritance, and includes not only reproductive differences, but also physiological and psychological differences.

Gender, on the other hand, consists of the different qualities, interests, attitudes, behavioural patterns and affiliation with social norms that we acquire as part of our maturation process. As we are socialized during our childhood by our parents, siblings and others, we begin to think and develop in a certain way as a result of that socialization. In childhood, a young boy may be encouraged to play rugby, to join a boxing club or to participate in mountaineering. Another boy may be socialized into hobbies such as embroidery or dressmaking. The socialization process may encourage one boy to act in a manner more associated with masculinity, whereas the other boy may develop values and norms that are considered typically more feminine. Masculine and feminine genders thus develop from the social context in which the individual is reared and socialized.

Alternatively, we can argue that gender is socially constructed. It is important to appreciate, however, that sex and gender do not necessarily operate in parallel. Someone of male reproductive sex may reflect the normally accepted behaviour patterns of someone of male gender, but this may not be the case. A male may reflect female gender qualities.

Key idea: Sex and gender

The essential distinction between sex and gender is that sex reflects the biological inheritance of an individual, whereas gender is a function of the role acquired through socialization.

Many feminists have argued that the way in which women understand and experience the world may be very different from the way in which men understand and experience their surroundings. Men may not pause to consider the realities of the lifestyles of women in the home. They may not internalize the reality of the washing, cleaning, ironing, cooking and childcare carried out by women. This kind of work may very often be done in isolation, separating women from the kinds of social interaction that enrich the lives of men. This division of labour in the household has a negative effect upon the quality of the lives of women. Moreover, it can also prevent women and girls from attaining a form of fulfilment that provides them with a sense of meaning in their lives. This is often termed 'self-actualization' or 'self-fulfilment'. We may also think of this failure to achieve personal fulfilment as a form of oppression created by men. Under these circumstances, women live out their lives under a regime of inequality, involving not only unfairness, but also a serious form of subjugation.

Key idea: Division of labour

The gendered division of labour in the household can have a negative effect upon the social life experienced by women.

Women and education

Since the end of the Second World War a great deal of time and research has been devoted to inequality in education. For most of the 1960s attention was focused upon social class and the consequences of this for the unequal distribution of opportunity. During the 1970s researchers tended to move their attention to the question of gender. Among the issues that concerned them was, first, that boys and girls tended to opt for different subjects at school. Frequently, boys tended to study mathematics, sciences and engineering, while girls opted for the social sciences and humanities.

Did you know?

Jane Addams (1860–1935) was an American sociologist, philosopher and social worker who was awarded the Nobel Prize for Peace in 1931, the first American woman to gain this honour. Although a leading sociologist who had connections with the department of sociology at the University of Chicago, she preferred to devote her attentions to social work. In fact she has come to be regarded as the person who established the profession of social work in the United States. Despite being a prominent intellectual, she preferred not to devote her time to the conduct of academic research and the writing of academic papers. Rather, she preferred to concentrate on areas in applied social science where she felt she could do more good in the world.

During a period when there was an increasing awareness of the significance of technical subjects for the economy, governments became aware of the importance of involving girls in these disciplines. There was a recognition that the socialization of girls in the broader society and at home contributed to a reluctance on the part of girls to take part in scientific and technical studies. The school system also came under criticism because of frequent implicit assumptions about the aspirations of girls, and also their likely levels of achievement.

Teachers tended to assume that girls would be more suited to non-technical subjects, and that they simply would not be as successful as boys in subjects such as mathematics and physics. These assumptions have subsequently been shown to be fallacious, with girls often outperforming boys, and showing more academic potential. Schools have now become more sensitive to the dangers of what became known as the hidden curriculum, a complex set of assumptions on the part of teachers that girls would be unlikely to be high achievers, particularly in some subjects, and would set their sights much lower.

In the 1960s and 1970s it was very often the case that both the school system and the society outside school encouraged the development of gender stereotypes, such that girls had little opportunity in reality of having a career in such areas as laboratory science. It may not have been that teachers deliberately tried to exclude girls from certain careers on the grounds of skills and aptitudes. It may have been that they thought they were giving relevant advice on actual gender divisions in society. Nevertheless, the result was that girls often had limited aspirations, which in turn affected the frequently negative impression they gave about their potential for higher education.

However, as we moved towards the 1990s and the turn of the century, there was a much more sophisticated understanding of the sociology of the school, and the way in which the educational system could have an effect upon the aspirations and achievements of girls. In terms of gaining five or more A–C grades at GCSE, girls have continued to do better than boys. Moreover, teachers were beginning to be aware that the behaviour patterns of teenage boys in school often militated against a good performance in school assessments. The reasons for these gender differences appear to be very complex, and it is important to develop strategies to address all aspects of underachievement.

Women and employment

One of the major factors that traditionally had an adverse influence on the employment of women was that they were usually expected to take responsibility for children and family duties, besides being able to work and contribute to the family income. Men, on the other hand, had the relative luxury of concentrating on their job or career, and not having to divide their time with family duties.

A lack of education and training was also a major handicap for women, whereas men did receive some training in the workplace. Up to the middle years of the 20th century men often had mixed feelings about their wives working. On the one hand, they liked to be seen as the one who earned the money and assumed the financial responsibility. On the other hand, they recognized that their wife's income made a very useful contribution to the family. It however resulted in their wife having to divide her time between household duties and employment. Men also took a pride in being able to carry out work roles that were heavy or dangerous, thus reinforcing their masculinity. Women were excluded from such jobs either for social reasons or because they were not considered capable of carrying them out. Little by little, heavy industrial jobs were replaced by jobs requiring a greater cognitive content, which enabled women to compete on more equal terms with men. However, the ultimate success of women in the workforce required the developing equality in educational opportunities. There was also a gradual social awareness that greater provision was required in terms of child care, so that women would be able to seek a career in jobs that were professional in nature.

There remained, however, a number of factors that continued to affect the success of women in the workplace. One of the most pervasive of these was discrimination. Much gender discrimination was founded upon stereotypical assumptions, which helped to sustain the viewpoint that women were only suited to certain categories of job. During the period when the first challenges to sex discrimination were being made, it was assumed, for example, that women were unsuited to such jobs as lorry drivers, fire officers and pilots. With the passing of the Sex Discrimination Act in 1975 there was a gradual reduction in the amount of sexism in employment. Women began gradually to be accepted in jobs where they had previously found it very difficult to be accepted.

Nevertheless, as we moved towards the end of the 20th century and into the 21st century, there was still a great deal of room for improvement in terms of work-based sexism. In terms of enabling women to gain access to professions in which they had not worked before, a number of different strategies were tried. In some cases one or two clearly well-qualified women would be employed in a particular job. It was argued by some that these women would then act as role models and would implicitly persuade other girls and women to enter the same profession. Such practices, however, were often known as 'tokenism', in that some argued that they were merely a gesture towards gender equality, and did not reflect a substantive change in the gender balance of that job.

Key idea: Stereotypes

Gender discrimination is often founded upon stereotypical assumptions about the roles of women, and the functions they should have in society.

Another feature of the gender balance of some occupations was, and is, that women are often employed in the lower echelons of the hierarchy of a profession but find it extremely difficult to progress beyond the level of middle management. There is said to exist a 'glass ceiling' that prevents women progressing higher up the hierarchy. The reasons for this lack of progression are probably varied and complex.

Direct discrimination may continue to play a part today, even after considerable equal opportunities legislation. Men often have access to widespread business, commercial and professional networks that gives them broad scope to access possible candidates for senior jobs. They also mix in a variety of social settings where they are able to facilitate business connections.

The assumptions made about the female gender are also likely to have effects on women in employment. The continued use of gender-biased language, such as the use of the male pronoun for senior executives on the assumption that they will indeed prove to be men, can have a negative effect on the aspirations of women. The use of female models in adverts can often be said to objectify women, treating them as objects to look at, rather than as human beings who are as talented as men, and should be considered as competent professionals in their own right.

The treatment of women

Unfortunately, women have very often been treated extremely badly, more often than not as a means to force them to act in the way in which men wanted them to act. Much of this treatment has involved murder, rape, sexual violence of various kinds, and many different types of physical violence. In many parts of the world, including the UK, women are subjected to physical threats and violence within the institution of marriage. This is usually to ensure that the husband retains power within the household. In some societies in which it is assumed that men will dominate and oppress women, sometimes murder has been the extreme consequence of women attempting to liberate themselves from the autocratic, male-dominated system.

Other forms of violence in some cultures include female genital mutilation, which is at once a form of oppression and domination of women by men, and also of patriarchal control over the sexual lives of women.

Key idea: Women and violence

In many cultures women are subject to considerable violence, often because they refuse to adopt a submissive role in a patriarchal society.

Women had a long journey in order to gain the right to vote in parliamentary elections. One or two British colonies gained the vote for women in the 19th century, but as with a great deal of social change it took the traumatic events of the First World War to persuade politicians to grant women's suffrage. Women gained the vote in Germany in 1918, in the Irish Free State in 1922, and in the UK for women over 21 years, in 1928.

Equal pay

One of the greatest unfairnesses for working women is the difference between average pay for men and average pay for women. Irrespective of whether we compute pay differentials for full-time workers or part-time workers, the mean female pay is considerably less than the mean male pay. The key principle here is that people should be paid equally for work of a broadly similar nature, irrespective of extraneous variables such as gender. There are, however, many factors that conspire such that women earn less than men while performing work that is roughly similar in nature.

When women are pregnant, for example, they will normally take maternity leave. However, during that period they do not add to their total experience time in a job; they are not able to gain further training to enhance their skills; and nor are they able to gain for themselves the kind of experience that will enable them to apply for and gain promotions in their particular field. When women resume their careers after taking maternity leave, they often find that there are no full-time posts available just when they want them. They may have to take a part-time version of their original job, or perhaps accept a part-time post that is not as appropriate as their first job. In either case they are considerably disadvantaged. For some of these reasons women's work is perceived as low status and therefore deserving of less pay. Of course, not all women have children and yet the pay differentials also continue for women free from children – the mere suggestion/hint that they are potentially capable one day of having children sets them at a disadvantage from the start of their working careers.

However we look at the situation, women are normally disadvantaged. This disadvantage can also be related to a variety of social factors, not just gender. Ethnicity and class can also have significant effects. As Davis notes:

> '"Intersectionality" refers to the interaction between gender, race, and other categories of difference in individual lives, social practices, institutional arrangements and cultural ideologies and the outcomes of these interactions in terms of power.'
>
> Davis, Kathy (2008), 'Intersectionality as buzzword: A sociology of science perspective on what makes a feminist theory successful' (p. 68).

Dig deeper

Butler, J. (2006), *Gender Trouble: Feminism and the Subversion of Identity*. Abingdon, Oxon: Routledge.

Cochrane, K. (ed.) (2010), *Women of the Revolution: Forty years of Feminism*. London: Guardian Books.

Saul, J. M. (2003), *Feminism: Issues and Arguments*. Oxford: Oxford University Press.

Walter, N. (2010), *Living Dolls: The Return of Sexism*. London: Virago.

Walters, M. (2005), *Feminism: A very short introduction*. Oxford: Oxford University Press.

Test your knowledge

1 During the Second World War women were encouraged to leave the home and work in...?
   a factories and farms
   b the record industry
   c fishing
   d the fire service

2 Harriet Martineau produced a translation of the work of...?
   a Comte
   b Durkheim
   c Marx
   d Darwin

3 Mary Wollstonecraft travelled to Paris during the...?
   a French Revolution
   b Napoleonic Wars
   c 100 Years' War
   d reign of Louis XIV

4 Who was Mary Wollstonecraft's daughter?
   a Mary Smith
   b Mary Thomson
   c Mary Shelley
   d Alice Shelley

5 Which war did Simone Weil fight in?
   a Vietnam War
   b Korean War
   c Spanish Civil War
   d Algerian War of Independence

6 Where did Simone Weil die?
   a Yorkshire
   b Scotland
   c Wales
   d Kent

7 Jane Addams won the...?
- **a** Nobel Prize for Peace
- **b** Pulitzer Prize
- **c** Victoria Cross
- **d** Légion d'honneur

8 Jane Addams established the profession of...?
- **a** accountancy
- **b** law
- **c** medicine
- **d** social work

9 The first Sex Discrimination Act in the UK was passed in...?
- **a** 1961
- **b** 1970
- **c** 1971
- **d** 1975

10 Women gained the vote in Germany in...?
- **a** 1910
- **b** 1911
- **c** 1912
- **d** 1918

17

Law, crime and social order

Sociologists are interested in the process of social definition whereby an act is deemed contrary to the norms of a particular society or culture, and if it is so defined by the legislature of a society then it becomes illegal. There is often a close interaction between public opinion on an issue, the attitudes of politicians within the legislature and the final passing of legislation. For example, as social attitudes gradually evolved in the 1960s and 1970s, legislation was passed to make sex and racial discrimination illegal. Sociologists are interested in the processes whereby the opinion of the general public on a social question gradually gathers momentum, until it develops either a moral force of its own or it becomes politically expedient for the government of the day to try to enact legislation on the question. These sociological questions are related to that of deviance. Deviant behaviour may or may not be illegal, but what is regarded as deviant provides an interesting guide to the evolving values of a society. This chapter will analyse these questions.

Crime, deviance and social norms

It is worth bearing in mind that in most societies the majority of citizens are relatively conformist and adhere to the accepted norms and standards of their society. It is equally worth noting that what is normal behaviour in one society may in fact be deviant or even illegal in another. In other words, we might argue that deviant or criminal behaviour are socially constructed, with social norms evolving differently in different societies. Certainly, social norms are important in a discussion of human behaviour, as the following quotations suggest:

'Supporters of normative conceptions assume that in any given group, these rules or social norms are given; they exist, and group members uphold them.'

DeKeseredy, Walter et al (2015), *Deviance + Crime: Theory, Research and Policy* (p. 2).

'Descriptive norms provide a standard from which people do not want to deviate.'

Schultz et al (2007), 'The Constructive, Destructive, and Reconstructive Power of Social Norms' (p. 430).

Key idea: Deviancy

In many cases what is considered to be deviant is not an absolute, but depends upon the view of society and its contemporary norms. It is thus a social construct, and may change with time.

The nature of deviance is defined and re-defined depending upon the context and the people who are producing the definition. We are, for example, increasingly aware that we have to be careful of such differences when travelling abroad. When people are in a different culture or society they may inadvertently engage in illegal activity simply because of the existence of practices that are different from those in their own country. We may not normally think of such people as criminals or as deviant, but as perhaps imprudent. In this discussion we are more concerned with people in their home society who for various reasons act illegally.

In such circumstances there are two broad categories of reason for people acting in a deviant or illegal fashion.

First of all, some people may be more inclined to challenge authority, to reject accepted standards of behaviour, and to want to live their lives according to their own view of the world. If they want to adopt that pattern of behaviour, then it may be that for psychological or genetic reasons they are more inclined towards deviant or criminal behaviour.

Did you know?

It may be strange to think of it in such terms but deviance can be positive and useful in society. If everyone adhered very closely to the rules of society, then very few changes would come about. Society would always stay the same. Acts of deviance, however, cause people to think carefully about society's conventions and norms, and to try to change them when necessary. This view was originally proposed as part of Durkheim's conception of deviance.

The other broad type of explanation for deviant behaviour is that people – often younger people – are influenced by their surroundings and the people with whom they are in contact, to behave in an antisocial manner. On this environmental theory, antisocial, deviant or criminal behaviour is acquired through intimate contact with subcultures that display this type of behaviour pattern. This process is sometimes known as 'enculturation' or the process whereby people acquire some of the features of the culture with which they are in intimate contact.

Key idea: Enculturation

People often acquire patterns of behaviour through contact with a social group. The term enculturation can be used to describe this process.

On this basis people are not considered to have been born as criminals, but to have developed criminal practices through being influenced by criminals with whom they are in contact.

Of course, one might argue that some people have a stronger disposition than others to developing deviant tendencies, or perhaps to copying deviant behaviour. This would then be a combination of psychological and sociological explanations of the development of criminal tendencies.

Acculturation

This social process takes place when two distinct cultures meet and influence each other. It is possible that each group will influence the other relatively equally. However it is more likely that one group will be able to exert more influence over the other. There are a number of different reasons for one group to influence the other. The first group may be more powerful in a number of ways, for example economically, militarily or in terms of numbers. One group may be much better established in terms of having their own housing, means of transport and financial savings. One group may also have a strong cultural identity. When a migrant group settles near an established social group, the immigrant group will generally be less well established than the host group. This may result in the immigrant group acquiring some cultural features of the host group. If a criminal subculture lives near a non-criminal group, then any transfer of cultural identity will depend on the degree of assertiveness shown by one of the groups. Enculturation, as opposed to acculturation, is the transfer of cultural identity within a group, rather than between groups.

Environmental explanations of crime

It can be argued that criminal tendencies are more likely to develop or flourish in areas of a city that are, in general, poorer and more disadvantaged, with inadequate housing and employment. In such areas there are usually tensions between more affluent residents, who perhaps live in adjoining areas, and less affluent groups.

When some social strata are finding it very difficult to improve their social status, and to develop the quality of their lives, there can often be conflict when those people can see the lifestyles of more affluent neighbours. When more disadvantaged people are aware of the differentials between them and their richer neighbours, it can lead to the development of criminal activity because of the desire to enhance their financial status. Often, financial tensions can override other forms of social tension. When young people fail to gain a good career, or to have a good income through legitimate means, they may look to other possibilities in order to improve their financial circumstances. In these contexts they may start to mix and become integrated with criminal youth gangs. They may then in effect serve a criminal apprenticeship, and develop close social ties with the members of the criminal gang.

Many young people who have been unable to develop a career, and have few financial resources, perhaps existing on social benefits, have little status in society. Membership of a criminal gang can help them gain such status.

Key idea: Gang participation

When young people do not have the resources to improve their lives and acquire a sense of status, they may resort to crime in order to do this. One method that has an appeal for some is to join a criminal gang. In some contexts this enables them to gain social status, which may not be available to them in any other way.

Criminal activity can help to enhance their financial status, and also to be engaged in the type of activity that brings them esteem within certain sectors of the community. If there is a correlation between low socio-economic status and delinquent or criminal behaviour, then it is worth considering why all young people living in poverty with few possibilities of advancement do not become criminals. Some clearly do, but there are many who appear to be able to resist the tendency to act in a dysfunctional way. It may be that the most accurate explanation of the development of criminality is that a number of variables are operating, including both environmental and genetic factors.

The origins of crime in social conflict

Developing an analysis of the origins of crime that has an explanatory function in most situations is not easy. While it is tempting to assume that people living in deprived inner-city areas may be drawn into crime because they see it as the only way to gain money to buy the material goods they want, it does not explain why many people living in poorer areas never become involved in delinquency or crime.

When a young person begins to realize that their life is not progressing or improving, they will no doubt start to reflect upon their options. They could, of course, join a criminal gang and try to earn money illicitly, or they could try other legal approaches. They could try to improve their education, go on a training course or apprenticeship, seek employment or start a small business enterprise.

As an alternative strategy, some young people drop out of conventional society, and lead a countercultural existence, although living within the law. In fact, even in a deprived area, it is a minority of young people who adopt a criminal lifestyle, and hence it is necessary to try to explain why this is so. To take the contrary situation, crime still exists in very affluent areas of cities, and certainly among people who are employed for large companies, on high salaries, and who have an extremely affluent lifestyle. The actual number of people who are involved in crime may be less than in deprived areas, but the amount of money involved, or lost to conventional society, may in fact be much more. Hence the correlation between deprivation and crime may be difficult to sustain. Crime seems to take place irrespective of the affluence of the environment.

Hence it seems difficult to sustain an argument that crime and deviance are caused by a lack of money, although that may be a factor in some cases.

A different, although related hypothesis, is that crime has its origins in a situation where people feel that they lack the power and influence needed to control their lives. It may be more precise to argue that people who are deprived and have fewer life chances consider turning to crime not because of lack of money, but because they feel they have few realistic opportunities to transform their lives.

Did you know?

Stokely Carmichael (1941–98), who was a member of the Civil Rights movement of the 1960s, referred to the concept of 'institutional racism'. This was the notion that the practice of racism was deeply embedded in some organizations, such as the police. In other words, it was not simply a case of one or two isolated individuals who were racist, but the racism of the entire collective culture of the organization. Among other things, this concept has been employed to explain the disproportionate number of black people who are 'stopped and searched'. See the following quotation:

> 'Nevertheless, the concerns and the lack of confidence of black and minority ethnic communities in policing – and the consequences of this – have been highlighted in more recent official reports since the Macpherson and Scarman inquiries.'
> IPCC (2013), 'Report on Metropolitan Police Service handling of complaints alleging race discrimination' (p. 3).

On the other hand, people who work for a large company may also feel powerless, not because they have little money, but because they feel trapped in a large, impersonal system, doing a job that seems to them to be ultimately fairly pointless. They perhaps want a job that gives them a greater sense of meaning in life, but they feel trapped in their present employment. They may also feel trapped because they have extensive financial commitments commensurate with their large salaries, and do not feel they can resign and take a less well paid job. They may lack control over their lives, and this inner tension may lead them into criminal activity.

Did you know?

In much of Western society, children are brought up to work hard at school, to get a good job and to try hard to attain the material things of life, such as a house and a car. These goals are related very much to a culture that aspires to material success. The generally accepted method for attaining these goals is to gain education and training, which are the route to a good job and financial success. Now if for a variety of possible reasons a person is unable to attain their goals, they may feel frustrated with their lives and experience a sense of tension. Robert K. Merton (1910–2003) referred to this as 'strain' and argued that it sometimes led to deviant or criminal behaviour.

Marxist viewpoints on crime and deviance

The views of Marxist thought towards crime start with the nature of capitalism. For Marxists, capitalism is an unfair system. The capitalist system oppresses working-class people because it tries to extract as much labour as possible from them for as little remuneration as possible. This leads to a profound sense of exploitation among working people. Since the bourgeoisie try to extract as much work for as little pay as possible, people working under a capitalist system tend to experience greater levels of poverty.

Capitalism also tends to encourage a sense of competition, often between the members of the bourgeoisie. One result of this is that in order to try to develop a more efficient company, employers pay their workers as little as possible so as to generate more profits.

Marxists argue that the origins of crime can be found in the economic system operated in a society. Capitalism, they suggest, encourages feelings of greed, and hence because the people working within capitalism want to acquire more and more wealth and material goods, many of them turn to criminal ventures in order to gain them.

Some Marxist criminologists would argue that crime is simply a manifestation of people trying to correct the wrongs and injustices of capitalism. The structure and power of capitalism makes it very difficult for people to combat the unfairnesses of the system. Therefore, Marxists argue, people turn to crime. Within this analysis a great deal of crime is a statement of political ethics. It may not necessarily be for personal gain, but rather to point out to society that the present political system is implicitly or de facto supporting the bourgeois class. In some cases, Marxists may also wish to use criminal activity to redistribute wealth.

Key idea: Marxist analysis of capitalism

Marxists argue that the values and ethics of a society can be identified within its economic system. They argue that capitalism is so profoundly unfair that it is in effect a criminal system. It advantages a minority in society, at the expense of the majority.

It can be argued, according to Marxists, that the system of capitalism is so profoundly loaded against poorer working people that it is a type of social crime. Not only that, but some would argue that it also causes criminal activity by making people want some of the material goods that a capitalist economy generates. On this analysis, criminals may be perceived as people who do not accept capitalism as fair, and want in some way to demonstrate their feelings about it. In addition, since one of the features of capitalist economics is the accumulation of wealth and property, people perpetrating vandalism or graffiti are, in a sense, making a comment about their view upon the ethics of amassing property.

For Marxists, the institutions of capitalism tend to work to the advantage of the institutions of the state. Marxists would seek to make out a case that when people break the law through small-scale theft, including shoplifting or making false claims in relation to social security benefits, they can sometimes receive a greater level of punishment than people who carry out much larger scale financial crime. In other words, the judicial system, while not perhaps being overtly biased towards economic or financial crime, appears to act in a manner that favours white collar crime.

The relationship between the media and crime

It is important to remember that the public perception of crime rests to a large extent on the nature of crime reported in the press, on television and radio and in popular fiction. Of the many crimes that are committed, only some are selected by the media for detailed reporting. In addition, only some features of crimes are selected for detailed reporting and examination.

Crimes that are selected for detailed attention may contain elements of violence, they may have implications for large sectors of the public, or they may involve wealthy or famous personalities. The fact that crimes may be newsworthy in some way justifies a detailed reporting and may give the impression that crimes of that type are widespread.

The role of the media in reporting some types of crime is very important in that it warns the public about them, and enables people to take evasive action where necessary. Equally, it can cause people to think that some types of crime are much more prevalent than they really are, and create a form of obsession with some crimes. As newer types of crime evolve, it is important that the media raise awareness of these.

Computer-related crime is an example of this. Computers enable criminals to intrude into the lives of people through, for example, identity theft or stalking, and awareness raising by the media can help reduce this type of crime. Although a description of such crimes may inform criminals of new methods they can use, on the other hand it does alert the public to ways of being on guard in order to protect themselves.

Crime and statistics

Positivist methods are widely used to try to investigate the nature of crime. However, statistics can tell us very little about perceptions of the morality of crime, about the way in which people analyse the nature of crime, and about the factors that influence crime. If a researcher wants to investigate the mental processes behind a person deciding to commit a crime, then statistical methods would not be of a great deal of use. The researcher could use interview techniques, and try to explore the factors that influenced the potential criminal. However, society is very often interested in the potential effects of social variables upon crime rates, and indeed rates of different kinds of crime.

Among the many social variables that might have an influence upon crime rates are: population density; age; ethnicity; gender; alcohol consumption; educational attainment; and levels of education. Politicians are very interested in the connections between variables such as education level and crime. As crime levels are very sensitive politically, politicians are keen to know how their political policies appear to have affected crime rates. If the rate of crime appears to have increased when the rate of unemployment increases, then we can speak of a positive correlation between crime rate and unemployment. However, this does not mean that we can assert that unemployment causes crime, or in other words that there is a 'causal connection' between unemployment and crime. The reason for this is that there may well have been a third variable that caused both unemployment and crime rate to increase.

When evaluating correlation or causation between variables such as unemployment or crime rate it is important to measure variables accurately. Alternatively, we could say that it is important to understand the parameters used to measure variables. For example, if we are measuring the number of robberies committed within a particular period of time, we should be able to define clearly what we mean by a robbery. Does, for example, pickpocketing count as a robbery, or do we only count theft from houses or from jewellery shops? Alternatively, should robbery be defined in terms of the value of goods stolen? The recording of crime statistics is equally problematic, and it is important that the same defining and recording techniques should be employed.

The defining of crime is complex. One can, for example, seek to define crime using criteria related to the perpetrator, or by using criteria related to the crime itself. So-called 'white collar crime', for example, is principally defined in terms of the type of people who become involved. They are normally professional employees, well-educated and working for large corporations. Typically, the crimes involved would be in the financial or business sectors, and might involve stocks and shares, and insider dealing. The normal motivation for the crime would be to gain money for the criminal, who would often be a person who was highly thought of in the community and within his or her profession. The criminal might bear all the external appearance of being a pillar of society.

This begs the question of why someone in such a social category would wish to carry out a crime that might result in their being confined to prison. In general terms it might be that the potential criminal is spending more money than they are earning, even though they might be earning a considerable amount of money. In sociological terms the person may have been drawn into a profligate lifestyle, where the subcultures to which they belong place a great deal of emphasis upon wealth and material goods.

So-called 'blue collar crime', on the other hand, is normally perpetrated by members of the working class or more impoverished social classes. As they are likely to be less well educated, such criminals may well commit less sophisticated crimes, such as armed robbery, theft from houses or people, and car theft. Many of these offenders may be unemployed, and not be able to remedy their social situation in conventional ways. Very often, those who have been unemployed for a long period may become involved in what may be termed public order crime. This is a form of activity that very often may be thought of as being on the borderline between crime and legitimate activity. It is sometimes considered a crime without victims, since it may not appear to do any harm to anyone, except people who are willing participants.

Organized crime on the other hand certainly does have victims. Organized crime has many of the features of a large legitimate business, in that it has a clearly defined hierarchy and precise division of labour. The key difference is often the use of violence to achieve and sustain its ends, and its involvement in activities which are definitely illegal.

Finally, corporate crime involves illegal activities carried out by large business organizations. The illegal activity is generally for the benefit of the organization rather than for the individual. Nowadays, one tends to hear of the concept of corporate responsibility when there is an accident, and some of the victims try to ensure that the corporate body accepts legal responsibility for the accident or damages.

Dig deeper

Downes, D. & Rock, P. (2011), *Understanding Deviance* (6th ed.). Oxford: Oxford University Press.

Hale, C., Hayward, K., Wahidin, A. & Wincup, E. (2013), *Criminology* (3rd ed.). Oxford: Oxford University Press.

Jones, S. (2013), *Criminology* (5th ed.). Oxford: Oxford University Press.

Joyce, P. (2011), *Criminology and Criminal Justice – A Study Guide*. London: Routledge.

Newburn, T. (2007), *Criminology*. Cullompton, Devon: Willan Publishing.

Test your knowledge

1 When deviant behaviour is defined in terms of society's norms we say it is...?

   a contingent

   b subversive

   c definitional

   d socially constructed

2 Deviant behaviour can sometimes help society to...?

   a grow

   b change

   c become conservative

   d expand

3 Deviant behaviour can be developed in people by contact with groups that are...?

   a deviant

   b close

   c random

   d differentiated

4 The latter process is known as...?

   a empathy

   b synthesis

   c parallelism

   d enculturation

5 When people cannot attain status by normal means they may resort to...?

   a investment.

   b self-defence

   c crime

   d travel

6 There is no necessary connection between social deprivation and...?

   a illness

   b hospitalization

   c crime

   d infection

7 What grouping was Stokely Carmichael a member of?
- **a** Right wing federation
- **b** Freedom party
- **c** Conservative party
- **d** Civil Rights Movement

8 Robert Merton developed a theory of deviance known as...?
- **a** strain theory
- **b** capital theory
- **c** sympathy theory
- **d** generational theory

9 Marxists view capitalism as a form of...?
- **a** crime
- **b** empathy
- **c** sympathy
- **d** development

10 White collar crime is normally perpetuated by...?
- **a** technicians
- **b** apprentices
- **c** young people
- **d** professionals

18

Sociology and citizenship

This chapter analyses the concept of citizenship from a sociological point of view. Being a citizen of a country implies a relationship between the individual citizen on the one hand, and the state on the other. There are duties and responsibilities on both sides. The citizen, for example, may be required to take up arms in time of war to defend the state. On the other hand, the state has a responsibility to organize itself so that the life and liberty of the individual are protected. In a democratic system, citizens may have a duty to participate in the democratic process by voting in elections, for example. Yet many citizens do not exercise their right to vote. A sociological analysis of citizenship seeks to understand the types of responsibility that citizens feel towards the state, and how this is demonstrated.

The concept of citizenship

Citizenship is a difficult concept to clarify or define, partly because there are a number of other related ideas that overlap citizenship. For example, we may describe ourselves as an American citizen, a British citizen or a European citizen. Some people even like to think of themselves as a citizen of the world. In each case, the term citizen denotes a sense of belonging to either a country, a continent or the world itself. Besides giving us a feeling of belonging, citizenship also implies a sense of responsibility, which may include a number of different responsibilities. Citizenship has a very real sense of meaning, particularly as it is supported by documentary evidence in the form of a passport.

Did you know?

The two key means by which people gain citizenship are *jus soli* and *jus sanguinis*. The former refers to the idea that a baby born within the borders of a country gains citizenship of that state. *Jus sanguinis* refers to a situation where a baby is born to parents who are themselves citizens, and the baby thus becomes a citizen of the same country.

In contemporary times we live in such a multicultural and diverse society that there are generally very few characteristics that can be said to link a diverse population to the state in which it exists. For example, a state may contain different tribal groups, religious groups, ethnic groups, indigenous and immigrant groups. Yet if all of these hold citizenship of that country, then that can be a major factor in ensuring a measure of coherence and uniformity in the country.

Key idea: Citizenship tests

Countries are increasingly employing citizenship tests to try to define the knowledge and skills someone must possess in order to be accepted as a citizen of a country.

Yet the fact that everyone in a state may hold citizenship does not mean that everyone is equal in other senses. Citizens may not have access to the same benefits of health care, or of education, employment and housing. The distribution of such benefits equally among citizens may be a social ideal, but in practice it may not happen. However, the right to vote and to select a government democratically that citizens feel can best represent their social and economic needs is a feature of citizenship as we now perceive it in many countries. As Turner suggests:

> 'In this area political citizenship required the development of electoral rights and wider access to political institutions for the articulation of interests.'
>
> Turner, Bryan (1990), 'Outline of a theory of citizenship' (p. 191).

Key idea: Citizenship equality

Just because people are citizens of a country does not necessarily suggest they are equal. They may be equal in a philosophical sense, but not in a sociological sense, having for example equal access to social resources.

Duties and rights

To be a citizen of a state is on the one hand to be granted a number of rights, and on the other to acknowledge that as citizens we have a number of duties. In a sense, the nature and extent of these duties and rights fluctuate with changing social circumstances, including the prevalent political leadership. The competing nature of rights and duties are particularly noticeable during times of threat to the country, such as when warfare is imminent. On such occasions, citizens may for instance be conscripted into the armed forces; they may be forced to take up certain types of occupation, such as mining or working in engineering, which are useful to the war effort; or they may be required to hand over their property or material possessions to the state in order to assist in the war.

Did you know?

It is possible to be registered as the citizen of more than one country, a situation often known as 'dual citizenship'. This can arise very often because countries may have different regulations and legislation governing citizenship and nationality. Dual citizenship can give rise to difficult legal situations, placing competing obligations upon citizens. It is partly for this reason that some countries do not permit their citizens to hold the citizenship of another state.

It is on such occasions that many citizens may feel that their individuality is being threatened, and that the state is encroaching upon their freedom and liberty. Thus although the state may concur with its citizens that the latter have a right not to have their lives intruded upon by the state, in times of war, the state may feel that in the interests of overall security it has the right to place limitations upon individual rights.

The opposite type of situation occurs in periods when the state exists within conditions of economic and political stability. When there is a relatively high level of employment, and when citizens are able to live a life characterized by high levels of opportunity and security. Under these circumstances, citizens are generally able to exercise relatively high levels of personal liberty, freedom and autonomy.

Key idea: Citizenship and freedom

Citizenship implies that certain limitations may be placed upon the rights and freedoms of individuals. Citizens have to accept this as a necessary concomitant of the privileges of citizenship.

Citizenship and the movement of people

We have only to watch the television news to begin to appreciate the type of circumstances from which many people in the 'South' or developing countries are fleeing. So complex and harsh are these circumstances that it is difficult to categorize people and say that some should be given entry to a country and others not. When we see people taking serious risks for themselves and their families in order to seek sanctuary in a European country, we can begin to build up a picture of the hardships they have faced.

The immediate question that is raised is one of the grounds upon which such refugees are entitled to be given access to a new country of which they are not formally citizens. There are first of all ethical grounds when people are suffering for them to be given help and sustenance. Some would argue that it is part of the nature of being a citizen that one should be willing to assist citizens of other countries when they are in extreme difficulties. It is a similar argument to the idea that since we are all human beings we should behave with empathy towards other human beings.

Some might argue that many migrants are in such difficult circumstances because their home countries – the countries of which they are formally citizens – have been very badly administered and governed. The implication of this argument for some is that the primary moral responsibility therefore lies with the government of the host country and not with a European country with whom the migrant may have no historical contact. However, the political situation in many developing countries is so disorganized that we cannot realistically expect their citizens to be able to rectify it in order to be able to lead relatively normal lives. They are not therefore able to function in their home countries in the manner of what we would regard as normal citizens.

Key idea: Failures of citizenship

The situation in many developing countries is so lacking in organization that it is very difficult to envisage the citizens being able to improve the situation without large scale external aid. They are therefore often unable to exercise what we would normally regard as the normal functions of citizens.

The fact of the matter is that the conditions of poverty, malnourishment, civil war and chaotic administration in many developing countries are not exclusively the result of internal issues, but in reality explicable by the way the developing world is – and has been – treated by the developed world.

Many developing countries have historically been subject to colonial powers in the 19th century which exploited their resources and did not give any priority to the education and development of their citizens. It is scarcely surprising then that in the contemporary world such countries have great difficulty in establishing democratic systems within which their citizens can exercise their normal duties and responsibilities. In fact, in such countries, it is sometimes doubtful whether those purporting to be citizens actually have an allegiance to the state as their prime sense of loyalty. More often than not, people look to their tribal group, ethnic group or perhaps simply to a local powerbroker as the locus for their loyalty. This can hardly lead to a true sense of citizenship.

When such people are confronted by very unfortunate circumstances where the lives of their family are threatened, and the quality of life becomes so fragile that they have to seek sanctuary elsewhere, many would argue that they are not in reality seeking any special favours. The circumstances of colonialism and other forms of exploitation mentioned above mean that many refugees could be regarded as simply trying to rectify the many unfairnesses of the past. The logic of this argument is that they should certainly be assisted in trying to find a more congenial life in Europe. However, there are others who would argue that the developed countries of Europe have a distinct moral claim to be able to retain the security of their borders, and to prevent their penetration by people from a wide range of developing countries.

One of the most contentious issues in relation to the migration of refugees is the attempt by refugees to obtain employment in the developed world, and indeed to work for levels of salary that would be rejected by indigenous workers. With regard to the latter, one might argue that it is one of the responsibilities of citizens to contribute economically to the financial welfare of their home country. One of the commonest ways of doing this is to be in employment, and to contribute by paying taxes. If people opt not to do this, because perhaps they feel that the level of remuneration is too low, then some people might feel that they have failed in terms of one of the basic requirements of a citizen. On the other hand, one of the principal arguments in favour of migrants from other countries is that for various reasons they are willing to work for such relatively low salary levels. Not only that, but they are often eager to work very hard indeed in areas of work sometimes shunned by indigenous workers. As Colic-Peisker and Tilbury argue:

> 'In metropolitan areas, where the majority of recent refugees have settled, they seem to be significantly concentrated in certain low-skilled service "niches" such as cleaning services, care of the aged, transport (especially taxi driving) and the security and building industries.'
> Colic-Peisker, Val & Tilbury, Farida (2006), 'Employment Niches for Recent Refugees: Segmented Labour Market in Twenty-first Century Australia' (p. 204).

In terms of economic and political migrants, some of the people who are in the worst situation are so-called stateless migrants. If a person is described as 'stateless' it means that he or she is not normally recognized as a citizen or national of any country. This situation often arises when a group of people live within a particular country, and would normally be recognized as citizens of that country, but they are overtaken by traumatic events. There may be major ethnic or racial conflict in the country, with one ethnic group eventually taking precedence. In this situation, the members of the weaker group may no longer find that they have the support of the new administration. They may be refused travel documents, passports or documents relating to economic status. The people who are excluded from the new state may find that they are in effect now stateless.

Subversion of the normal structure of a state may happen for many reasons, including the destruction of an entire state through warfare or insurrection. The situation of stateless people can be very precarious. They will not be able to avail themselves of health care provided by the state, nor will they be able to fall back upon the state for protection in time of invasion or misfortune.

Key idea: Statelessness

A stateless person is one who cannot lay claim to being a citizen of a country. This may arise, for example, when the infrastructure of a country collapses and a person loses evidence of previous citizenship.

Did you know?

Around the world there are millions of people who are stateless. This is an enormous disadvantage in their lives since it is normally very difficult for them to travel from one country to another, and even trying to be accepted in a higher education institution can pose many problems. Statelessness can occur when countries such as the former Soviet Union split up and restructure, leaving some people without a defined nationality. Sometimes countries do not have very precise legislation when it comes to nationality, and hence some people lose their proof of citizenship. This can be further exacerbated when the parents of some children are not known, or where legislation does not allow women to transmit their own nationality to their children.

An increasing number of migrants are having to move from their home area or country because of environmental factors. Some areas of Africa are subject to greater levels of drought, which results in the death of livestock, the destruction of large areas of crops, and the subsequent impossibility of sustaining life in traditional areas of habitation. The rising sea levels across the world are having a disastrous impact on such low-lying areas as Bangladesh and the Ganges delta. It is difficult to grow crops in the traditional way, and villagers are finding that migration is the only realistic solution. Sudden meteorological events that result in flooding and the destruction of food stocks are having a deleterious effect on the capacity of developing countries to feed themselves. The migration of village peasant farmers is the commonest result, but it is very difficult for them to identify a rural location in which they can farm in their traditional manner without the dangers of living in their previous location. They therefore often move to an urban location, where they may not be able to pursue their traditional occupations. As Morton et al argue:

> 'Most environmental migrants move and settle in urban centres within their home countries, with a smaller proportion migrating to neighbouring countries ("South–South Migration").'
> Morton, Andrew, Boncour, Philippe & Laczko, Frank (2008), 'Human Security Policy Challenges' (p. 6).

Sub-Saharan Africa

The large area of Africa to the south of the Sahara desert is one of the least developed parts of the world, and one that places the greatest pressures upon its citizens to create a tolerable quality of life. When the pressures of hunger, water shortage and health problems become too severe people inevitably consider migrating. Such displaced people often lose evidence of their citizenship, and find it difficult to establish themselves in a new country. Sub-Saharan Africa is seriously affected by a shortage of water for irrigation in rural areas, and the resulting failure of crops can lead to malnutrition and starvation. Climate change also has serious consequences in the region with unanticipated climatic events leading to drought on the one hand and serious floods on the other. The difficulties of maintaining their lives in rural areas lead many people to migrate to cities in their own country, or even to travel further afield to try to reach Europe.

At present, the largest proportion of the population of the region lives in rural areas, although for the reasons mentioned urbanization is likely to double during the next 15 to 20 years. However, the movement to the cities is not likely to be a panacea for the problems of rural living. Approximately three quarters of people in cities live in slum conditions without access to regular safe drinking water. Life in urban shantytowns is extremely precarious. Quite apart from health problems, the temporary housing that people erect is subject to damage by the extremes of climate. Parents do not have the resources to ensure that their children are well nourished and well educated. Given this minimal quality of life, it is understandable that some people risk all to reach an imagined better life in the northern hemisphere. However, by dislocating themselves from their roots, there is the danger that some may be unable to sustain evidence of their citizenship, and may continue to find themselves in very difficult circumstances.

Dig deeper

Blitz, B. K. & Lynch, M. (Eds.) (2011), *Statelessness and Citizenship: A Comparative Study on the benefits of nationality.* Cheltenham: Edward Elgar.

Cesarani, D. & Fulbrook, M. (Eds.) (1996), *Citizenship, Nationality, and Migration in Europe.* Abingdon, Oxon: Routledge.

Cook-Martin, D. (2013), *The Scramble for Citizens: Dual Nationality and State Competition for Immigrants.* Stanford: Stanford University Press.

Edwards, A. & van Waas, L. (Eds.) (2014), *Nationality and Statelessness under International Law.* Cambridge: Cambridge University Press.

Pittock, M. G. H. (2001), *Scottish Nationality.* Basingstoke, Hants: Palgrave.

Test your knowledge

1 When people want to apply for nationality of a country they may be required to...?
   a take a citizenship test
   b speak a foreign language
   c take a driving test
   d be a qualified professional

2 Citizens of a state have rights but also...?
   a money
   b pleasures
   c privileges
   d responsibilities

3 If a person is a citizen of two countries at the same time they can be said to hold...?
   a gender
   b ethnicity
   c dual citizenship
   d multiculturalism

4 People living as citizens in the developing world may not be able to...?
   a purchase a car
   b get a driving licence
   c join a tennis club
   d vote in a democratic way

5 Colonial powers may not have prepared developing countries...?
   a for a democratic existence
   b for advanced technology
   c for a mining industry
   d to farm correctly

6 A stateless person is not recognized as...?
   a an expatriate
   b a citizen of any country
   c a professional
   d a politician

7 When a federation of countries divides, people are often left...?

   a without an education

   b without a vote

   c poor

   d stateless

8 The movement of people to cities, and the expansion of cities, is known as...?

   a emigration

   b exclusion

   c urbanization

   d immigration

9 Sub-Saharan Africa is affected by...?

   a industrialization

   b drought

   c vegetation

   d wealth

10 Many people in Sub-Saharan Africa live in...?

   a suburbs

   b shantytowns

   c a large metropolis

   d agricultural communes

19

The sociology of educational achievement

A range of complex issues are raised by the sociology of education, and will be discussed in this chapter. For some, Western education systems are meritocracies, with the most intellectually able students being high achievers. For others, there is a transmission of middle-class values through a hidden curriculum, which serves to support middle-class students to the detriment of working-class students. Other analysts point to the mode of transmission within our educational system as favouring the middle classes, while at the same time the curricular selection process favouring elite knowledge enhances this differential process. Some argue that the initial social status of students is a more significant factor in educational attainment than sheer intellectual ability, and that social mobility through education is more limited than many advocates of our education system would prefer to acknowledge.

The causes of educational achievement

There could scarcely be a more complex issue than unravelling the causes of educational attainment. Of course, children inherit different intellectual abilities, and clearly this plays an important role in their ultimate achievement levels in education. However, quite apart from inherited abilities there are very many social factors that appear to play a significant part in attainment levels. So important are these social factors that political parties of all complexions devote a great deal of time to developing new policies that they hope will make an obvious difference in the educational performance of children and young people.

In particular it is desirable for politicians to be able to demonstrate that it is possible to improve the performance of children irrespective of the level of poverty or affluence of the child's family. Let us therefore examine in detail some of the most important social factors that can affect the educational performance of children, and by implication explore the kind of strategies that could be introduced to improve educational achievement.

One of the most general factors affecting educational under-achievement is poverty. Low family income has an insidious effect on the educational performance of children in a wide variety of ways. When children are born into a poor family, this appears to have a significant effect upon their own earning potential when they are older, and in effect the consequences of poverty are replicated when they themselves have children. Moreover, family poverty seems to have a major effect upon the range and type of educational experiences of both young children and adolescents.

Key idea: Educational achievement

Poverty and the consequent social deprivation are arguably the key factors that have an impact upon the educational achievement of children.

There is not the money to help them join sports clubs, to purchase sports equipment, to go on school trips, to buy books and computers, or to visit places of educational and cultural equipment. Unlike their wealthier peers, they will probably not be able to travel abroad and hence to experience the cultural richness that comes from speaking a foreign language in its indigenous context. When children have available a wide range of cultural and educational experiences from an early age this has a positive effect upon their intellectual development, which is lost to children from poorer families. As pointed out by Goodman and Gregg:

> 'There are big differences in cognitive development between children from rich and poor backgrounds at the age of 3, and this gap widens by the age of 5.'
> Goodman, Alissa & Gregg, Paul (eds.) (2010),
> 'Poorer children's educational attainment:
> how important are attitudes and behaviour?' (p. 5).

Children from wealthier families will normally have much wider and varied educational experiences in the family home than children from poorer families. Parents will be likely to be in professional jobs, and much of their employment lifestyle will spread over into home life. It is true that they may have to work very long hours and may consequently see less of their children, but when they are at home their children will see them in a variety of activities that will support the educational enterprise. Parents will make work phone calls from home; they will bring work-related documents home; they will be interacting with computers in the home; and will have visitors who, like them, are in professional jobs. Their children will therefore be likely to develop a wider spoken and written vocabulary, and will also acquire wider computing skills, simply because their parents are using these either in work-related tasks or in home-based activities.

Key idea: Cultural and educational experiences

The children of wealthier parents in professional jobs will normally be exposed to a greater range of cultural and educational experiences compared with children from poorer families.

The hobbies, sporting pastimes and non-work-related activities of parents will also have a considerable effect on the children of wealthier parents. For example, parents may be members of golf clubs, tennis clubs, bridge clubs, chess clubs or rowing clubs. They may participate in amateur dramatics, light opera or family history societies. All of these activities will open wider horizons for children. However, such activities are likely to be missing from the lives of children of poorer parents, and their home-based educational experiences will be all the more limited because of this. In addition, the children of wealthier parents not only gain from experiencing the wider activities of their parents, but also from meeting the friends of their parents who are involved in such activities. These advantages are even greater when the children reach adolescence and want to extend the range of their own activities. They then have a list of contacts who they can use to extend their own knowledge of certain sports or activities.

Wealthier parents have often experienced a university education themselves, a factor that has probably led them to acquire a well-remunerated job and a good career. Almost inevitably they will encourage their children to also try to attend university, and will emphasize the advantages of gaining higher-level qualifications. There would appear to be a correlation between the wishes of their parents that their children attend university, and the children's success in external examinations.

Key idea: Educational aspirations

Professional parents often have high aspirations for their children in terms of continuing to higher education, and this tends to have a positive effect on the success of their children in educational assessments.

There appears to be a connection between the fact that children who are born of poorer parents do not seem to achieve as well in academic terms. There are also several associated connections, such as that neither the children nor the parents may think that academic results are very important.

Did you know?

A number of people have produced a critique of the orthodox educational system and its role in helping poorer children to learn effectively. Many of these critiques have argued that the 'Western', formal education system as we know it is essentially dysfunctional for many groups of children, including children living in the developing world, and the children born into poorer families. One of the best known of such educationalists and philosophers was Ivan Illich (1926–2002).

A main criticism of our education system and also of society was the role of institutions. He felt that schools, colleges and universities had fixed ideas of what amounted to a valid pedagogy, a valid curriculum and a valid means of assessment. He did not feel that it was necessarily appropriate to always teach students in disciplined classrooms where they all had to conform to fixed modes of teaching and learning. He felt that at times it was more appropriate for students to determine the approach to learning that would suit them best. Equally, students might feel it was better for them to learn subjects that they defined as relevant for themselves, rather than topics defined by teachers. Finally, Illich was often critical of the assessment procedures in our contemporary education system.

The grading system frequently resulted in teachers having to teach in such a manner that students could gain high grades. He felt it was more important for teachers to encourage enthusiasm for a subject. Another way of summarizing this approach to education was that it should be a system that was influenced as much by students as by teachers. In this way students would be more motivated to learn in their own fashion.

Many of Illich's notable ideas were analysed in his book *Deschooling Society*. Illich was also critical of the notion of the 'expert', as he felt that such an individual was in a position to impose a single view of the world, rather than encouraging a debate about the nature of reality. Nor was he particularly in favour of the treatment of educational qualifications as a commodity. While accepting that to some extent education had to be treated as something to be bought and sold, he thought it was preferable in many ways to encourage students to exchange knowledge, by people acting first as the teacher and then changing to the role of the student. In relation to education in developing countries, he considered it important that such countries were able to act with autonomy in evolving their own approach to education.

Children appear to have the lowest levels of academic achievement when they are part of a family that demonstrates recurrent poverty. That is, if a family that demonstrates poverty and deprivation appears not to be able to rectify the situation from generation to generation, then the children of that family are unlikely to succeed academically.

The work of Paulo Freire (1921–97)

Paulo Freire was a philosopher and radical educationalist who was born in Brazil, and who experienced considerable poverty in his early life. These experiences helped him to appreciate the great difficulties in trying to acquire an education when one is born into a poor family. He eventually managed to gain a university education but never forgot the experiences of his childhood.

As he continued his academic career he reflected more and more upon the nature of traditional education systems and whether these really helped the poorer people of the world. He was particularly critical of what is often termed the 'banking' approach to education, where children are taught a range of facts that are assumed to reflect the truth and reality of the world. Within this type of pedagogical system, people rarely tend to challenge the construction of the curriculum and ask who defines the nature and content of what is taught. Freire was critical of this type of teaching because it rarely seems to question the inherent values that determine what is taught. He argued that all too often this type of curriculum tends to be defined by those in power, and hence reflects the values and attitudes of the dominant classes in society. In this context Freire particularly analysed the difference in education between the oppressor and the oppressed. In terms of education the oppressor adopts policies that militate against young people, and particularly poor young people, in being able to give a voice to their own view of the world. Freire's view was that those who were learning, whether children or adults, should be able to work with their teachers in exploring the nature of the world and developing an understanding of it.

Freire was aware that in many countries of the world, especially former colonies of European powers, the education system reflected that of the colonizers. This could be in terms of the language that was the medium of instruction; the religion of the colonizers; and the political system and values that were disseminated through the educational system. Freire argued that if learners of any age permitted themselves to accept the values and ideas of the dominant class, then they would essentially be dehumanized. Students needed to become aware that the educational process was capable of transforming them, and helping them become aware of their own sense of social consciousness. This process was termed 'conscientization' by Freire. Many of these ideas were discussed and analysed in Freire's book *Pedagogy of the Oppressed*. This book went on to become an extremely influential work around the world.

In conclusion, it is worth noting that for Freire to be involved in education was essentially a political activity. For a person to decide to become educated was to try to understand the world and at the same time to seek, if necessary, to try to transform it. For Freire, educational action and political action were both part of the same activity.

One can imagine, for example, that if children have little or no experience of the adults in the extended family having a responsible career, then many of the advantages we have discussed in previous paragraphs will be missing from their academic and social development. It is understandable that if children have little experience of family members gaining

academic qualifications then they will be less likely to
grow up to appreciate the value of such things. As Palmer
points out:

> 'More generally, success in acquiring formal qualifications
> bolsters children's self-esteem, and enhances development of
> self-identity.'
>
> Palmer, Guy (2011), 'Educational attainment at age 16'.

Family factors affecting achievement

Most evidence appears to suggest that there are two factors
that have the most influence upon the performance of children
within the education system. These are the financial status of
the family into which the children are born, and in addition
what we might term the social influence or social capital of
the family. Financial status is important because it enables the
family to purchase many of the educational resources to which
we have alluded previously. Social capital is important also
because it enables the parents to offer accurate and relevant
advice to their children, and also to relate effectively with
the most important figures in the child's education. These
include educational professionals such as headteachers and
teachers, careers officers, gatekeepers to sixth form colleges and
universities, and employers. However, besides the importance
of social and financial factors, it is also important that the
parents have a strong sense of the importance of education as
a process, so that they can use their potential influence in this
area to help their children.

Key idea: Social skills

Professional parents often have a wide range of social skills that
enable them to relate effectively with key people in the lives of their
children, and hence maximize opportunities for them.

Did you know?

Some educators have specifically advocated the idea of children learning at home rather than at school. One such writer was John Holt (1923–85). Holt argued that many children did not succeed at school because they were frightened of many aspects of the educational system. Many children were afraid of not understanding what they were taught; of doing badly in tests and examinations in comparison with their peers; of the pressures put on them by their teachers; and of needing to study subjects and material which not only did not interest them, but which they knew they could not master. In his book *How Children Fail* and in subsequent works he recommended a radical review of the school system, and an exploration of the possibility of more education carried out in the home.

Educational achievement is one of the key factors that contributes to the social mobility of children. If children are born into families with high levels of financial and social influence then they will commence their lives with considerable social status. This does not mean, however, that they do not need to think about educational achievement since social mobility implies the possibility of a downward movement as well as an upward movement. The social and financial status of a family does not in any way guarantee educational success for the children of the family, but it certainly makes it easier for the children and a good deal more likely. About one quarter of children in the United Kingdom are born into families that we might generally describe as poor, and within which the prospects of high educational attainment are slender. This has considerable implications for the type of life that such children are likely to experience in the future. As Perry and Francis argue:

'However the literature shows that the increasingly segregated education system, driven via a market in which the wealthy have better purchasing power (via both financial and social capital) mitigates against the narrowing of the social class gap for attainment.'

Perry, Emma & Francis, Becky (2010), 'The Social Class Gap for Educational Achievement: a review of the literature' (p. 3).

Strategies to improve the achievement of children from poorer families

It is one thing to identify the factors that appear to correlate with poor educational achievement, particularly for children from less wealthy families, but it is arguably more difficult to develop a range of strategies that are effective in improving the performance of children. The role of parents is critical in this regard. If parents have had little experience of progressing very far in the educational system, then they are less likely to be able to offer meaningful advice to their children.

Key idea: Educational achievement

High educational achievement is one of the key factors affecting the upward social mobility of children.

Did you know?

The American thinker and writer Paul Goodman (1911–72) was critical of our compulsory Western education system. He felt it was inappropriate to make children learn facts from set books, and that education should be much more innovative and exploratory. He was an advocate of children and young people learning more in the external society, rather than in formal educational institutions. His ideas were explored in his books such as *Growing Up Absurd*.

Parents may feel that the educational system has failed them, and hence they may have little enthusiasm for the system. Such parents may be unfamiliar with more recent changes to the curriculum, and hence feel that they are at a disadvantage when it comes to helping their children with homework. In addition, they may feel that because they do not have an effective track record of success in education they will be less likely to be able to help their children with grammar, spelling, essay writing and basic mathematics. This can lead to a form of inferiority complex in some parents, whereby they do not feel confident or competent in talking about the education system with other parents, or with teachers and headteachers.

Schools can play a very useful role in informing parents about the education system. They can arrange talks on new elements in the curriculum, so that parents can keep up to date on developments. They can also provide evening discussions on new developments in assessment, and the different ways in which parents can encourage their children to improve performance. Developing a wider knowledge can help parents to have more confidence in discussing the educational system, which in turn can help them to provide meaningful advice to their children. Once poorer parents have enhanced their knowledge of the education system, they will hopefully have more confidence in talking to the teachers of their children. If children see their parents and their teachers having meaningful discussions about education, it may well encourage them to try harder at their work.

There are now many opportunities for adults to extend their education, and if their children see them undertaking further study, then it may well create more enthusiasm in the children for the process of education. Above all, if parents could show a commitment to the future education of their children, then it is likely that children would make greater and greater efforts.

With regard to children it is very useful if they can be encouraged to see education as the route to a better and more fulfilled life. They need to be helped to see the relationship between education and a good career. In particular, they should be helped to expand their horizons in terms of employment, so that they come to realize that simply because they come from a poorer family, they do not need to feel that they have to restrict their life and career aspirations.

Dig deeper

Freire, P. (trans. M. B. Ramos) (2014), *Pedagogy of the Oppressed*. London: Bloomsbury.

Goodman, P. (2011), *Growing up Absurd*. New York: New York Review Books.

Holt, J. (1964), *How Children Fail*. New York: Pitman.

Holt, J. (1995), *How Children Learn*. Boston: Da Capo Press.

Illich, I. (2000), *Deschooling Society*. London: Marion Boyars.

Test your knowledge

1 Educational under-achievement is most affected by...?
   a   language style
   b   text-books
   c   poverty
   d   writing patterns

2 Ivan Illich argued that our formal, compulsory education system was...?
   a   unphilosophical
   b   full of errors
   c   essay oriented
   d   dysfunctional

3 Illich felt students should be more...?
   a   autonomous
   b   hard working
   c   casual
   d   literate

4 Illich did not like educational...?
   a   progress
   b   institutions
   c   writing
   d   contexts

5 Illich did not like education to be treated as a...?
   a   commodity
   b   study
   c   subject
   d   form of escapism

6 Paulo Freire was born in...?
   a   Canada
   b   England
   c   Spain
   d   Brazil

7 Freire was critical of educational systems influenced by former...?

  a professors

  b schools

  c colonial powers

  d journalism

8 John Holt was in favour of more...?

  a home teaching

  b study

  c exams

  d handwriting practice

9 Paul Goodman did not like the compulsory learning of...?

  a proverbs

  b theories

  c metaphors

  d facts

10 Who wrote *How Children Fail*?

  a Durkheim

  b a consortium of students

  c Holt

  d Illich

20

Postmodern society

The end of the Second World War acted as a significant watershed in world culture, and some have suggested that postmodernity can be dated from this time. Whether we accept a specific point of transition from modernity to postmodern society, or whether we prefer to think of a process of evolution, some such as the French philosopher Lyotard have tried to summarize postmodernity. He has argued that it is characterized by the rejection of metanarratives. Sweeping theories such as Marxism or progressive historical development leading inexorably to social progress are rejected by Lyotard on the grounds that they simply cannot encompass the diversity of human thought and experience. Postmodern sociologists see contemporary society as unpredictable and uncertain, and not susceptible to rational planning. They view postmodernity as being often chaotic, diverse and irrational, partly at least because individuals espouse so many different perspectives and viewpoints on society.

Chapter 20 will examine the validity of this theory of micronarratives, and end the book by posing the question whether this is just yet another metanarrative!

The nature of postmodernity

The use of the term 'postmodern' has become almost trite, so extensive is its use in discussing contemporary society without attempting to define its characteristics. It is an extremely complex term to define, and to some extent changes with our evolving society. As Jameson argues:

'Postmodernism is not something we can settle once and for all, and then use with a clear conscience.'

Jameson, Fredric (1991), *Postmodernism, or, The Cultural Logic of Late Capitalism* (p. xxii).

Arguably the most insightful of the thinkers who have discussed the subject of postmodernism was the French sociologist Jean-François Lyotard (1924–98). Lyotard's analysis was largely based upon the concept of what he termed 'metanarratives'. For Lyotard the period of modernism, which he conceived of as existing largely before and just after the Second World War, was characterized by a faith in large-scale, all-embracing world views, which were generally regarded as reflecting an absolute truth. For example, up to the 1950s and 1960s there tended to be an almost unshakeable faith in the progress of science. Advances in science were providing almost unparalleled improvements in the material quality of life of citizens in the West, and the United States was developing technology to explore our solar system, and indeed the further limits of the universe.

Did you know?

Daniel Bell (1919–2011), writing in the 1970s, very effectively predicted major changes in society, which were then only beginning to take hold. He predicted the decline of manufacturing industry as the principal means of generating wealth in Western societies giving rise to a post-industrial society. The latter term can to all intents and purposes be used synonymously with postmodern society. Bell pointed out that service industries would gradually start to be the predominant sector in Western countries. The primary change that would take place, however, would be the significance of human knowledge, technological awareness and digital understanding, the combination of which would constitute the principal vehicle for wealth generation.

There seemed to be no challenge to the metanarrative that the inexorable progress of science was a good thing for humanity. However, the Vietnam War, pitting as it did the advanced technology of the United States against a developing country, showed that science was not the sole factor in gaining international respect.

Key idea: Failure of science and technology

America's failure in the Vietnam War did much to challenge the metanarrative that science and technology would always succeed.

It also became evident that the unrestricted expansion of science was leading to industrial pollution and other damage to the environment. In other words, the metanarrative of the virtues of scientific progress came under attack in the latter decades of the 20th century. As Bernstein put it:

'On the one hand, the primary rhetorical gesture of the "postmodern" movement is to be critical – of Western rationality, logocentrism, humanism, the Enlightenment legacy, the centred subject etc.'
Bernstein, Richard (1992), *The New Constellation: The Ethical–Political Horizons of Modernity/Postmodernity* (p. 7).

The period of the 1950s and 1960s was also one of competition between two political grand narratives. The centralized economic system of Marxism in the Soviet Union was in opposition to that of liberal capitalism in the Western economies, particularly the United States. The 'fall' of the Berlin Wall and the collapse of the Soviet Union demonstrated the limitations of centralized political systems. Equally, the effects of unlimited capitalism were often to demonstrate that the pursuit of profit for large corporations did not always result in improvements for society.

Did you know?

Prior to the Second World War and for the first 20 or so years after the War, capitalist production was typified by the Fordist model, named after Henry Ford (1863–1947), the founder of the Ford Motor Company. Ford developed a particular model of industrial production based on the concept of providing a relatively small number of products for the consumer. The products to be made were defined by the producers based upon their analysis of the needs and wishes of the consumer. One might even argue that through processes of marketing and advertising, needs and desires were created in the minds of consumers. By limiting the range of products, the Fordist model could opt for a process of large-scale production, thus lowering overall costs. The repetitive nature of the manufacturing process also enabled factories to analyse the different elements of manufacture, and thus to allocate workers to specific and specialized tasks. For Fordist capitalism to function well, however, there needed to be a large market available which matched the products being manufactured.

However, as we moved into the later decades of the 20th century, there was a greater tendency for consumers to define the kind of products that they required. This postmodern period was typified by what is usually called a Post-Fordist means of production. The variety of products required by consumers made it difficult to use mass production techniques, and in the postmodern era computerization made the manufacturing process much more flexible. Equally, the monitoring of sales, for example in supermarkets, enabled manufacturers to stock their distribution outlets to the optimum level. It was no longer necessary to maintain large stock levels that were traditionally expensive to retain.

Key idea: The nature of goods

During the modernist era, the nature of goods to be made was largely defined by the producer; while in the postmodernist era they were increasingly defined by the consumer.

Lyotard's essential argument was that postmodern society had recognized that a commitment to grand narratives could be shortsighted, and that society had already begun to recognize the limitations of such a commitment. Lyotard argued that postmodernism was characterized by significant doubts about grand narratives, and that the acceptance of the benefits of more limited, restricted views provided a greater flexibility of thought.

The transition from modernity to postmodernity

The Second World War was won through the possession of superior technology, and the quantity of that technology. It was also won, at least in the Far East, through the possession and application of nuclear technology. When the war ended, there continued the belief that the possession of scientific knowledge was the key condition for the continued expansion and enhancement of the quality of life.

This philosophy continued during the 1950s and 1960s. The major boost to science and engineering during this period was the successful launch of the *Sputnik* spacecraft in 1957 by the Russians. A key aspect of the Cold War between the United States and the USSR was thus the so-called 'Space Race'. The Russians gained even greater prestige when in 1961 Yuri Gagarin became the first person in space. The Americans responded in 1969 when Neil Armstrong walked on the Moon. One of the consequences of the competition in science between the West and the USSR was the increased emphasis on the teaching of science subjects in schools both in England and the United States. A related feature in the West was the rapid expansion of university opportunities, and also a diversification in the range of courses.

In the UK in the early 1960s only a small percentage of young people were able to obtain a place at university. In addition, there was a restricted range of subjects available to study. In the modern world of the early 1960s it was normally sufficient to possess a university education in order to obtain a professional career. Gradually, however, courses became more specifically related to vocational and professional areas. The nature of higher education courses became more and more to be determined by the needs of the consumer. The increasing use of computers by students, along with global communication via the Internet, put the baby boomer generation and their children in contact with the planet in a way denied to their forebears. The postmodern generation was able to make choices about their lives and careers normally denied to their parents and grandparents within modernity.

Postmodernity, power and knowledge

One of Lyotard's main criticisms of metanarratives is that they tend to rely for their existence upon people who are in positions of power. For example, he argued that liberal capitalism was supported by rich investors who contributed wealth to large companies and had much to gain from the success of those companies. The senior executives of such companies also had a great deal to gain from this economic system. As the acquisition of profit is the main raison d'être of such companies, those in charge of large companies are not necessarily concerned about peripheral damage that may occur as a result of the pursuit of such profit. Some would argue then that the pursuit of such a system is not necessarily based upon a profound belief in the validity of the system, but simply because the system generates profit for certain individuals. The same argument can be made in relation to Marxist economic and political systems, where a relatively small number of political bureaucrats have a great deal to gain from the existence of the system. Their support of it is not therefore necessarily indicative of a commitment to it, other than to the benefits that it provides for them.

> **Key idea:** Power and influence
>
> One criticism of metanarratives is that they tend to be related to people who are in positions of power and influence.

In fact, Lyotard pointed out that the world is not structured in a neat, concise manner, so that a single grand narrative can be used to explain our observations about the world. The reality is that everything seems to be much more complex than this. If we take as an instance, the treatment of illnesses. In the case of a particular complaint, one person may recommend surgery, another radiotherapy, another naturopathic treatment, and yet another psychotherapy. The selection of a certain form of treatment may depend to a large extent upon one's ideological world view, rather than a collection of empirical data concerning the treatment of a particular illness. The reality of the postmodern world is that there tends not to be a single all-encompassing theory, but a variety of what we might call micronarratives. These smaller-scale models of the world compete for our attention and commitment. In the postmodern world we tend to increasingly accept that the universe is too complex to be explained using one all-embracing model. We realize that there are choices to be made, and that we must exercise our critical faculties in order to make those choices.

Furthermore, the advent of information technology has brought this multiplicity of explanatory models to our attention, and invited us to make a selection in order to make sense of our existence. Some may argue that we are left with a profusion of micronarratives, and that this merely creates a confusion in our minds about how to understand the world. However, it can equally be argued that order and uniformity are not really part of the true nature of the world. An explanation of the world that is closer to reality is one based upon a lack of order, and one that calls upon us to select a single narrative from a plurality of models. Freedom of choice has consistently been a factor that has run through much of Lyotard's thinking.

Key idea: Micronarratives

The postmodernist era is arguably characterized by a wide range of micronarratives.

After studying at the Sorbonne in Paris, Lyotard taught in Algeria during the 1950s. This was during the period of French colonialism, when many Algerians were fighting for their independence. Lyotard tended to take a left-wing orientation towards issues, and during the 1960s was part of the broad student and trade union protest movement that led to the 1968 challenge to the French establishment. He was a key personality in the university reforms that followed the 1968 riots.

The university system in France had traditionally supported a curriculum that was committed to what we might term 'high' culture. The postmodern movement at the time started to challenge the idea of a singular cultural model, and argued that the many diverse elements of popular culture could, to different degrees, be integrated and combined with classical culture, giving a much richer range of subjects to be studied. This movement was strengthened by the increased development of computers, which made available to young people the diversity of knowledge, theories, models and structures that could be employed to make sense of the empirical world. In the past, students had been brought up to rely upon their teachers and professors whom they deemed to be authorities in their field. With the advent of computers, however, students had access to such a wealth of knowledge that they could begin to think of themselves as experts.

Although the approach of postmodernism appears to be well established, there remain some grounds upon which it can be challenged. A fairly general argument against the principles of postmodernity is that of the grounds upon which one might argue for many micronarratives rather than a single grand narrative.

If there are very many different accounts of the world, then people are left with a great deal of uncertainty. It becomes very difficult to reach a consensus for action within society because of the proliferation of perspectives on the world. In any case, one might also question the basis for selecting a society in which there are many different visions of the world. Ultimately, there might be a unique vision for every single human being. It is difficult then to see how people could plan and resolve issues in society.

There is a tendency then, within a postmodern society, to reject attempts to understand reality or 'truth' based upon a rational analysis of empirical data. Rather there are attempts to compare, contrast, discuss, analyse and reflect upon a range of observations, until people arrive at a subjective version of reality. Such a version will not normally be an absolute picture of the world, but will instead be a plural, subjective impression that represents many different kinds of culture. Postmodernity is characterized by a vast array of popular culture, including journalism, television, radio, music, electronic games and cinema. These cultural forms are transmitted in a variety of different ways, but most notably through computers and electronic means. The means of communication are so extensive that, in many cases, it almost appears as if it is the communicative process that is more important than the content.

Did you know?

Manuel Castells (1942–), the Spanish sociologist, has written about the 'information age', arguing that the postmodern world is distinguished not by productivity and the manipulation of raw materials, but by the use and control of information and knowledge (see also quotation by Lyon, below). The period of industrial manufacture of the latter part of the 20th century is being transformed into a society that uses information. Furthermore, the advances in the use of information, it is argued, will not be made by individuals but by groups of people who are able to work in an integrated manner, using their intellectual abilities to work together in intelligence-based networks of creativity.

One of the distinctive features of the postmodern world is the extent to which people travel. The physical movement of people favours interactions of various kinds, but also an exchange of ideas between social and cultural groups where this would previously have been difficult. Not only is this physical movement mediated through, for example, low-cost airlines, but also through the movement of whole ethnic groups across far and inhospitable tracts of land, in order to try to improve their standard of living. This large-scale movement is also a key element in the world economy, which moves raw materials, goods, components and part-assembled products to locations where they are most needed, or where the infrastructure of production is most amenable.

Key idea: Information and knowledge

The postmodern world is characterized by the importance of advances in information and knowledge.

And thus we are left with a postmodern world characterized by enormous diversity, widely different opinions between which there seem to be few established procedures to differentiate. Indeed, in this lack of methodological process for analysing the range of world views, we are to some extent left wondering whether the supposed validity of variety and chaos is simply a new grand narrative of the type readily consigned to modernism.

Dig deeper

Bauman, Z. (1997), *Postmodernity and its Discontents*. Cambridge: Polity.

Bauman, Z. (2007), *Liquid Times: Living in an age of uncertainty*. Cambridge: Polity.

Butler, C. (2002), *Postmodernism: A Very Short Introduction*. Oxford: Oxford University Press.

Harvey, D. (1990), *The Condition of Postmodernity*. Oxford: Blackwell.

Lyotard, J.-F. (1984), *The Postmodern Condition: A Report on Knowledge*. Manchester: Manchester University Press.

Test your knowledge

1 Lyotard argued that postmodernism was characterized by the decline of...?
   a investment
   b capital
   c metanarratives
   d micronarratives

2 The decline of manufacturing industry is a feature of...?
   a Marxism
   b post-industrial society
   c capitalism
   d bourgeois society

3 Service industries are a feature of...?
   a postmodernist society
   b manufacturing
   c construction
   d Europe

4 During the Cold War, the USSR and the United States were...?
   a in cooperation
   b in competition
   c working together in space
   d launching rockets together

5 Fordism required a small number of products and...?
   a good engineering
   b a few workers
   c a small market
   d a large market

6 The 'Space Race' of the 1960s increased the amount of science...?
   a in the sky
   b on rockets
   c discussed
   d taught in schools

7 Metanarratives are frequently related to...?

   a   mass media

   b   power structures

   c   education systems

   d   law and order

8 Lyotard was a supporter of French student protest in the...?

   a   1960s

   b   1980s

   c   1870s

   d   1890s

9 What was the nationality of Manuel Castells?

   a   French

   b   German

   c   Spanish

   d   Dutch

10 Postmodernism is typified by a merger of 'high culture' and...?

   a   'low culture'

   b   classical music

   c   ecclesiastical art

   d   Shakespeare

Answers

CHAPTER 1	CHAPTER 3	CHAPTER 5
1 b	1 b	1 c
2 a	2 a	2 a
3 c	3 d	3 c
4 d	4 c	4 c
5 d	5 a	5 d
6 a	6 a	6 c
7 c	7 d	7 a
8 a	8 a	8 b
9 b	9 b	9 d
10 c	10 c	10 a

CHAPTER 2	CHAPTER 4	CHAPTER 6
1 b	1 b	1 a
2 a	2 a	2 c
3 d	3 d	3 b
4 c	4 c	4 d
5 a	5 d	5 a
6 d	6 a	6 b
7 b	7 a	7 d
8 b	8 d	8 a
9 d	9 b	9 c
10 b	10 c	10 a

CHAPTER 7	CHAPTER 9	CHAPTER 11
1 b	1 c	1 b
2 d	2 a	2 c
3 d	3 a	3 d
4 c	4 d	4 b
5 a	5 b	5 a
6 d	6 d	6 d
7 a	7 b	7 a
8 c	8 c	8 d
9 b	9 b	9 a
10 c	10 b	10 c

CHAPTER 8	CHAPTER 10	CHAPTER 12
1 d	1 c	1 b
2 a	2 b	2 a
3 b	3 d	3 d
4 c	4 a	4 d
5 b	5 d	5 b
6 b	6 a	6 a
7 b	7 d	7 c
8 a	8 b	8 a
9 d	9 a	9 a
10 c	10 d	10 a

CHAPTER 13

1 d
2 b
3 b
4 b
5 a
6 c
7 a
8 b
9 a
10 a

CHAPTER 14

1 a
2 c
3 c
4 a
5 d
6 d
7 a
8 a
9 d
10 b

CHAPTER 15

1 c
2 d
3 c
4 a
5 b
6 c
7 d
8 c
9 d
10 b

CHAPTER 16

1 a
2 a
3 b
4 c
5 c
6 d
7 a
8 d
9 d
10 d

CHAPTER 17

1 d
2 b
3 a
4 d
5 c
6 c
7 d
8 a
9 a
10 d

CHAPTER 18

1 a
2 d
3 c
4 d
5 a
6 b
7 d
8 c
9 b
10 b

CHAPTER 19	CHAPTER 20
1 c	1 c
2 d	2 b
3 a	3 a
4 b	4 b
5 a	5 d
6 d	6 d
7 c	7 b
8 a	8 a
9 d	9 c
10 c	10 a

References

CHAPTER 1

Arendt, H. (1977), *On Revolution*. London: Penguin.

Brooker, W. (1998), *Cultural Studies*. London: Hodder Headline.

Ward, G. (2010), *Understand Postmodernism*. London: Hodder Education.

CHAPTER 2

Blumer, H. (1986), *Symbolic Interactionism: Perspective and Method*. Berkeley: University of California Press.

Heywood, A. (2007), *Political Ideologies: An Introduction* (4th ed.). Basingstoke: Palgrave Macmillan.

Kuhn, T. S. (2012), *The Structure of Scientific Revolutions* (4th ed.). Chicago: University of Chicago Press.

CHAPTER 3

Aldridge, A. & Levine, K. (2001), *Surveying the Social World: Principles and Practice in Survey Research*. Buckingham: Open University Press.

Flick, U. (2006), *An Introduction to Qualitative Research* (3rd ed.). London: Sage.

Glaser, B. G. & Strauss, A. L. (1967), *The Discovery of Grounded Theory: Strategies for Qualitative Research*. Chicago: Aldine.

Gray, D. E. (2004), *Doing Research in the Real World*. London: Sage.

CHAPTER 4

Allen, J. (1992), 'Post-industrialism and Post-Fordism' in Hall, S., Held, D. & McGrew, T. (Eds.), *Modernity and its Futures*. Cambridge: Polity, pp. 169–220.

Wirth, L. (1938), 'Urbanism as a way of life', *The American Journal of Sociology*, Vol. 44 Issue 1 pp. 1–24.

Yearley, S. (1992), 'Environmental Challenges' in Hall, S., Held, D. & McGrew, T. (Eds.), *Modernity and its Futures*. Cambridge: Polity, pp. 117–68.

CHAPTER 5

Bilton, T. et al (2002), *Introductory Sociology* (4th ed.). Basingstoke: Palgrave Macmillan.

Goffman, E. (1956), *The Presentation of Self in Everyday Life*. Edinburgh: University of Edinburgh.

Matthewman, S., Lane West-Newman, C. L. & Curtis, B. (Eds.) (2007), *Being Sociological*. Basingstoke, Hants: Palgrave Macmillan.

CHAPTER 6

Busino, G. (2000), 'The signification of Vilfredo Pareto's sociology', *European Journal of Social Sciences* XXXVIII -117/2000, placed online 17 Dec. 2009, consulted 27 Nov. 2014. URL: http://ress.revues.org/730

Sterne, J. (2005), 'C. Wright Mills, the Bureau for Applied Social Research, and the Meaning of Critical Scholarship', Cultural Studies – Critical Methodologies, Vol. 5 Issue 1 pp. 65–94.

Sweetman, B. (2005), 'Lyotard, Postmodernism and Religion', *Philosophia Christi*, Vol. 7 No. 1 pp. 141–53.

CHAPTER 7

Gallagher, E. V. (2004), *The New Religious Movements Experience in America*. Westport, CT: Greenwood.

Keysar, A. (2014), 'Shifts along the American Religious-Secular Spectrum', *Secularism & Nonreligion*, Vol. 3 No. 1 pp. 1–16.

Tabor, J. D. & Gallagher, E. V. (1995), *Why Waco? Cults and the Battle for Religious Freedom in America*. Berkeley, CA: University of California Press.

CHAPTER 8

Gans, H. J. (2003), *Democracy and the News*. Oxford: Oxford University Press.

Gans, H. J. (2005), *Deciding What's News: A Study of CBS Evening News, NBC Nightly News, Newsweek and Time* (2nd ed.). Evanston, Illinois: Northwestern University Press.

Habermas, J. (trans. T. McCarthy) (1984), *The Theory of Communicative Action. Vol. 1. Reason and the Rationalization of Society*. Boston, MA: Beacon Press.

Habermas, J. (trans. T. Burger) (1989), *The Structural Transformation of the Public Sphere: An Inquiry into a Category of Bourgeois Society*. Cambridge, MA: MIT Press.

Lanson, G. & Stephens, M. (1994), *Writing and Reporting the News* (2nd ed.). Oxford: Oxford University Press.

Marcuse, H. (1968), *One-Dimensional Man: Studies in the Ideology of Advanced Industrial Society*. Boston, MA: Beacon Press.

McLuhan, M. (1964), *Understanding Media*. London: Routledge and Kegan Paul.

McLuhan, M. & Powers, B. R. (1989), *The Global Village: Transformation in World Life and Media in the 21st Century*. New York: Oxford University Press.

CHAPTER 9

Di Stefano, V. (2006), *Holism and Complementary Medicine: Origins and Principles*. Crows Nest, NSW, Australia: Allen and Unwin.

Gjernes, T. (2013), 'Work, Sickness, Absence and Identity-work'. *Nordic Journal of Working Life Studies,* Vol. 3 Issue 3 pp. 175–93.

Parsons, T. (1951), *The Social System*. Glencoe, Illinois: The Free Press.

United Nations (2013), World Population Ageing 2013. ST/ESA/SER.A/348. New York: United Nations.

CHAPTER 10

Chesterman, J. & Galligan, B. (1997), *Citizens without Rights: Aborigines and Australian Citizenship*. Cambridge: Cambridge University Press.

Hartmann, D. & Gerteis, J. (2005), 'Dealing with Diversity: Mapping Multiculturalism in Sociological Terms', *Sociological Theory*, Vol. 23 Issue 2 pp. 218–40.

Thomas, H. (1997), *The Slave Trade: The Story of the Atlantic Slave Trade 1440–1870*. New York: Simon and Schuster.

CHAPTER 11

Abella, M. & Ducanes, G. (2009), 'The Effect of the Global Economic Crisis on Asian Migrant Workers and Governments' Responses', *Asian and Pacific Migration Journal,* Vol. 18 Issue 1 pp. 143–61.

Benjamin, S. (2000), 'Governance, economic settings and poverty in Bangalore', *Environment & Urbanization,* Vol. 12 Issue 1 pp. 35–56.

George, K. K. (2011), 'Kerala Economy: Growth, Structure, Strength and Weakness'. Kochi: Centre for Socio-Economic and Environmental Studies.

Selznick, P. (1998), 'Foundations of Communitarian Liberalism' in Etzioni, A. (ed.), *The Essential Communitarian Reader*, (pp. 3–14). Lanham, Maryland: Rowman and Littlefield.

CHAPTER 12

Braverman, H. (1998), *Labor and Monopoly Capital: The Degradation of Work in the Twentieth Century*. New York: Monthly Review Press.

Burke, R. J. & Ng, E. (2006), 'The Changing Nature of Work and Organizations: Implications for Human Resource Management', *Human Resource Management Review,* Vol. 16 pp. 86–94.

Perlow, L. A. (1999), 'The Time Famine: Toward a Sociology of Work Time', *Administrative Science Quarterly,* Vol. 44 No. 1 pp. 57–81.

Sullivan, S. E. (1999), 'The Changing Nature of Careers: A Review and Research Agenda', *Journal of Management,* Vol. 25 No. 3 pp. 457–84.

CHAPTER 13

Beck, U. (2010), 'Climate for Change, or How to Create a Green Modernity?', *Theory, Culture & Society,* Vol. 27 No. 2–3 pp. 254–66.

Ishizaka, S. (2009), 'What has the Chipko Movement brought about?: Forest Protection Movement and Environmentalist Network Formation in India'. Shiga: Afrasian Centre for Peace and Development Studies, Ryukoku University, Japan.

Matten, D. (2004), 'The Impact of the Risk Society Thesis on Environmental Politics and Management in a globalizing economy – principles, proficiency, perspectives', *Journal of Risk Research,* Vol. 7 Issue 4 pp. 377–98

CHAPTER 14

Labonté, R., Mohindra, K. S. & Lencucha, R. (2011), 'Framing international trade and chronic disease', *Globalization and Health,* Vol. 7 No. 21 pp. 1–15.

Movius, L. (2010), 'Cultural Globalization and Challenges to Traditional Communication Theories', *PLATFORM: Journal of Media and Communication,* Vol. 2 Issue 1 pp. 6–18.

Stiglitz, J. E. (2007), *Making Globalization Work.* London: Penguin.

CHAPTER 15

Cohen-Scali, V. (2003), 'The Influence of Family, Social, and Work Socialisation on the Construction of the Professional Identity of Young Adults', *Journal of Career Development,* Vol. 29 No. 4 pp. 237–49.

Grattet, R. (2011), 'Societal reactions to deviance', *Annual Review of Sociology,* Vol. 37 pp. 185–204.

Reay, D. (2006), 'The Zombie stalking English schools: Social class and educational inequality', *British Journal of Educational Studies,* Vol. 54 Issue 3 pp. 288–307.

CHAPTER 16

Davis, K. (2008), 'Intersectionality as buzzword: A sociology of science perspective on what makes a feminist theory successful', *Feminist Theory*, Vol. 9 No. 1 pp. 67–85.

Hemmings, C. (2005), 'Telling Feminist Stories', *Feminist Theory*, Vol. 6 No. 2 pp. 115–39.

MacKinnon, C. A. (1983), 'Feminism, Marxism, Method and the State: Toward Feminist Jurisprudence', *Signs*, Vol. 8 No. 4 pp. 635–58.

CHAPTER 17

DeKeseredy, W. S., Ellis, D. & Alvi, S. (2015), *Deviance + Crime: Theory, Research and Policy* (3rd ed.). Abingdon, Oxon: Routledge.

IPCC (2013), 'Report on Metropolitan Police Service handling of complaints alleging race discrimination'. London: Independent Police Complaints Commission.

Schultz, P. W., Nolan, J. M., Cialdini, R. B., Goldstein, N. J., Griskevicius, V. (2007), 'The Constructive, Destructive, and Reconstructive Power of Social Norms', *Psychological Science*, Vol. 18 No. 5 pp. 429–34.

CHAPTER 18

Colic-Peisker, V. & Tilbury, F. (2006), 'Employment Niches for Recent Refugees: Segmented Labour Market in Twenty-first Century Australia', *Journal of Refugee Studies*, Vol. 19 Issue 2 pp. 203–29.

Morton, A., Boncour, P. & Laczko, F. (2008), 'Human Security Policy Challenges', *Forced Migration Review*, Issue 31 pp. 5–7.

Turner, B. S. (1990), 'Outline of a theory of citizenship', *Sociology*, Vol. 24 No. 2 pp. 189–217.

CHAPTER 19

Goodman, A. & Gregg, P. (Eds.) (2010), 'Poorer children's educational attainment: how important are attitudes and behaviour?'. York: Joseph Rowntree Foundation.

Palmer, G. (2011), Educational attainment at age 16. (The Poverty Site). Available online at: www.poverty.org.uk/26/index.shtml

Perry, E. & Francis, B. (2010), 'The Social Class Gap for Educational Achievement: a review of the literature'. London: RSA.

CHAPTER 20

Bernstein, R. J. (1992), *The New Constellation: The Ethical-Political horizons of Modernity/Postmodernity*. Cambridge, MA: MIT Press.

Jameson, F. (1991), *Postmodernism, or, The Cultural Logic of Late Capitalism*. Durham: Duke University Press.

Lyon, D. (1999), *Postmodernity* (2nd ed.). Buckingham: Open University Press.

Index

Aboriginal Australians, 158–9
accidents, industrial, see industrial
	accidents
acculturation, 252
Addams, Jane, 240
advantages of geography, see
	geography, disadvantages of
agenda-setting, 123–4
Ambedkar, Dr B. R., 223
Amin, Idi, 155
anthropology, 46–7
anti-globalization, 206–7
antipositivism, 28, see also
	interpretivism
Applewhite, Marshall, 113
Arendt, Hannah, 8
Arkwright, Richard, 60
Australian colonization, 158–9,
	see also British colonialism;
	colonialism

Bangalore, 167–8
Barker, Eileen, 114
Becker, Howard, S., 227
Bell, Daniel, 208, 292–3
Berger, Peter, 117
Besant, Annie, 111–12
Bessemer, Henry, 62
Beveridge, William, 165
Bhopal incident, 194
Blavatsky, Helena, 111–12
blue-collar crime, 260
Bourdieu, Pierre, 10–13
bourgeoisie, 8, 218, 256
Brahmins, 220
brainwashing, 112–14
Branch Davidians, 116–17
branding, 210
Braverman, Harry, 184

British colonialism, 155–6, see also
	colonialism
Burgess, Ernest, 65
Burns, Mary, 63

call centres, 201, 203
capital (per Bourdieu), 10–11
capitalism, 63, 75, 96, 111, 189, 192,
	195, 200, 256, 294, see also
	Marx, Karl; Marxism
Carmichael, Stokely, 255
Carson, Rachel, 195
caste system, 217–18, 219–23
Castells, Manuel, 208–9, 299
Chicago School of Sociology, 6
church elite, 92
Church-Sect Continuum, 115
church vs state, see secularism and
	religion
Cicourel, Aaron, 82
citizenship, 265–74
	and migration, 268–74
	and refugees, 268–74
	definition of, 266–7
	dual, 268
	tests, 266
closed organizational system, 74–5
colonialism, 200, see also British
	colonialism
communitarianism, 170
Comte, Auguste, 4, 5, 38, 234
Concentric Zone Model, 65–6
Concordat, 108
constructionism, see social
	constructionism
corporate crime, 261
cottage industries, 60
crime, 252–6, 261
crime and statistics, 259–61

criminal behaviour, 7
critical theory, 28–9
cults, 116
cultural capital, 12–13
culturalist theory, 125
cultural relativism, 152
culture, affecting education, 279–80
curriculum, hidden, 241

Dalits, 221–3, see also
    'untouchables'
data analysis, 49–51
de Beauvoir, Simone, 32–3, 233
denomination, 115
dependency theory, 124
deprofessionalization of teaching,
    182–3
descriptive analysis, see data
    analysis
deviance, 226–7, 250–2
  definition of, 136
diaspora, 153–6
differential opportunity, 164–72
disadvantages of geography, see
    geography, disadvantages of
division of labour, 239
Drucker, Peter, 209
dual citizenship, 268
Du Bois, Dr W. E. B., 152
Durkheim, Émile, 6–7, 38–9, 67,
    109–10, 251
duties and rights, 267–8

economic capital, 11
economic opportunities, 163–72
ecotourism, 189
educational achievement, 277–87
  causes of, 277–84
  family factors, 284–5
  improving, 286–7
educational aspirations, 280
educational streaming, 227–8
elites, see political elites

emigration, see migration
empirical data, 42
employment, 5, 15, 60, 61, 65, 67–9,
    96–7, 139, 150–1, 178, 209,
    216–17, 259, 271, 279, see also
    social class and employment;
    women and employment
enculturation, 251
Engels, Friedrich, 62–3
Enlightenment, the, 4, 5
environment:
    and equilibrium, 194–6
    risk and the, 192–4
environmental accidents, 194
environmental exploitation, 188–92
environmentalism, 194–6
equal pay, 245–6
ethnocentrism, 157
ethnographic research, 46–7
ethnomethodology, 81
Etzioni, Amitai, 170
European territorial expansion,
    156–9, see also British
    colonialism; colonialism
existentialism, 33, 97, see also
    Sartre, Jean-Paul
extended supply chain, 204

factory working, 61, 141–2
family roles, traditional, see
    traditional family roles
female religious leaders, 111–12
feminism, 234–9
feminist theory, 31–3
Ford, Henry, 180, 294
Fordist model, 294
Foucault, Michel, 16, 17, 98,
    99–100
framing, 124
Frankfurt School, 29
Freire, Paulo, 282–3
French secularism, 108
functionalism, 75–6, 135–9

Gandhi, Mohandas, 195, 219, 221
gang participation, 253
Gans, Herbert J., 127–8
Garfinkel, Harold, 81–2
Gemeinschaft, 64
gender, 233–46
    inequality, 32–3
gentrification, 66–7
geography, disadvantages of, 164–6
Gesellschaft, 64
globalization, 200–10
    and commodification, 209–10
    and communication networks,
        201
    and new technology, 201–2
    and risk, 201–2
    and the knowledge society, 207–9
    description of, 200
Goffman, Erving, 83
Goodman, Paul, 286
grounded theory analysis, 49–51

Habermas, Jürgen, 128–9
Hall, Stuart, 125, 126
harijans, *see* 'untouchables'
health, *see* sociology of health
health care and ageing, 137–8
Heaven's Gate, 113
hidden curriculum, 241
Holt, John, 285
Hume, David, 4
Husserl, Edmund, 34, 78

ideology, 27
Illich, Ivan, 281–2
illness, *see* sociology of health
immigrant labour, 166
immigration, *see* migration
Indian partition, 153
indigenous cultures, 157–9
industrial accidents, 194
Industrial Revolution, The, 5, 60–3,
    91, 96–7, 176

industrialization, 5, 39, 61
inferential analysis, *see* data
    analysis
information age, 299
information technology, 208
Innis, Harold, 126–7
insanity, nature of, 16–17
institutional racism, 255
international trade, 202–3
Internet, the, 125, 130
interpretivism, 41–2, 44, 45–6,
    49
interviews, 45
Iranian Revolution, 109
Irish diaspora, 154
IT industry in India, 167–8

Jones, Jim, 116
jus sanguinis, 266
jus soli, 266

Kerala, 169
knowledge:
    and work, 182
    construction of, 84–5
    social basis of, 15–17
Kshatriyas, 220

latent functions, 76–7
life history research, 46
Lyotard, Jean-François, 98–9, 292,
    295, 296–8

manifest functions, 76–7
Marcuse, Herbert, 129–30
marine pollution, 190
marriage, 32–3
Martineau, Harriet, 234
Marx, Karl, 7–9, 10, 63, 97–8, 110,
    218
Marxism, 10, 96–9, 135, 141, 142,
    293–4, 296
    and analysis of capitalism, 257

and viewpoints on crime and
deviance, 256–8
and workers' health, 135
mass media, 122–30
McLuhan, Marshall, 127
Mead, George Herbert, 31
mechanical solidarity, 67
media:
and crime, 258
and political control, 100–2
meritocracy, 93, 217
metanarratives, 292, 293, 296, 297
Michels, Robert, 96
micronarratives, 297–8
migrant workers, 154–6, 166–7, 169
migration, 6, 149–59, 200, 272–3
origin and causes, 150–2
Mills, C. Wright, 92, 94
Moonies, 114
Morton, Robert K., 76
Mosca, Gaetano, 96
multiculturalism, 151, 152

Narayanan, K. R., 221–2
National Health Service, see NHS
native Americans, 157–8
Nettles, Bonnie, 113
New Age Movement, 114
Newcomen, Thomas, 61
new religious movements, 112–17
New School, The, 79
news, 122–8
analysis, 124
creation, 127–8
reporting, 126
NHS, 171
North–South divide, 164–5
nuclear accidents, 194

occupational health, 140–3
open organizational system,
74–5
organic solidarity, 67–8

organizations and society, 74–7
organized crime, 261

paradigm, definition of, 23–5
Pareto, Vilfredo, 95–6
Parsons, Talcott, 75, 136–7
participant observation, 45–7
partition of India, see Indian partition
patriarchy, 234–9
Peoples Temple, 116
perspective, definition of, 26, 28–30
phenomenology, 33–4, 78–80
pluralism, see political pluralism
political elites, 90–5
political engagement, 98
political pluralism, 91
political power, 90–5
positivism, 38–40, 43–4
postmodernism, 98–9
and travel, 300
postmodern society, 291–300
post-structuralism and political
power, 97–100
poverty, 170–2
affecting education, 278–9, 282
pressure groups, 91
probability sample, see sampling
proletariat, 8
public sphere, 128–9
pull migration factors, 150–1
purposive sample, see sampling
push migration factors, 150–1

qualifications, 12
qualitative research, 14–15, 28,
41–2, 48
quantitative research, 14–15, 28,
40–1, 46, 48
questionnaires, 43–4

racism, institutional, see
institutional racism
Rana Plaza building incident, 204–5

reductionism, 40, 44
refugees, 152–6
    and citizenship, 268–74
religion, 106–7, 109–117, *see also*
        secularism and religion
remote working, 177–9
research methods, 37–52
rural environments, 63–4

sampling, 47–8
Sartre, Jean-Paul, 32, 97–8
Schütz, Alfred, 79–81
sects, 115–16
secularism and religion, 107–9
Shudras, 220
sick role, 136–9
Silent Spring, 195
Singapore, 166
Sloan, Alfred, 189–90
snowball sampling, *see* sampling
social:
    action and organizations,
        77–84
    action theory, 77–8
    capital, 11–12, 225
    class and education, 223–9
    class and employment, 216, 217
    class and politics, 96–7, 216–17
    classes, 7–9, 218–19
    constructionism, 16, 17, 84, 117
    media, 101–2
    mobility, 10–13, 217
    reproduction, 8–9
    research ethics, 51–2
    sciences, 13–15
    status, 39, 40–2, 219–21
    stratification, 216–18, *see also*
        social classes
    theory, 21–34
socialization, 76–8, 238
sociology:
    as a scientific discipline, 4
    definition of, 13–14

of health, 134–43
    origins of, 4–7
Space Race, 295
statelessness, 271–2
structuralism, 96–7
sub-Saharan Africa, 273–4
suicide:
    and religion, 110
    rates, 7
supply chains and outsourcing,
    203–6
symbolic interactionism, 30–1

Taylor, F. W., 176
teaching, deprofessionalization of,
    182–3
technological change, 167–70
theory, definition of, 23, 25
Theosophical Society, The, 112
time and motion, 183
Tönnies, Ferdinand, 64–5
totalitarianism, 27
traditional family roles, 235–9
typifications, 80

Ugandan Asian diaspora,
    154–5
Unification Church, *see* Moonies
'untouchables', 220–1, *see also*
    Dalits
urbanization, 5, 62, 63–70, 150
urban social development, 69

Vaishyas, 220
Vietnamese boat people, 154
Vietnam War, 293
virtual teamworking, 178–9
Voltaire, 4–5

Washington, Booker T., 150
Watt, James, 61
Weber, Max, 9–10, 41–2, 77,
    110–11, 115, 218–19

Weil, Simone, 237
welfare state, 165
white-collar crime, 260
wild species reintroduction, 188
Wirth, Louis, 69–70
Wollstonecraft, Mary, 236
women:
    and education, 239–41
    and employment, 241–3
    treatment of, 244–5
women's suffrage, 244–5

work:
    and women, 179–80
    changing nature of, 175–84
    in the electronic age, 177–80
    tasks, nature of, 180–4
worker disparity, 165–8
work-life balance, 179
work-related stress, 142–3
world view, definition of, 25–6

Yugoslav conflicts, 153